Introduction to Rwandan Law

This book explores key innovations in Rwandan law, exploring how the country has tried to combine the homegrown legal system with the civil law and common law legal systems to create a new hybrid legal system.

The author explores the history of Rwandan law through the pre-colonial, to the colonial and post-independence periods, and examines the homegrown legal and justice approaches, such as *Gacaca*, *Abunzi*, and *Imihigo*, introduced to deal with legal problems that could not be dealt with using the western legal system in post-genocide Rwanda. The book highlights the innovative Rwandan approach to incorporating international law in the domestic legal system; it also covers the evolution of Rwandan constitutional law and constitutionalism since independence, and the development of family law from a legal system that oppressed women to one that promotes the rights of girls and women. Finally, the book explores the combination of common law and civil law systems in the development of the new Rwandan criminal law and in the transformation of the organization, jurisdiction, and functioning of Rwandan courts.

This book will be of interest to scholars and students of African law, international law, and the legal system in Rwanda.

Jean-Marie Kamatali is a tenured professor of law and director of the Center for Democratic Governance and Rule of Law at Ohio Northern University Law School. Between 1998–2002, Professor Kamatali served as Dean and Professor at the National University of Rwanda, the only law school in Rwanda.

Routledge Contemporary Africa Series

The International Criminal Court and the Lord's Resistance Army
Enduring Dilemmas of Transitional Justice
Joseph Otieno Wasonga

African Intellectuals in the Post-colonial World
Fetson A Kalua

National Healing, Integration and Reconciliation in Zimbabwe
Edited by Ezra Chitando

Africa's Elite Football
Structure, Politics, and Everyday Challenges
Edited by Chuka Onwumechili

Social Licensing and Mining in South Africa
Sethulego Matebesi

The Everyday Life of the Poor in Cameroon
The Role of Social Networks in Meeting Needs
Nathanael Ojong

Introduction to Rwandan Law
Jean-Marie Kamatali

State Fragility and Resilience in sub-Saharan Africa
Indicators and Interventions
John Idriss Lahai and Isaac Koomson

For more information about this series, please visit: www.routledge.com/Routledge-Contemporary-Africa/book-series/RCAFR

Introduction to Rwandan Law

Jean-Marie Kamatali

United States Agency for
International Development

Routledge
Taylor & Francis Group
LONDON AND NEW YORK

First published 2020 by Routledge

2 Park Square, Milton Park, Abingdon, Oxon OX14 4RN
605 Third Avenue, New York, NY 10017

Routledge is an imprint of the Taylor & Francis Group, an informa business

First issued in paperback 2021

Publisher's Note

The publisher has gone to great lengths to ensure the quality of this reprint but points out that some imperfections in the original copies may be apparent.

British Library Cataloguing-in-Publication Data
A catalogue record for this book is available from the British Library

Library of Congress Cataloging-in-Publication Data
A catalog record has been requested for this book

ISBN: 978-0-367-41000-1 (hbk)
ISBN: 978-1-03-217574-4 (pbk)
DOI: 10.4324/9781003004721

Typeset in Sabon
by codeMantra

Contents

Preface

Between 1998 and 2002, I had the privilege of being Dean of the only law school in Rwanda at that time. As a young Rwandan newly awarded with a PhD in law, I had returned home to make my modest contribution to the challenging rebuilding of my country, which had been devastated by the Genocide against the Tutsi. During my tenure as Dean and professor in Rwanda, I had the opportunity to work with such brilliant minds as Professor Samuel Rugege, who later served as Chief Justice in Rwanda, and Professor William Schabas. Both inspired and supported me in my academic and service goals. One of the concerns I shared with them was the lack of coursebooks and other legal publications on Rwandan law. Law books, usually thicker than other books, had been burned by soldiers and militias either to provide warmth in the evening or for other evil purposes. There was, therefore, a strong need not only to acquire books but also to write more books on Rwandan law.

In 1997, Professor Schabas had taken the lead and published, with the support of the United States Agency for International Development (USAID), the "Introduction to Rwandan Law." For many years, this book remained the main publication on Rwandan law. Rwandan laws, however, continued changing, especially after the initiative launched in 2000 to reform the constitution and most laws in force at that time. Although this reform inspired and offered me an opportunity to start working on writing on Rwandan law, the government was slow to complete it.

After I left Rwanda to continue my teaching career in the United States, I felt the burden of having done little to support the development of Rwandan law. Once I finished navigating the tenure road of American law schools, I was finally able to begin paying my dues.

When, in 2017, through my law school at Ohio Northern University, I approached the USAID for a grant to support the publication of a new book on Rwandan law, they were very generous and supportive. After all, it had been more than 20 years since Professor Schabas's publication of the introduction to Rwandan law, a publication that had never been updated and therefore could no longer serve its initial purpose. A new book introducing

Rwandans and non-Rwandans to key Rwandan laws was therefore more than needed.

Many individuals and institutions have helped, directly or indirectly, in the preparation and publication of this work. First and foremost, I am grateful to the USAID for its generous grant (Award number: AID-686-F-17-00002). Thanks are due to officers in the USAID Office in Kigali, particularly Gloria Jean Garland, Director, Office of Democracy and Governance, for her support and dedication in promoting Rwandan legal capacity building and this book in particular as well as Guillaume Bucyana, who managed this award. Of course, the work is the exclusive responsibility of its author and does not necessarily represent the views or opinions of the USAID or the United States Government.

I am also grateful to my research assistants Emily Hudson, Cassidy Galbreath and Alan Embree, without whom this work could not have been successful. My thanks go also to Denis Bikesha, Dean of the law school at the University of Rwanda, and Robert Turyahebwa, Dean of the law school at the University of Lay Adventists of Kigali, for their advice and support in writing this book. Jean-Marie Olivier Rukundakuvuga, Chief Registrar at the Rwanda Supreme Court, and Ahmed Gakuru, registrar at the Rwanda Supreme Court, were also instrumental in finding me cases that I used in this book.

Finally, I must thank Ohio Northern University Pettit College of Law, where I am a law professor, for allowing me to work on this project and my wife Aline, who put up with my regular and sometimes long trips to Rwanda doing research on this book.

The law is up to date as of August 2019.

Jean-Marie Kamatali
Professor of Law
Director, Center for Democratic Governance and Rule of Law
Ohio Northern University, Pettit College of Law

Introduction

"Ubi societas, ibi ius." Wherever there is society, there is law. In the early eleventh century, Rwanda was founded as a small kingdom known as *Rwanda rwa Gasabo*, marking the start of its existence as a society with an identifiable people, culturally distinct from others. Since then, it has expanded by conquering and creating alliances with its neighboring communities while also creating centralized institutions and cementing them with a set of general rules that protect and guarantee social order, succession of power, national defense, and economic organization.

Unlike most African countries that were created by colonialism, when the first European colonialist officially entered it in May 1894,[1] Rwanda, as a nation-state with a common culture, language, values, and institutions cemented by contractual and binding norms, had already been founded. The first agenda of colonial powers was therefore to discredit and dismantle the institutions and norms of the Kingdom of Rwanda, which, although not perfect, had for more than five centuries helped in keeping the country together and organized.

Germany, the first power to colonize Rwanda, did not stay long enough to leave a significant impact on Rwandan institutions. Belgium, which took over from Germany after its World War I defeat, was the power that most shaped the Rwandan institutions and legal system. During its first phase of colonization, which started with occupation, Belgium began degrading and destroying the institutions and laws it had found in Rwanda with no specific plan or vision on how to replace them. In the second phase, which started with the United Nations (UN) trusteeship system, Belgium, under UN pressure, rushed to pass on to Rwanda institutions and laws copied from the then Belgian Congo without first checking on their relevance and fitness to Rwandan realities. These institutions and laws placed the leaders, meaning colonial authorities, above the law and divided the society for the benefice of divide and rule.

Thus, once Rwanda gained independence, its new leaders had nowhere else to look for inspiration about leadership and building institutional and legal foundation but their colonial masters. They copied and continued with the laws and leadership style they had learned from colonialism. Looking back, one can easily see that the newly independent Rwandan society built on the colonial foundation of divide and rule, with institutions and laws with no basis in Rwandan realities and with little concern about this nuance, contributed in planting the seeds that led to the 1994 Genocide against the Tutsi.

Since the end of the 1994 Genocide against the Tutsi, the government has been looking for better ways to build institutions and laws that are rooted in Rwandan realities and needs. In early 2000, the overhaul of the Rwandan legal system began. Its objective was to build a system that maintained the best parts of the existing legal system, a system mainly based on the civil law system inherited from colonial power, while introducing new laws that reflected Rwandan realities and values. Rwanda's location and its membership in the East African Community and Commonwealth meant that it had to incorporate some elements of the Common Law System into its legal system; also, as the 2003 Constitution as amended in 2015 puts it, Rwandans needed to initiate homegrown mechanisms to build the nation, promote national culture, restore dignity, and deal with matters that directly concerned them.

The current Rwandan constitutional and legal system combines the civil law system with elements of the common law system but mainly seeks to ground them on Rwandan realities and values. With regard to the civil law system, the Rwandan legal system remains dominated by statutes and legislative acts. As it purges old laws and rules from the colonial period from its legal system, this system is moving toward giving courts more powers in creating rules through *stare decisis*.[2] After all, courts are better positioned than parliaments to balance the need for change with the need for stability, and to understand the purpose of law in society and therefore help the law to achieve it.[3] Additionally, Rwanda's traditional legal concepts, such as *Gacaca*, *Abunzi*, and *Imihigo*, are being reintroduced to serve as homegrown solutions to problems specific to Rwanda that cannot easily be addressed by laws modeled on Western legal systems.

This book does not intend to exhaustively study all the laws of Rwanda. Instead, it focuses on key laws that describe and reflect the above-mentioned realities of the Rwandan legal system. It is presented in seven chapters covering the following topics.

Chapter 1 discusses the history of Rwandan law. It explains its development through three key phases: Pre-colonial, colonial, and independent Rwanda. It shows a pre-colonial legal system that, though not perfect, was organized and centralized, and created a solid homegrown rule of law under which the institutions of the Rwandan kingdom and society found their roots. It further shows how colonialism destroyed this system but failed to replace it with a "civilized" legal system, and how the post independent Rwanda maintained the colonial laws and institutions. This chapter concludes by noting that, since early 2000, Rwanda has been taking steps to create a system built on the basis of civil law, common law, and homegrown legal concepts and solutions.

Chapter 2 discusses the systems of *Gacaca*, *Abunzi*, and *Imihigo* as homegrown legal concepts and solutions. The first part studies the concept of *Gacaca* as well as its origins and developments. It illustrates how this traditional practice functioned in pre-colonial Rwanda and explains why and how it was reintroduced and improved as a solution to the challenges of post-genocide justice. In discussing *Gacaca* courts, the chapter explains how their laws have evolved and improved with time, and concludes by making a short assessment of their achievements. The second part discusses the *Abunzi* system as a traditional pre-colonial conciliation system, reintroduced in post-genocide Rwanda to respond to the country's realities and needs. This section explains the organization and functioning of the *Abunzi* system as well as its impact on reducing litigations between citizens while building peace and harmony in society. The last part discusses the concept of *Imihigo*. Like *Gacaca* and *Abunzi*, it finds its origins in pre-colonial Rwandan legal tradition. It is studied as a legal concept and solution that combines elements of contract, covenant, and competition in achieving one's goal while also benefitting community and society as a whole.

Chapter 3 discusses the evolution and development of the Rwandan Constitution from independence through to today. It discusses the following Rwandan Constitutions: That known as the "Constitution of Gitarama," which was the very first written Rwandan Constitution; the 1962 Constitution that is considered the very first constitution of the independent Rwanda; the 1978 Constitution that legitimized the one-party dictatorial system; and the 1991 Constitution that reopened the multi-party system but came also to be known as the constitution under which Rwanda collapsed into genocide. It further discusses the 1995 Fundamental Law which was made up of scattered documents that included the amended 1991 Constitution, the peace agreement between Rwandan Patriotic Front (RPF)and the Rwandan Government, the protocol agreement between the Rwandan political parties, and the RPF declaration. Rwanda remained under this fundamental law until 2003, when it adopted a new constitution. This chapter discusses how the 2003 Constitution was drafted and adopted, and different amendments it underwent until 2015. The final part of this chapter elaborates more on this constitution as the fundamental law into force today. The study of the 2015 version of the Constitution highlights its respective amendments since 2003 as well Supreme Court cases that sought to challenge some of its provisions.

Chapter 4 is about international law in Rwanda. It covers the process of creating, incorporating, and positioning international law in the country's legal system. It discusses in detail three key fields of international law to which Rwanda has recently made stronger contributions: Human rights law, International Court of Justice (ICJ), and international criminal law. The chapter presents an overview of key international and regional human rights treaties ratified by Rwanda and human rights bodies that Rwanda is actively participating in. With regard to ICJ, the chapter discusses key cases this Court has heard that involve Rwanda and highlight them as well as their contribution in the development of international law. The last part of this chapter discusses the contribution of the International Criminal

Tribunal to Rwanda (ICTR) as well as that of domestic courts in prosecuting and punishing genocide, war crimes, and crimes against humanity.

Chapter 5 covers the organization, jurisdiction, and functioning of courts in Rwanda. It mainly summarizes and explains the law regulating the organization and functioning of the Judiciary in Rwanda as well as that determining the jurisdiction of courts. More particularly, it discusses the composition and organs of the High Council of the Judiciary, the role and composition of the Judicial Organ Bureau, as well as the key structure and jurisdiction of the Rwandan courts system. This includes the Supreme Court, Court of Appeals, High Court and its Chambers, Commercial High Court, Military High Court, Intermediate Courts, Commercial Court, Military Tribunal, and Primary Courts.

Chapter 6 covers laws related to persons, family, matrimonial regimes, and succession. It first summarizes the historical development of these issues in Rwandan law from colonialism to the present. The subsequent parts of this chapter discuss laws governing the legal personality, marriage, legal separation, divorce, adoption, matrimonial regimes, family donations, and succession.

Last but not least is Chapter 7, which discusses Rwandan criminal law. It first summarizes the historical development of Rwandan criminal law from pre-colonial to present-day Rwanda. This summary discusses key elements of criminal law under traditional Rwandan law, colonial law, and the very first criminal code of the independent Rwanda. The chapter presents the dilemma of the 2012 Penal Code that sought to incorporate all scattered Rwandan criminal law provisions under one umbrella and how this approach failed, leading to the adoption, in 2018, of a new law on offenses and penalties. The main section of the chapter studies this law in detail, covering general provisions applicable to all offenses and penalties as well as detailed offenses and their respective penalties. Wherever necessary, the chapter includes Supreme Court rulings that either tried to challenge the constitutionality or explain some provisions of this law.

Notes

1 Byanafashe, D. and Rutayisire, P., *History of Rwanda, From the Beginning to the End of the Twentieth Century* (Kigali: National Unity and Reconciliation Commission, 2016), 167.

2 For example the Law N° 020/2019 of 22/08/2019 repealing all legal instruments brought into force before the date of independence (Official Gazette N° 37 bis of 23/09/2019) provides that effective the date of its publication in official Gazette "all legal instruments, brought into force before the date of independence of Rwanda, are repealed." As the explanatory note that accompanied the adoption of this law reveals, the gap left by the repeal of 1000 legal instruments by this law, opened up further the opportunity for judges to legislate in addressing an issue not contemplated by written legislation, a practice that was absent in Rwanda when it was still under civil law system.

3 Barak, A., "The Role of Judges in a Democracy," in *Human Rights, Democracy and Rule of Law*, ed. Liber Amicorum and Luzius Wildhaber (Zurich: Dike Verlad, 2007), 942.

1 History of Rwandan law

Introduction

Ubi societas, ibi ius. Wherever there are human activities and wherever there are politically organized societies, there are rules and laws: meaning regimes that order "human activities and relations through systemic application of the force of politically organized society, or through social pressure, backed by force, in such a society."[1] This applies to both contemporary and ancient Rwanda.

A number of authors have observed that before colonialism in Africa, "territories occupied by communities organized in kinship followed legal rules that derived from rules of law issued by indigenous authorities by either jurisprudence or customs."[2] More specifically, it is said that powerful pre-colonial kingdoms and empires, such as Monomotapa, Ashanti, Buganda, Rwanda, and Burundi, had well-organized state structures.[3] According to Vanhove, an attaché at the Belgian Ministry of Colonies who studied Rwandan customary law, Europeans who analyzed the early customary organization and laws of Rwanda were surprised by how similar they were to the European feudal system. This was particularly the case with land and cattle tenure, and customs regulating persons and families, which were governed by thorough, stable, and predictable regulations.[4]

There is no requirement that a rule must be written to qualify as law. Laws have existed and continue to exist in both literate and illiterate societies. Rwandan law might have evolved, been updated, and been modified throughout key phases of the country's history, but it did not start with the introduction of literacy in Rwanda, or with colonization. To understand the history of Rwandan law, one must examine its development through the four key phases of Rwandan history: (1) the pre-colonial period, (2) the colonial period, (3) the periods encompassed by the first and second republic, and (4) the period post-1994 genocide against the Tutsi.

It should be noted that each of these periods was governed by a specific legal regime. However, the end of a period did not necessarily mean the end of the legal regime that governed it. Sometimes, as we will see in the following sections, elements of one legal regime remained applicable beyond their corresponding historical period, creating layers that overlapped both new and old legal regimes. For example, some colonial and even pre-colonial laws particularly regarding family matters, continued to be applicable in the post-independent Rwanda.

With this in mind, this chapter explores how what we know as Rwandan law has evolved from pre-colonial Rwanda up to the present day. Further, it examines the contribution of colonialism, independence and post-independence dictatorship, and the post-1994 genocide regime toward the development of existing Rwandan law.

Section 1. Pre-colonial Rwandan law

Although its modern-day borders were drawn in the early 1900s, Rwanda formed as a politically organized society around the tenth and eleventh centuries, when it was known as the *Nyiginya* Kingdom.[5] The starting point of the kingdom was a tiny territory known as *Rwanda rwa Gasabo* (Rwanda of *Gasabo*), located on the shore of Lake *Muhazi*, near the present capital city of Kigali. Its initial extension started as a confederation between *Rwanda rwa Gasabo* and four other small territories: *Bwanacyambwe*, *Buriza*, *Busigi*, and *Busarasi*. In this confederation, the King of Rwanda, the *Umwami*, was the unifier of those autonomous territories governed by *abatware* (chiefs). In 1378,[6] King Cyirima Rugwe put an end to the confederation by removing the autonomous chiefs of the federation from their respective offices and replacing them with his own appointed chiefs. After this, Rwanda became an authentic autonomous state and entered its phase of military expansion by conquering other kingdoms around it. Where military occupations were impossible, alliances were made with powerful kingdoms through negotiations and marriages. In the five centuries that followed, Rwanda became a large kingdom. By the eighteenth century, the initial tiny territory of *Rwanda rwa Gasabo* was three times the size of present-day Rwanda, stretching in the north to include a sizable territory of what is now Uganda; in the west, it included a large portion of the present-day Democratic Republic of the Congo; and in the east, it included small portions of land that are today located in Tanzania.[7]

The Kingdom of Rwanda could not have survived for more than eight centuries without strong institutions and legal tools to cement them. As Alexis Kagame put it in his compilation of the laws of the pre-colonial institutions of Rwanda, the early legal system had two key objectives: (1) to create a strongly hierarchized society with an absolute monarchy at its summit, and (2) to create a customary law that balances the requirements of the "social army" and those of a community justice that transcends kinships.[8] Under this system, no one was above the law, not even the king. As one Belgian governor of Ruanda-Urundi conceded, "[the Rwandan] Royal institution relied entirely on custom and tradition. The king himself was in a way a slave of tradition because what the ancestors had declared had to be respected."[9]

Because the pre-colonial Rwandan legal system was based on oral tradition, its laws cannot be examined independent of the institutions that created it, preserved it, or applied it. The pre-colonial Rwandan politico-legal system finds its sources in (1) *Ubwiru*, comparable to the constitutional codes in modern states; (2) the king's decrees and precedents; and (3) the *umuco* or "custom."

1. Ubwiru

The *Abiru*, comparable to the Egyptian priests at the time of Pharaohs,[10] had a very important role. They were the depositories of the "esoteric code" known as *Ubwiru*, which was the fundamental law of the dynasty. The *Ubwiru* contained all the secrets about the rituals and traditions that dictated how the king was chosen, enthroned, exercised his powers, and was removed. As Jacques Maquet has observed:

> the traditional body was not unlike a constitution in a modern state, and the *Abiru* institution can be said to have had a role similar to that of a supreme court judging whether a new rule is compatible with the fundamental charter of the country.[11]

This is also confirmed by many other authors, who observed that the *Ubwiru* was a code, comparable to a constitution in modern state, and the *Abiru* played the role of a constitutional court.[12] As Paul Del Perugia has argued, the institutions and constitutionalism of pre-colonial Rwanda functioned so well because, mainly, of the wisdom and knowledge of the *Abiru*.[13]

The following section on *Ubwiru* is mainly based on Kagame's unique inside knowledge of their contents and procedures.[14] The *Abiru* were placed above any civilian or military authorities in the country's hierarchy. Also, unlike those authorities, who were appointed and removed by the king, the position of *Abiru* was hereditary. Before assuming their functions, the *Abiru* had to take a special oath as a guarantee to keep the secrets of the esoteric code. After the oath, they had to swallow a special mixture known as *igihango* or "compact of blood." The brew was believed to be a strong and efficient guarantee against any indiscretion. Indiscretions, even those committed inadvertently, constituted *gutatira igihango* or "serious betrayal of the compact," and this breach automatically triggered the punishment provided in the sibylline formula pronounced during the swallowing of *igihango*.[15] The fact that *Ubwiru* were kept secret may be puzzling in today's legal philosophy, which teaches that laws have to be public. However, in a legal system based on oral tradition, this was an effective method to protect the fundamental rules against any potential challenges and amendment, and to guarantee the separation of powers between the ruler, on the one hand, comprising the king and his court, and the guardians of the constitution, on the other. The *Abiru*'s role as the sole repository and enforcers of the Rwandan fundamental law can be compared to a situation in which the knowledge of a constitution is entrusted only to Supreme Court judges, who can only reveal and interpret its provisions when called to prevent or resolve a constitutional issue.

Some authors have argued that the entire content of the esoteric code entrusted to the *Abiru* had to be kept secret from everyone, including the king and the queen mother.[16] However, Father Kagame, the only researcher who was ever entrusted with the responsibility of transcribing the records of *Ubwiru*, argued that the king was the only person to whom the *Abiru* could reveal the contents of *Ubwiru*. It was, however, forbidden for an *Umwiru* to talk to the king about these contents alone. At least one *Umwiru* witness had to be present during any such conversation.[17]

The content of the esoteric code was categorized into three parts: (1) the *irage ry'abami* or "the kings' last permanent wills or legacies," (2) the *umurage w'ingoma* or "the testament on the succession of the throne," (3) the *Inzira z'Ubwiru* or "the esoteric procedures." In addition to these three parts there was the *intekerezo z'ubwiru* or the "history and comments on the previous three parts." *Ubwiru* were presented in the form of poetry memorized by *Abiru*.[18]

The *Abiru* highest in the hierarchy were known as *Abiru b'ijambo* or "the *Abiru* of the big secret." These three personalities held the highest position in the country, with only the king above them, and held the secrets of the royal succession powers. When the king passed away, they were the ones to know who the crown prince was, the process of his coronation, etc. The first of this trio came from the clan of *Abatsobe*. He was the great priest in charge of announcing the newly crowned king to the nation. The fact that there was no first born right to the throne in Rwanda, gave enormous constitutional power to this *Umwiru* in shaping and balancing the power in Kingdom.[19] The royal name that the king received at his coronation defined whether he would be, for example, a warrior king (whose mission would be to expand the territory of Rwanda) or a cattle king, or some other type. The royal name also predicted the priority of the country during that king's reign and determined his residence and the territories he could not travel to. The second member of the *Abiru b'ijambo* trio came from the great family of *Batege* and was captain of the royal army, known as *Abaragutsi* and *Abakaraza*. He was the priest in charge of ceremonies related to announcing the death of the king. This announcement marked the beginning of nationwide rituals that included the suspension of all activities for eight days and the suspension of conjugal relations for two months.[20] The third member was from the family of *Baheka* and was the chief of the bovine army known as *Insanga*.[21] His role was to designate the bulls (*inyambo*) to coronate with the new king and designate the residence of the new king. In addition to these three *Abiru*, there were at least ten other members of the *Abiru* institution. They included, for example, the *Umwiru* of the royal drum *Kalinga* and the *Umwiru* known as *Mwiru-king* of the clan of *Abakono*, whose role was to keep the secrets of how clans rotated in offering who should be coronated as queen mother. The power of *Mwiru-king* should not be underestimated because the role of queen mother, and, likewise, her clan and family, had very important constitutional significance. The enthroning of the king had to occur simultaneously with that of the queen mother, and she and the king were collectively addressed as *Abami* (kings).[22] In addition, if the king was enthroned at a very young age, the queen mother exercised the king's powers by regency.

The fact that *Abiru* came from powerful clans or families and that they held constitutional knowledge that no other administrative or military authorities had created a system of separation of powers and checks and balances between different powerful clans and families as well as different institutions of the kingdom, such as the king, *Abiru*, army chiefs, and territorial chiefs. The checks and balances also existed between *Abiru* themselves because no *Umwiru* possessed the entire knowledge of the esoteric code.[23]

By the nineteenth century, after many years of practice and improvement, the system of *Ubwiru* had been accepted as part of the Rwandan politico-legal system. It represented the codification of the constitutional rules and procedures governing various aspects of rituals and political practice. As such, it legitimized the institutions of royalty in Rwanda,[24] guaranteed a ruled and peaceful transfer of power, and created stability and trust in the kingdom.

2. The king's decrees and precedents

The king in pre-colonial Rwanda was an extremely powerful and absolute monarch, only bound by the esoteric code. He incarnated the supreme legislator, the supreme administrative chief, and the supreme judge.

Insofar as legislative power was concerned, the king exercised it alone. In his capacity as *Nyamugira Ubutangwa*, meaning "the one who does whatever pleases him and whose orders everyone must follow,"[25] the king could adopt a new law, abrogate any law, and suspend or order an exception to any law. His legislative power was exercised through the mechanism of *Guca iteka*, meaning a solemn and special ceremonial act by which he introduced a new custom or abrogated an old one. During the ceremony, the population was called to, a public place, *ku karubanda,* and the king, surrounded by the chiefs, publicly declared the decision or rule he intends to become a formal and general law. This decision was accompanied by a particular rhythm of a special drum known as *Rucabugome*, meaning literally "anti-rebellion," which signaled a new era in which the acts or behaviors forbidden by the king's decree would not be tolerated. The chiefs, in turn, using local authorities, had to disseminate this law to the people under them, down to the lowest level of the administrative structure.[26] *Iteka* could be permanent or temporary.

A permanent decree or *itegeko* was of general application. It was introduced with a special formula, stating that it was to be observed *ingoma ibihumbi*, literally meaning "for thousands of reigns" or now and forever.

This meant that, unless specifically abrogated, the permanent decrees were binding for present and future kings. The oral tradition made sure that kings' decrees were well kept and enforced throughout the country and throughout successive reigns, ensuring the continuity and predictability of the rule of law. The king's decrees touched issues of both public and private law. A temporary decree, however, was a provisional measure taken by the king for a transitional issue, such as an order not to cross into a zone demarked as disease-stricken, a ban of a specific individual, or a state of emergency in times of famine or armed conflict. The act by which the king revoked a temporary decree was known as *gutanga ihumure* or "appeasement." It authorized the individual or people affected by the temporary decree to resume activities as they were before the adoption of the emergency decree.

As said earlier, only the king exercised legislative power. Anyone else who attempted to assume this power could be condemned to death. Moreover, anyone who acted contrary to the king's laws and decrees, which in Kinyarwanda was called *guca mu iteka ly'umwami*, could face severe punishment, even the death penalty. This practice also played a role in the separation of powers under traditional Rwandan law because administrators only had the power to execute the king's decrees and other general rules, not to create their own. It also helped citizens feel like they were living under a system in which the rules were general, public, prospective, stable, clear, consistent, and administered by an authority other than the one who created them. The breach of laws, even by the administrative authorities, opened recourse to judicial intervention.

The bulk of the judicial system of pre-colonial Rwanda was introduced by the decrees of King Cyilima I Rugwe, who reigned between 1345 and 1378. It was through his decrees that the hierarchy of courts made of family mediation, the *Gacaca* hearing, *Abunzi* mediation and the Royal Court were introduced, guaranteeing everyone the right to appeal, from the lowest level (family mediation) to the highest level (the Royal Court).[27] The resolution of every issue had to start with family mediation; issues that could not be solved this way, or that involved more families were referred to *Gacaca* conciliation, which was made up of the heads of the families involved. Issues that failed to be solved by *Gacaca* were sent to *Abunzi*. At this level, the resolution of issues moved beyond families to involve the community at large, which is why *umutware w'umusozi* ("the chief of village") was the one to head the *Abunzi* bench. It was also a decree of Cyilima I Rugwe that introduced the system of witnesses known in Kinyarwanda as *gutanga umugabo* or "presenting evidence," putting an end to the old practice that sought truth through different traditional rituals.[28]

The judicial system, especially the supreme justice placed in the hands of the king, limited its ruling to specific cases and specific parties involved in such cases. It created precedents and *stare decisis*. Through a specific ruling, the king issued general decrees with legislative powers. Principles, drawn from the ruling, became binding as general rules. For instance, the principle that nobody was above the law was developed in a ruling by the king in the *Semakamba wa Shumbusho* case. This case was initiated by Semakamba when he challenged a king's order that violated the royal decree that was in force at that time. Semakamba was accused of shooting King Rwabugiriri's son, Cyitatire, with an arrow. The latter was wounded, but survived. King Rwabugiri, in his anger, ordered that Semakamba's family be exterminated. Semakamba, who survived, argued before the king's court that the extermination order was in violation of the royal old decree that allowed the king to order that a family be exterminated only if the criminal act that one of the family's members was accused of had caused the death of an upper-class victim or victims. After hearing the case, the king's court, presided over by King Rwabugiri himself, ruled that the king's order of extermination had been illegal and ordered the king to pay eight cows to the surviving members of Semakamba's family and to give his own daughter (Cyitatire's sister) to them in marriage.[29]

Torture and cruel punishment was also outlawed in Rwanda through a precedent set in the famous *Kamegeri* case, rendered by King Mibambwe Sekarongoro Gisamura, who ruled Rwanda between 1609 and 1642.[30] After hearing a treason case involving a citizen who had plotted against him, the king approached his advisors and asked them what would be an appropriate punishment for the offender, given the severity of his crime. Kamegeri, one of the king's closest advisors, came up with an idea he thought brilliant. He advised the King to heat a rock to the highest possible temperature and, once it was red hot, throw the offender on it to be burned alive. The king ordered that the rock be heated, then invited the people to witness the execution of his sentence. To their surprise, he then ordered that Kamegeri be thrown on the burning rock instead of the person who had been found guilty of plotting the assassination. Through that act, the king issued a decree ordering all chiefs in the country not to practice torture and inhuman punishments again.[31]

3. *Custom* (umuco karande)

The term *umuco* or *umuco karande* in Kinyarwanda could be defined as "custom" in the sense of an old practice that, through common adoption and long, unvarying habit, has come to have the force of law.[32] Unlike *Ubwiru*, the king's decrees and precedents that found their binding forces in the authorities of the *Abiru* or the king who imposed them, *umuco* found its binding force from the breadth and length of their application, and acceptance as law by those who practiced them. In Kinyarwanda, *guta umuco*, meaning "losing customs," means being outside the norms and values. A person who ignores customs is stigmatized as an outlier. It is the fear of this psychological stigma that makes one observe *umuco* and gives it the *opinio juris* that makes it binding.

Customs can come from practices that are started by the higher authorities of the country, region, or community, creating something like public customary law. They can also emerge and evolve horizontally in a community that accepts and applies them broadly as law, creating private customary law. Rwandan customary law has evolved from both these sources.

A. Customary public law

The key public law customs of pre-colonial Rwanda are those regulating the social army, the institution of *ubuhake*, and the administrative institution. These customs are often the sources of the rights and duties of pre-colonial Rwandans. They also regulate labor and administrative issues.

Customs that contribute to the development of public law often comes from the top elite or leadership. This allows them to move quickly down to those who will put them in practice and to be broadly accepted. However, in a country where laws are communicated orally, it is difficult to know whether the binding force of a custom resulted from the length and acceptance of the practice that initiated it, or the authority who started it attached some binding authority to it. In the specific case of Rwanda, it is difficult to know which provisions of the military code, pastoral code, or administrative code compiled by Father Kagame, in his code of pre-colonial Rwandan institutions[33], started as royal decrees or precedents and which ones started as top-down practices.

a. Social army as a source of citizen's rights and duties

In traditional Rwanda, the army was not only a military but also a social, political, and economic institution, connecting an individual and his patrilineal family to the king through the intermediary of their military chiefs.

Before colonization, each male Rwandan had to belong to a social army and had to have a military superior.[34] Social or economic status did not matter; even the king had to belong to a social army. An army was made up of patrilineage rather than individual members. A man was not affiliated with an army on his own; he was part of it with his sons (married or not), his brother and his brother's sons, and his paternal uncles.[35] Social armies were intermediary institutions between the people and the king.[36] Each one was divided into two wings: the military wing and the cattle herder wing.[37] The military wing was made up of warriors trained to defend the country and to invade and conquer new territories. The cattle herder wing was made up of the members in charge of the bovine army, meaning all cows owned by the members of a social army; those in charge of booty cows; the *inkoma mashyi*, meaning "royal cheerleaders or clappers"; and, finally, the detached warriors.[38] The rights and duties of each individual, family, and patrilineage depended on the membership and position of their social army. The organization of the social armies made every Rwandan an immediate vassal of the king, from whom he could seek recourse for protection against any injustice.

As soon as the new king was enthroned, all vassals attached to the crown through the contract of pastoral serfdom, *ubuhake*,[39] had to bring their sons who had not been recruited into the social armies of the previous reigns to be recruited into the first company, known as *itorero*.[40] This company of the personal army of the king, of which he was also a member, was put under the command of the chief of the royal palace (*umutware w'urugo rw'umwami*).[41] This company joined four or five other companies from throughout the country, each with a special name and under the command of a subordinate dignitary (*umutware w'Itorero*), appointed by the chief of the royal palace.[42] New members could come from different social armies of the previous reigns or directly from other kinships.[43] Each recruit had to give a cow to the chief of the royal palace as recognition of his authority.[44] Afterwards, the new army acquired customary legal personality and could be assigned to social duties exercised by similar institutions. The training given to the members of *itorero* included not only physical and warlike exercises but also literary, poetry, artistic, self-control, public debate, and rhetorical exercises and performances.[45]

On some occasions, different armies undergoing training were invited to the royal court for competitions.[46] These often involved the *Imihigo*, in which specific individuals or groups in an army set difficult targets and performed competitively to achieve them.[47]

Subordinates in a social army had to perform all the duties required of faithful vassals by their military chiefs. In return for the benefits he received from his subordinates, the military chief was obligated to assist and protect them, socially, economically, and even in any administrative or judicial hearings.[48] For instance, no case involving a member of a social army could be heard by the king unless the party is accompanied or assisted by his military chief. A subordinate without this assistance was considered obstinate and a draft-dodger. Such a person, with no support or trust from local authorities, was not considered worthy of the king's protection.[49] The military chief could not, however, abuse his powers. The power he had over his subordinates was balanced by the power of the latter to report to the king any abuses and violations of the social army ethics and values. Among the violations that could lead to an army chief's removal was his failure to protect his subordinates or represent them in court.[50] The king was often obliged to comply with requests from members of a social army to remove or destitute an army chief in cases where he breached their trust.[51]

The king was the supreme patriarchal chief of all families or kinships[52] in Rwanda. He was the eminent owner of all the movable and immovable properties shared by his immense family of Rwandans. As such, the king had to ensure that each citizen's personal property was well protected.[53] Personal property included agricultural land and royal cattle, meaning cows that the king had donated to a citizen in appreciation of his bravery or labor.[54] This justice was rendered under the rules of the social army.

In return for the protection received from the king, each member of the army had to demonstrate absolute obedience. This had to be reflected in their attitude toward his immediate superior chief and other subordinates. Any soldier who disobeyed any royal authority, even if the official occupied a lower rank, could face a severe penalty.[55]

The system of the social army was a complex but effective legal and political framework, creating a two-way connection between the king and his subjects through army chiefs and their assistants. It served as a tool to create patriotism, social control, and accountability for citizens and their direct leaders. It also assisted in creating a structure in which each citizen was guaranteed his rights, but those rights were also connected to his duties as a member a politically and legally organized society.

b. The institution of ubuhake

In addition to the social army, which was a contract connecting a citizen to his country and creating and defining his social, civil, and military rights and duties, there was the system of *ubuhake*, which looked more like a social employment contract.

The institution of *ubuhake* was defined as a contract of pastoral servitude in which a person known as an *umugaragu* (servant), who had an inferior social status and was less well off, provided cattle to, offered his services to, and asked protection from a person called a *shebuja* (master), whose status was higher and whose wealth was greater.[56] If the offer was accepted, the man in the superior position bestowed on the one in the inferior position one or several cows. This act placed them both in the institutionalized relationship of *ubuhake*. This has been compared to the notion of feudality, which existed in the European Middle Ages.[57]

The obligations of the *umugaragu* included paying visits to and respecting his master, accompanying him whenever he traveled, participating in military expeditions, carrying his messages, and building or repairing parts of his fences or houses. Some of the obligations of the *umugaragu* were different, depending on whether he was an upper-class (Tutsi) *umugaragu* or a lower-class (Hutu) *umugaragu*.[58] It should be reiterated here that Hutu and Tutsi were in no way ethnic categorizations; instead, they were flexible socioeconomic statuses of people or families. Thus, the Hutu servant had to cultivate for the master and join the night watch in his enclosure. The Tutsi servant was mostly an advisor, messenger, informant, and companion.[59] The *ubuhake* relationship was perpetuated even after the death of both parties. The *shebuja*'s heirs inherited their father's contract of *ubuhake*, vis-à-vis his servants, and the servant's heirs kept the cows given to their father.

In exchange for the services of the *umugaragu*, the *shebuja* owed him protection. This protection included legal and material support. For instance, the master provided milk for the servants' children if their father's cows did not yield enough and contributed to the payment of bride-wealth if the client and his lineage could not meet the expenses. If the client was murdered, and his lineage was unable to do anything about it, the *shebuja* was responsible for demanding justice from the king on the client's behalf, or even avenging his death by blood feud (*kumuhorera*), if required. Also, if the servant died, the master had to help his widow and children if there was no one to take care of them.

The client's or *umugaragu*'s rights involved enjoying the usufruct of the cattle given to him by his master, which included full rights of ownership over milk, bulls born from the herd and the meat and skin of cows that died or had to be slaughtered. Also, the servant could, in his turn, use the cows received from his master to start a new chain of *ubuhake* agreements, creating clientelism over people under him.[60]

The system of *ubuhake*, although not perfect, shows that elements of labor law, family law, and individual and collective rights and duties, as well the law of contracts, existed to a certain extent in traditional Rwandan law.

c. The administrative, tax, and judicial organization law

The king was the supreme chief of the civil administration. He exercised authority over zones inside the country and delegated functions to the chiefs of the armies of the various provinces, which were subjected to military invasions.[61]

The interior zones of Rwanda were divided into civil districts known as *ibikingi*.[62] This term could, however, also mean the localities conceded to the bovine armies[63] or sub-chieftaincies, or the pasture concessions to big cattle breeders.[64] At the district level, the king appointed three competing officials with complex responsibilities: the first was the bovine army chief or *umutware w'ingabo*. Such chiefs were the heads of pasture districts, which corresponded to the number of bovine armies in the country.[65] They had powers related to the military, including conscription and taxation related to the social army, and acted as advocates for members of their armies in matters heard by the king. The two other chiefs, also appointed by the king, were the chief of land (*umutware w'ubutaka* or *umunyabutaka*) and the chief of pasture (*umutware w'umukenke* or *umunyamukenke*). The chief of land, who was most often a Hutu, was responsible for taxes on food production, while the chief of pasture, who was most often a Tutsi, handled taxes on cattle.[66] In the districts under their jurisdiction, the two officials enjoyed equal territorial authority, each in his material competence.[67] They exercised their authority over inhabitants of the district without involving themselves in the institutions of the social army or the bovine army, which was headed by the chief of the bovine army.[68] The chief of the army, although a bit higher than the other two, had no supervisory power over them. This smart and competitive administrative structure allowed the king to exercise his powers while relying on the competing allegiances and intelligence of these chiefs.

The chief of land had the judicial powers to hear, in the first instance, cases related to land ownership, while the chief of pasture had the power to hear, in the first instance, cases related to pasture. Appeals of the decisions made by the two chiefs were made to the king with the assistance of the chief of the army.[69]

The district was also divided into hills (*umusozi*). At that level, the cattle and land chiefs had only one subordinate: the hill chief (*umutware w'umusozi*). Each hill typically included several neighborhoods. Each neighborhood was headed by a family head chosen by the hill chief, called the *umukoresha* (labor supervisor).[70] These authorities had both administrative and judicial powers.

Taxes applied to two key sources of income, which depended on the social class of the taxpayer. Tax on land was paid through manual drudgery (*corvée*) or any other activity. The deputy chief of the district had to deliver to his superiors the number of cultivators required as taxation proportional to the number of inhabitants of his district; the remaining cultivators worked for him.[71] Also, at the harvest, the chief required of his deputy a fixed number of baskets of a given product. Every family had to deliver the required quantity to the deputy chief. The latter, in turn, had to deliver the quantity of tax required to the chief, retaining the surplus for himself. The chief kept a third of the taxation, and the remaining two-thirds were delivered to the queen mother.[72] The queen mother was in charge of economic activities and tax collection at the king's palace.

As far as taxation on cattle was concerned, the cattle chief of the district, through his deputy, ordered each cattle owner to deliver a given number of jars of milk to the royal residence on certain days.[73] The chief, or his deputy, could not take their share of the taxation from the jars set aside for the royal court. Instead, they could reserve a number of cattle breeders that would deliver milk to them specifically.[74]

d. Criminal law and criminal procedure

In general, pre-colonial Rwanda had an elaborate and well established criminal justice procedures. Pre-colonial or traditional criminal law system and procedure have been studied in depth by Vanhove in his book *Essai de Droit Coutumier du Ruanda*,[75] which is discussed in detail in chapter 7 on criminal law.

The court system started at the hill level, which could hear both criminal and civil matters. Trials were held in public. In court, the victim was required to provide the chief with evidence of the offense (*igihanga*).[76] Each party was allowed to speak twice, starting with the applicant. The first time was when presenting the case or means of defense, and the second acted as a rebuttal. The losing party had the right to appeal either before the chief of the district or before the chief of the army. The king was the supreme judge. He heard cases and rendered his verdict in public, surrounded by eminent scholars of customs (*abahanga*) or high personalities of the court. Every Rwandan had the right to be heard by the king in cases of injustice or abuse by a chief. The king also had jurisdiction as the last source of appeal for cases involving parties from different districts. In most cases, parties had to be represented or assisted by their chiefs, who acted as their advocates.[77]

B. Customary private law

It was rare for customs that had developed horizontally or from the bottom up to become binding nationally. Such customs may have become known nationally, but they remained binding only in the regions or communities in which they were developed or primarily practiced. Some of these customs were mainly related to private law practices, such as marriage, succession, or inheritance. The Rwandan customary private law had three key characteristics: It was social, patriarchal, and pluralist.

In terms of its social aspect, Rwandan customary law sought to build family and community harmony. It put their interests above those of individual members, and it privileged mediation and conciliatory methods of conflict resolution over those promoting a winner-loser outcome.

The interest in familial and community harmony was illustrated, for example, by the law on marriage and matrimonial regimes. Marriage created a union not just between a bride and groom but between their two families. Family should be understood here not in the nuclear sense but in the extended sense. Marriage was not a simple contract but a union; a compact of trust between two families committed to make sure their children stayed together for better or for worse.[78] The matrimonial regime was based on patriarchal structure. Because the property belonged to the family under the leadership of its chief, property was transferred only through male descendants. A married woman could not inherit property from her parents because marriage placed her, and her children under the authority of her husband's family. As there was no individual land or cattle ownership rights but rather family property rights represented by the chief of the family, allowing a married women to inherit from her parents meant giving the property not to her but to the family of her husband.

Family interests and harmony also involved positioning the honor, image, and integrity of a family above those of its individual members. This was illustrated, for example, in the way a woman who became pregnant out of wedlock was treated. To avoid the humiliation of such an act on her family, the woman was sent away, sometimes to an island, where she would have to live alone.[79]

The primacy of mediation and conciliation mechanisms over adjudication in customary private law is reflected in conflict resolution methods, such as *Gacaca* and *Abunzi*. As in Japan[80] or China under Confucianism,[81] under Rwandan customary private law, the family and community honor and harmony took primacy over individual rights and freedoms. Dirty laundry had to be kept confidential and cleaned in the privacy of the family, and by elders in the community. Such issues were moved into the public court system only when all venues of mediation and conciliation had been exhausted or fruitless. For example, instead of divorcing her husband, a wife preferred to move in with her family or her husband's family (*kwahukana*). This move ignited a family mediation in which the husband was called to explain himself in front of the elders and, if found at fault, was required to pay a fine in the form of beer or gifts before being allowed to take his wife back (*Gucyura*).[82] A husband's fear of appearing before the family elders and explaining himself was a sufficient deterrence against abuse and mistreatment of his wife.

As a patriarchal law, customary private law sought to protect, maintain, and promote a society in which males held power and dominated in roles of political leadership, moral authority, social privileges, and control of property. For example, only male family members had the right to inheritance; chiefs of families, community, and all positions of leadership were held only by men, and conflict resolution mechanisms were male dominated.[83] The patriarchal privileges came, however, with heavy responsibilities of fairness and protection over those who were weaker and underprivileged, and over victims of abuse.

It should be repeated here that patriarchal private law was not unique to Rwandan society. Even when Belgian colonists introduced their own version of the law, it provided little recourse for women. After all, colonial law was inherited from Roman law, which itself was a patriarchal law per excellence.[84]

The pluralist characteristic of Rwandan customary private law results from the fact that the country developed by conquering other small kingdoms and communities with their own cultures and practices. The success of the centralized government in implementing the rules of public law on the conquered territories did not, however, mean forcing the new members of the Rwandan territory to abandon their local cultures and adopt new ones. Regions such as Bugoyi and Burera in the northern part of the country, Bushi and Kinyaga in the southwestern part, and Gisaka in the southeastern part kept their customary laws related to marriage, property law, inheritance, and succession. However, using Kinyarwanda as a common language throughout the entire territory of Rwanda made it possible for different communities to learn from each other and adapt and harmonize their customs, creating more communality over time.

The legal system of pre-colonial Rwanda may not have been perfect, but it had at least two advantages. First, it was homegrown and therefore reflected the values and history of Rwanda. It was not just imposed; rather, it was accepted as the result of a long trial and error process slowly formalized and rationalized as Rwandan. Second, the Rwanda model has often been praised as having features of state similar to those in modern political systems.[85] Unfortunately, as discussed below, colonialism degraded and destroyed this legal system; and worse, failed to replace it with another sustainable one.

Section 2. Colonial Rwandan legal system

The study of the history and the development of law in colonial Rwanda can be divided into four phases, corresponding to the four periods of colonization: (1) the German Protectorate (1897–1916), (2) the Belgium occupation (1916–1924), (3) the Belgium Mandate (1924–1945), and (4) the Belgian United Nations Trusteeship (1945–1961). Although the common denominator for these is the destruction of traditional Rwandan constitutionalism and political structures, the weight and impact of each period is different. The first three phases marked the degradation and destruction of the constitutionalism and legal regime of pre-colonial Rwanda. The fourth, particularly its later period, marked the realization by the Belgian colonial power and the United Nations that little had been done to build a sustainable legal and institutional system that could sustain independence. As a result, legal and institutional mechanisms were hurriedly patched, creating an artificial legal system that was unlikely to be sustainable in the long term.

The German Protectorate (1897–1916) began with the Berlin Conference in which European powers divided Africa into their individual areas of domination. During this conference, Rwanda was placed under the German zone of influence of East Africa. The act of German protection became official in January 1897 and was made official by captain von Ramsey, military commandant of the region, handing a German flag and a letter of protection (*schuzbrief*) to King Rwabugiri of Rwanda.[86] Under the protectorate system, or *schutzgebiete*, adopted by the German Empire during its colonization of East Africa, the fundamental law of the colonies and other principal laws were to be adopted by the Empire itself. According to the fundamental laws of the German colonies, at the apex of each colony was the governor appointed by the emperor. He was assisted by a number of civil servants, among whom was a *Kanzler* and a high judge *oberrichter*, as well as a civil servant in charge of finance, also appointed by the emperor.[87]

After the Berlin Conference, however, Germany expressed more interest in conquering Europe than in expanding its influence in Africa. Instead of developing a new legal and administrative system to sustain its occupation, it opted for an indirect rule, keeping both public and private customary law status quo. The Germans focused more on economic than legal and administrative transformation of the country: they opened the country for trade, favored the role of missionaries in the social and health development, introduced currency known as "rupies" and introduced capitation tax.[88] German's introduction of cash and taxes changed, however, the foundation of the Rwandan economy from a cattle-based to a cash and cash-crop system. Changing the economic structure of the country had unintended consequences on the legal foundation of the kingdom: First, citizens started cultivating cash crops such as coffee and tea, and selling their cows to make money to be able to pay tax; second, the obligation to pay capitation tax contributed in shifting allegiance from the kingdom to the colonial institutions. To pay a tax required acknowledging the power and authority of the institution that collected it. As paying tax is not only a duty but also a source of rights on taxpayer, the latter expects some obligations from the tax collector in exchange for the tax paid. In the case of Rwanda those who paid taxes to the Germans administration expected not only protection but more specifically the protection from obligations of the traditional rulers and laws.[89] This move marked, therefore the beginning of the weakening of the institutions such as *Ubuhake* and the social army that for long have served as the foundations of the Rwandan legal system. Fortunately for the kingdom of Rwanda the German colonialism did not last long because it ended with the defeat of Germany in World War I.

The second phase of the Rwandan colonization started with the Belgian occupation (1916–1924). In 1916, Belgium occupied a part of German East Africa that included Rwanda and Burundi.[90] Its entry into the scene marked the beginning of a serious assault on traditional Rwandan constitutionalism. Almost all acts taken by Belgium during its military occupation lacked any constitutional or legal foundation. As a matter of fact the only legal limitation on the Belgian military occupation was the terms of Article 43 of the Hague Convention that provides that "the authority of the legitimate power having in fact passed into the hands of the occupant, the latter shall take all the measures in his power to restore, and ensure, as far as possible, public order and safety, while respecting, unless absolutely prevented, the laws in force in the country."[91] The Ordinance Law No. 2/5 of 6 April 1917, which was the very first legal act adopted by Belgium to legitimize its occupation authority and actions, did little to move the country from a colonial dictatorship to a colonialism governed by law.[92] Although it reiterated interest in maintaining the indirect rule introduced by Germans, this ordinance insisted that the king could exercise his political and judicial powers only under the direction of the Belgian Resident, according to indigenous customary law and the instructions of the Royal Commissioner.[93] The Belgian military occupation dictatorship and interest in destroying the institutions they found in Rwanda can be illustrated by the following acts.

In their first year controlling Rwanda, the Belgians arrested many prominent figures of the Rwandan monarchy, including King Musinga, on the charge of attempting to poison the Belgian commander of the Rwandan zone. Although after an investigation, the king was found innocent,[94] this accusation and arrest achieved its intended goal of demystifying the king and the institutions of the kingdom and showing the superiority of the colonial authority. By jailing Musinga, the Belgians proved that they had assumed ultimate power in Rwanda, something that foreigners had never done.[95] Those who learned of the king's arrest began to see him as an ordinary man, liable, like themselves, to Belgian orders and punishment. From that time onward, most began paying court to the Belgians, who they believed had real powers. The king's arrest was followed in 1917 by the occupiers' decision to strip him of his judicial power to condemn anyone to death without the approval of the Belgian Resident.[96]

In 1922, the Belgian Colonial Administration appointed a Belgian Resident Delegate to supervise the king's judicial functions.[97] In 1923, the colonial authorities subjected the king's power to appoint or remove district chiefs, and to appoint or remove the district civil servants, to the approval of the colonial authority.[98] The assault on *Abiru* was performed in 1925, when restrictions were imposed on the king's ability to practice the rites of *Ubwiru*.[99] In 1926, Belgians abolished the system of checks and balances represented by the triple hierarchy of chiefs: the chief of pasture (*umutware w'umukenke or umunyamukenke*), the chief of land (*umutware w'ubutaka or umunyabutaka*), and the chief of the army (*umutware w'ingabo*). These were replaced by a single chief, reporting only to the colonial authorities.[100] By removing the institutions that served as the sources of law and practices, the Belgians erased the traditional legal system and made it irrelevant for the future. As one author has highlighted, it was only after the Belgians abolished the system of the social army and replaced the triple hierarchy of chiefs that they realized the fundamental values these had served in Rwanda's pre-colonial legal system.[101]

The Belgian occupation was followed by the Belgian League of Nations Mandate (1924–1945). In its 6 May 1919 meeting, the Supreme Council of Allies and their Associates decided that Great Britain would be given a mandate over Oriental German Africa. Belgium, which found itself excluded from this division, despite its contribution to defeating Germany in Rwanda, entered into negotiations with Great Britain to receive a mandate over Rwanda and Burundi. It was allocated control over Rwanda by the Orts-Milner Convention of 30 May 1919. The formalities related to Rwanda's status as a mandate territory under the League of Nations were, however, completed in 1924[102] and it was not until March 1926 that Belgium effectively ended its occupation over Rwanda.[103]

The Belgian Mandate over Rwanda was put into the Type B category.[104] It was granted to those communities that did not yet have autonomy and where a trustee was needed to manage the affairs for the benefits of the indigenous population. The major requirement was that Belgium administrate the mandate under the following conditions: (1) To guarantee freedom of conscience and religion without any limitations except those commended by public order and good morals, and (2) to prohibit some forms of abuse, such as slave trade, trafficking of arms and alcohol. Powers administering the Mandate were forbidden from setting up military or naval bases on the territories under them as well as giving military instructions to indigenous people, save for reasons of police or territorial defense.

On 1 March 1926, the Law of 21 August 1925 on the Government of Ruanda-Urundi,[105] entered into force.[106] This law, made up of only seven articles and the Belgian Colonial Charter,[107] officially marked the end of Belgian military dictatorship, provided the constitutional foundation for the colonial administration and set the legal system to be applied in Rwanda.[108] Three key contributions of the 1925 law merits to be highlighted: First, it created administrative union between the territory of Ruanda-Urundi and its Belgian Congo colony (Art. 1) but granted the former a distinct legal personality under the administration of a Vice-Governor General (Art. 2); second, it placed Ruanda-Urundi under the laws of the Belgian Congo (Art. 1) but provided that decrees and legislative ordinances of the governor general that had not been specifically adopted for Ruanda-Urundi would require an ordinance of execution by the Vice-Governor General to make them applicable (Art. 3); and third, it extended, the rights recognized to indigenous Congolese by Belgian Congo laws to the indigenous of Ruanda-Urundi (Art. 5) but it stressed that the extent of their application remains under the limitations of the terms of the UN mandate (Arts. 6). In brief, this ordinance created a legislative labyrinth that made it difficult to know exactly which laws were applicable in Rwanda. Even those who could manage to know the applicable laws they had difficulties accessing them. This situation was well exploited by the Belgian colonialists because it allowed them to create a system in which citizens, the overwhelming of which had no knowledge or direct access to laws, came to believe and accept that the law is that what administrator or the authority, who has the monopoly on knowing and accessing legal texts, says it is. This culture of Rwandans to perceive the law (*itegeko*) as whatever the administrative authority or leader (*umutegetsi*) says it is, whether it is a law, an order, or a recommendation; whether it is legitimate or not has remained hard to shake off even after independence.

The terms of the mandate legitimized and sealed the destruction of the Rwandan traditional institutional system undertaken during the Belgian occupation. By degrading and rendering powerless the three key sources of the pre-colonial Rwandan law – (1) the king, (2) the *Abiru*, and (3) the *umuco* or custom – and by installing a colonial dictatorial system, the colonial rulers created a system in which they, exclusively, were the source of law and institutional legitimacy. It is with this background that in November 1931, they did not fear to remove King Musinga, a destitution that had no foundation, neither in the written colonial law nor in the constitutional customary law.[109] With this destitution Belgians proved to Rwandans that what matters is not the sanctity of the rule and traditions but the ruler.

Highlighting the colonial agenda in destroying the Rwandan traditional constitutionalism should in no way be understood as romanticizing the traditional legal and institutional system of Rwanda. It is, rather to acknowledging that unlike that of Belgian colonialism, the Rwandan system though not perfect, was at least based on social contracts and checks and balances and had worked for centuries guaranteeing justice, rights, and obligations for each Rwandan and had promoted equality, and prevented injustice and dictatorship.[110] This observation is shared by both Rwandans and even some Belgians specialists on Belgian colonization, who have agreed that, Belgian colonial administrators in Rwanda were paternalistic, authoritarians holding legislative, executive, and judicial powers; accountable to no one and not interested in the rights of indigenous people.[111]

Not only did the period of the occupation and mandate affect the substantive public law of pre-colonial Rwanda; it also contributed to the destruction of the structure of its organization of courts and competence. The 1917 Ordinance did not make any significant changes to its existing judicial organization. It kept justice in the hands of the *Mwami* and his chiefs, though mostly in theory.[112] This court, although known as the Court of *Mwami*, was presided over by the Belgian Resident.[113] It was not until 1943 that there was a major legislative reorganization of the courts in Rwanda, this legislation came to cement the *de facto* reorganization of customary systems initiated since the Belgian occupation. For example, between 1925 and 1926, a *tribunal du territoire* was created at every chef-lieu of every territory, and a court of appeals and the Court of *Mwami* were created at Nyanza. The territorial tribunals were composed of a judge, a chief, two to five *assesseurs*, sous-chefs, and a registrar. The Court of Appeals and the Court of *Mwami* were composed of the same judges and *assesseurs*, also appointed by the Belgian Resident. The Resident, his deputy, or an administrator specifically appointed to the bench could act in lieu of the judges and *assesseurs* of these two courts.[114] The king who presided over the Court of *Mwami* could also preside over the Court of Appeals. In 1934, conciliatory courts were created at the territorial level to deal with less important cases.[115] The 1943 Ordinance confirmed this organization with some modification and clarified its jurisdiction. As a result, a three-level customary courts system was created: the *Tribunal de Chefferie*, the *Tribunal de Territoire*, and the Tribunal of *Mwami*.[116] Although these tribunals were called customary courts, they were still under the direct supervision of the colonial authorities, who not only had to approve their judges but also could sit on them whenever they wanted. This same structure was maintained when the indigenous courts were reformed in 1948.[117]

The assault on the traditional Rwandan legal system affected not only public law but also private law. For example, although Article 4 of the Ordinance Law No. 2/5 of 6 April 1917 provided that the king exercised, under the direction of the Belgian Resident, his political and judicial duties according to indigenous customary law and the instructions of the Royal Commissioner,[118] the Ordinance Law No. 45 of 30 August 1924 limited the field of application of customary law. It introduced a dualist but nonetheless confusing system. On the one hand, it provided that, in matters not regulated by legislative provisions of the Royal Commissioner, courts could decide civil and commercial cases according to local customs and general principles of law and equity (Art. 55); on the other, it reiterated the right of indigenous courts to decide cases under their jurisdiction according to customary law, traditions, or instructions of the Royal Commissioner (Art. 85). In other words, formal courts were required to first apply written law where it existed and only use customary law on matters not regulated by written colonial law. Even indigenous courts were not fully allowed to apply customary law because instructions from the Royal Commissioner, which often came as a simple administrative order, were superior to any customary rule, no matter how long it had been accepted by the local community.

The field of application of customary law was further limited when ordinance No. 34/Just of 25 August 1936 rendered applicable in Rwanda a significant number of provisions of the decree of 4 May 1895, creating the civil code of the independent State of Congo.[119] This code changed the customary law in many respects. The legislative ordinance No. 347/A.I.M.O. of 4 October 1943 shrunk the field of application of customary law in Rwanda even more. Article 20 of this 1943 Ordinance stated that when a legal or regulatory provision was adopted with the intent to substitute it for an indigenous customary provision, courts would apply the former. The same article provided that even in the absence of legal or regulatory provisions, the application of customary law would be accepted only if this was not contrary to a "universal public order." Obviously, what constituted universal public order could only be defined by the colonial authority, using their colonial lenses. As J. Vanhove, then attaché at the Belgian Ministry of Colonies in 1941, put it, the colonial preoccupation did whatever it could to get rid of as much of the customary law as possible.[120]

The Belgian UN Trusteeship (1945–1961) was the last phase in the destruction of the pre-colonial legal system and the building of the colonial legal system in Rwanda. The trusteeship was organized under Chapter XII of the 1945 UN Charter for, among other things, "territories held under Mandates established by the League of Nations after the First World War." It was in this context that the period of the Belgian Mandate over Rwanda and Burundi ended, with the approbation of the tutorship over these territories by the UN on 13 December 1946.[121] The trusteeship's objective was "to promote the political, economic, and social advancement of the Territories and their development towards self-government and self-determination." It also encouraged "respect for human rights and fundamental freedoms, and recognition of the interdependence of the people of the world."[122]

During its first visit in 1949, the UN Trusteeship Council questioned the intrinsic value of the Belgian indigenous policy and its indifference toward the political and economic development of Rwanda as well as its not involving indigenous leaders in the national decision-making process. The Council recommended that Belgium speed up this development. More specifically, it requested that the *Mwami* and local leaders be invested with more legislative and executive powers, and that the colonial powers consult more indigenous authorities in their decision-making.[123] The Council reiterated the same remarks on its 1951 visit.[124]

Thanks to this persistence, two legislations were adopted. The first was the Decree of 5 July 1948 on the reorganization of the court system in Rwanda.[125] Although this subordinated customary courts to colonial courts, it at least allowed a separation of powers between the colonial executive and the judicial powers. Another important legislation was the decree of 14 July 1952,[126] which handed more political powers back to the *Mwami* and local councils.

However, the intervention of the UN to encourage the Rwandan political and legal regime toward self-determination was too little too late. Belgium resisted the depth and the speed proposed by the Council, creating serious tensions with the UN.[127] As a consequence, Belgium focused on artificial, often rushed, and uncoordinated changes that resulted in more ethnic division, political unrest, and a patched legal system. Because of the United Nations' pressure to accelerate Rwanda's legal and political self-determination, during the trusteeship period, Belgium downloaded on Rwanda and Burundi, almost tripling ordinance rendering applicable in these countries' Belgian Congo laws.[128] But these rushed measures did little to fix the damage caused during the Belgian occupation and mandate period. Having a legal system disconnected from the Rwandan reality helped only the newly created Rwandan elite; teaching them to copy and duplicate foreign laws, and initiating them to the colonial governing approach of keeping laws in the books, using them only when they serve the politicians interests and ignore them when they do not.

The destruction of the legal and institutional system of pre-colonial Rwanda by the Belgian colonial administration and the failure to replace it with a solid and sustainable legal system are at the foundation of the failure of the independent Rwandan legal and institutional system; a challenge that continues to affect even the post-genocide legal and institutional reform.

Section 3. Post-independent and pre-1994 genocide Rwandan legal system

Rwanda gained its independence on 1 July 1962. Unlike most African countries, it did so without a constitution.[129] To ensure the continuity and necessity of legal order, a Presidential ordinance was adopted in September 1962, expanding the application of colonial law beyond the colonial period.[130] Article 1 of this ordinance provided that

> until the entry into force of the new constitution of the Republic of Rwanda, laws, decrees and legislative ordinances, as well as their executive measures and all regulatory provisions, in force as of June 30th, 1962, shall remain applicable as long as they are not expressly abrogated.

The new constitution, however, did little to stop the application of the colonial legal system in the newly independent Rwanda. The first post-independent Rwandan Constitution, adopted on 24 November 1962, provided in Article 108 that all legislation in force at the time would remain valid as long as it was not in violation of the present constitution or abrogated by new laws and regulations.

Not only did the 1962 Constitution ensure the continuation of the colonial legal order; it also did very little to initiate a new constitutionalism by restoring the Rwandan values and foundations destroyed by colonialism or creating a new social contract to serve as the foundation of the independent Rwandan legal system. Instead of being inward- and forward-looking, the drafters of the 1962 Constitution sought inspiration from outside of Rwanda and drafted a constitution with little connection to the country's realities. A comparative analysis of the 1962 Constitution found that it was inspired by the constitutions of France, the Republic of Guinea, Senegal, Madagascar, and the then Haute-Volta (currently Burkina Faso). The constitutions of France and Senegal were heavily relied upon, with provisions of the latter literally copied and pasted into the Rwandan constitution.[131]

The preamble of the 1962 Constitution talked about the need to "consolidate the liberation of Rwandans from the feudal-colonialist yoke by endowing the country with real democratic institutions." However, by importing the new Rwandan constitution and maintaining the colonial legal order, the leaders of the newly independent nation created a legal system that reflected the continuation of the colonial agenda of destroying the value-based legal system while importing, sometimes even without adapting, the colonial or Western legal and institutional system. In other words, the independence and its accompanying legal system seemed more interested in freeing the country from its legal and institutional monarchal system, a system already erased by colonialism, than from that of colonial system and its underlying rules. For the leaders of the newly independent Rwanda, the enemy was not external but internal, so the fight had to be directed inward. The colonial legal system offered a good weapon for this infighting. Although in its very early provisions, the 1962 Constitution provided that "the Mwami regime is abolished and can never be restored," and "the Mwami Kigeli V and all his dynasty are declared deposed from their royal prerogatives" (Art. 2), in its 111 articles, it did not once mention the word "colonialism" or its consequences in Rwanda. The choice of the term *Mwami* over "king" seems also to have been deliberate to make a distinction between the king of Rwanda, the *Mwami*, and the colonial power of Belgium.

The above shortcomings had a tremendous impact. First, with regard to public law, the colonial constitutionalism remained dominant. After destroying the imperfect but at least homegrown and rooted constitutional system of checks and balances, and legal and justice guarantees set up by the pre-colonial institutions, the colonial powers introduced "an authoritarian, bureaucratic and non-constitutionalist executive with uncontrolled full powers."[132] This was the constitutionalism that the newly independent Rwanda inherited. The 1962 constitution, with its imported provisions and its submission of the executive to legislative and judiciary control, was therefore doomed to fail, not only because it was alien and ran against the existing constitutional order but also because it was not accompanied by a comprehensive overhaul of the legal order that had served as the foundation of the colonial regime. Second, with regard to private law, the blanket adoption of the colonial legal order led to laziness among the political leaders of the newly independent Rwanda in conducting a thorough legal revision and reform.

The contents of the 1962 Constitution will be analyzed in the chapter 3 on the Rwandan Constitution; here, though, it is worth mentioning that it created three powers of government – executive, legislative, and judiciary – and guaranteed their separation and cooperation (Art. 45). The executive power lay in the hands of both the president, who was the head of state and government, and his appointed cabinet (Art. 49). The legislative power was placed in the hands of both the National Assembly and the President of the Republic (Art. 73). The judiciary was placed in the hands of the courts, which were guaranteed independence from the legislative and executive powers (Art. 98). After declaring that all Rwandans are equal without distinction based on sex, or other characteristics (Art. 16), the constitution allowed only male citizens the right to be elected as president of the Republic (Art. 54). The president was the chief supreme of the state (Art. 51). He was elected by direct universal suffrage and a simple majority (Art. 52) for a 4-year term, renewable only three times (Art. 53). The president was assisted by his ministers in the execution of government policies (Art. 62). Although the legislative power was exercised by the National Assembly through legislative means, when it was impossible for them to meet, this power was temporarily delegated to the president, who exercised it in the cabinet through law decrees (Art. 75). Although the initiative to introduce a bill belonged to members of the parliament and the executive, bills introduced by the former could not pass if they had budgetary consequences, unless they also contained the means of covering these expenses (Art. 93). The Supreme Court guaranteed the constitutionality of laws by, for example, offering opinions on their constitutionality and providing authentic interpretation of written and customary laws. With regard to the position of customary law in the post-independent legal system, Article 109 of the 1962 Constitution provided that "an organic law shall determine the procedure through which customary laws are to be codified and harmonized with the fundamental principles of this constitution."

The problem of the post-independence Rwandan legal system was not the lack of legal provisions; it was the gap between constitutional provisions and practice, on the one hand, and the laziness of the legislative to change or adapt colonial laws, on the other. Although in 1963, the parliament adopted 24 laws, this number dropped to 6 in 1965 before jumping to 14 in 1967, only to drop to 1 in 1969, 1972, and 1973.[133] These laws were more related to the national and administrative sectors[134] than the other sectors of Rwanda, which remained under colonial law.

However, like the colonial powers they had replaced, the new independent government quickly learned that the existence of laws does not mean the existence of the rule of law.

The biggest test to the primacy of the rule of law came in late 1960s when the constitutional power of the parliament to control the action of the government was challenged. The 1962 Constitution had introduced a solid system of checks and balances by the parliament on the executive. The Executive inspired by the colonial style of unaccountable leadership fought zealously to undermine this control. It began by seeking to remove the members of parliament who seemed likely to question or oppose its policies and agenda, thereby creating more of a rubber stamp parliament.[135] This practice led to a *de facto* powerful executive system dominated by one party: MDR Parmehutu. This system undermined the political debate and participation not only by imposing a one-candidate presidential election but also by removing the constitutional presidential term limit to allow him to be president indefinitely.[136]

On the other hand, the judiciary was weakened by its lack of independence. This was mainly due to three factors[137]. First, although the constitution stated that the judiciary was independent of the executive and the legislative (Art. 98), there was no legislation organizing the practical framework of this independence on issues like the tenure of judges. Judges, including those of the Supreme Court, were appointed and removed with no consideration whatsoever to their tenure, and this affected their independence. The second factor was their lack of expertise and experience. Until 1977, when the first cohort of law students graduated from the National University of Rwanda, the judiciary was dominated by a few Supreme Court judges trained in Belgium, who often read and interpreted Rwandan law with a Belgian mindset and education. The rest of the country had no legally trained judges. This lack of confidence and experience in laws made them vulnerable to the government's intimidation and influence. The third factor was the politicization of the judiciary. Often, the political ambitions of the successive presidents and vice presidents of the Supreme Court since 1962 meant they were more political actors than independent judges. For example, in 1965, the president of the Supreme Court ran for the presidency of the ruling political party, Parmehutu.[138]

The 1970s and 1980s did very little to change the deterioration of the Rwandan legal system. As a matter of fact, following the military Coup by General Juvenal Habyarimana in 1973, the constitution was suspended, and the government was ruled by decrees until 1978, when a new constitution was adopted. The constitution of 1978 pushed the deterioration even further by legalizing the dictatorship through a one-party system and concentrating powers in the hands of the president. Article 7 of the 1978 Constitution provided that "all Rwandan people are politically organized within the National Revolutionary Movement for Development, a unique political formation outside which no political activity is permitted … every Rwandan is automatically a member of the National Revolutionary Movement for Development."[139] Although the constitution removed the requirement that the president be a male citizen, it provided that only the president of the National Revolutionary Movement for Development (MRND) could be a candidate for president of Rwanda (Art. 40). It also gave the candidate unlimited powers during their five-year term (Art. 40), both executive and legislative powers (Arts. 35 and 51), and the ability to dissolve the parliament (79), and made him the supreme guardian of the constitution (Art. 46) and protector of the independence of the judiciary (Art. 81).

Constitutional law was not the only field of public law that suffered in post-independence Rwanda. As said earlier, there was unwillingness, incompetence, or laziness in overhauling the Rwandan law and adapting it to post-independence realities. For example, until 1977, criminal law in Rwanda was regulated by a Belgian decree dating from 30 January 1940.[140] The legal regime governing private law was even worse than that of public law. Private law was governed by archaic Belgian ordinances as well as a multitude of scattered and limited laws, decrees, and regulations that sometimes contradicted each other. Also, until the late 1980s, persons and family issues were mainly governed by the Belgian decree of 4 May 1895, instituting the Civil Code.[141] Until 2011, contract law was governed by a Belgian decree dating as far as 30 July 1888.[142] Until the early 2000s, most issues related to commerce and business were governed by laws and regulations that dated to before independence was achieved.[143] Also, until very recently, issues of property law remained regulated by Belgian decrees adopted before 1920.[144]

The development of post-genocide Rwandan law is discussed in mainly discussed in chapters 2 and 3 of this book specific to each area of law. It is worth highlighting here, however, that the Government of Rwanda seriously considered the need to assess and overhaul its law in the early 2000s. Between 2000 and 2004, an ad hoc law reform commission was created, mainly to deal with constitutional reform. In 2013, however, the Rwanda Law Reform Commission was created with the mission to "review Rwanda laws with a view to ensuring their development and reform."[145] In an effort to combine the civil law system based on statutes and the common law based on precedents, Rwanda seems determined to use statutes while also allowing courts to create laws where necessary.[146]

Notes

1 *Black's Law Dictionary*, 8th ed., s.v. "Law."

2 A. Sohier, "Le marriage en droit coutumier Congolais," Institut Royal colonial Belge, Section des Sciences Morales et Politiques, Memoires, T.XI, fasc. 3, 1943, p. 39.

3 M. Mamdani, *Politics and Class Formation in Uganda* (London: Heinemann, 1976), 21; W. Bgoya and G. Hyden, "State and the Crisis in Africa: In Search of a Second Liberation," *Development Dialogue*, No. 2 (1987): 8–10.

4 J. Vanhove, *Essai de Droit Coutumier du Ruanda, Memoire couronne au Councours Annuel de 1940* (Brussels: Library Falk fils, 1941), 3–4.

5 Alexis Kagame, *Un abrégé de l'Ethno-Histoire du Rwanda* (Butare: Editions Universtaires du Rwanda, 1972), 39; L. Delmas, *Généalogies de la Noblesse*

du Rwanda (Kabgayi: Vicariat apostolique du Ruanda, 1950), 41; Bernard Lugan, *Histoire du Rwanda, de la Préhistoire à nos jours* (Paris: Editions Bartillat, 1997), 65.

6 This date is provided in Kagame, *abrégé de l'Ethno-Histoire*, 39, but, according to Vansina, the reign of Cyilima corresponds to the period of 1506. For more information, see J. Vansina, *L'évolution du royaume rwanda des origines à 1900* (Bruxelles: Académie Royale des Sciences d'Outre- Mers, 1962), 56.

7 For more details on wars and alliances that led to the expansion of Rwanda, see Alexis Kagame's *Un abrégé de l'Ethno-Histoire du Rwanda* and Bernard Lugan's *Histoire du Rwanda*, de la Préhistoire à nos jours, pp. 77–111. For details on how Rwanda lost its territories following the colonial borders scramble, see J.M. Kamatali, "State-Building in Rwanda," in *Reconstructing the Authoritarian State in Africa*, ed. George K. Kieh, Jr. and Pita O. Agbese (London: Routledge, 2013), 163.

8 Alexis Kagame, *Code des institutions du Rwanda precoloniale* (Brussels: Institute Royal Colonial Belge, 1952), 4.

9 Postiaux, interview notes from 19th August 1929 between Musinga and his mother Nyirayuhi, C.P.I, cited in Deo Byanafashye and Paul Rutayisire, *History of Rwanda From the beginning to the end of the Twentieth Century* (Kigali: National Unity and Reconciliation Commission, 2016), 246.

10 Paul Del Perugia, *Les derniers rois mages* (Paris: editions Phebus, 1993), 243–244.

11 Jacques J. Maquet, *The Premise of Inequality in Rwanda* (London and New York: Oxford University Press, 1961), 61

12 Filip Reyntjens, *Pouvoirs et Droit au Rwanda: droit public et evolution politique, 1916–1973* (Tervuren: Musée royal de l'Afrique centrale, 1985), 25.

13 Perugia, *Les derniers rois*, pp. 243–244.

14 According to this study, the king ordered *Abiru* to reveal the contents of *ubwiru* to Father Kagame, so he could record them in writing on the conditions that (1) the text of the Code could never be published in Kinyarwanda during the lifetime of the *Abiru* who revealed it to him; (2) it would never be translated into a foreign language that could be understood by Rwandans; and (3) a study that provided a general idea of *ubwiru* with no particular details would be allowed. For more information, see Ibid., p. 364.

15 F.X. Hagenimana, *La séparation des pouvoirs et l'histoire constitutionnelle Rwandaise* (Kigali: INR, 1990), 21.

16 Donat Murego, "La Revolution Rwandaise 1959–1962, Essa d'interpretation" (master's thesis, University of Louvain, 1975), 122; Hagenimana, *La séparation des pouvoirs*, 21.

17 A. Kagame, "Le Code Esotherique de la Dynastie du Rwanda," in Zaire, *Revue Congolese* (Bruxelles, April 1947), 364 and 374.

18 Ibid., pp. 374–376.

19 Vanhove, *Essai de Droit Coutumier du Ruanda*, p. 97.

20 Ibid., p. 96.

21 For details on the Bovine Army, see infra.

22 Vanhove, *Essai de Droit Coutumier du Ruanda*, p. 88.

23 According to Fatehr Kagame, only four *Abiru*, the *Mwiru*-king of Batsobe, the great-priest *Umwiru*, the *Mwiru* of Karinga, and the *Mwiru*-king of *Nyamweru* possessed the entire content of the esoteric code. Kagame, *Le Code Esotherique*, p. 373.

24 Alison Des Forges, *Defeat is the only Bad News: Rwanda under Musing, 1896–1931*, ed. David Newbury (Madison: University of Wisconsin Press, 2011), 23.

25 Kagamge, *Le Code Esotherique*, p. 376.
26 Ibid., p. 377.
27 "Rwaciriwe I Mutakara, ubutabera bubereye u Rwanda Twifuza," a white paper developed by the Rwandan Justice Sector (Kigali: September 2017), 17 (unpublished).
28 Ibid., p. 19.
29 Ibid.
30 Ibid., p. 20.
31 Ibid.
32 *Black's Law Dictionary*, s.v. "custom."
33 Kagame, *Code des institutions.*
34 Ibid., Art. 13.
35 Maquet, *Premise of Inequality*, p. 110.
36 Kagame, *Code des institutions*, Art. 82.
37 Ibid., Art. 49.
38 Ibid., Art. 49(b).
39 See section infra on *ubuhake.*
40 Kagame, *Code des institutions*, Art. 16.
41 Ibid., Arts. 16–17.
42 Ibid., Arts. 19 and 22.
43 Ibid., Arts. 29–32.
44 Ibid., Arts. 23 and 33b.
45 Ibid., Arts. 25, 27 and 28.
46 Ibid., Art. 36.
47 The *Imihigo* contract is discussed in the chapter on "Homegrown Legal Concepts and Solutions."
48 Kagame, *Code des institutions*, Arts. 68–72.
49 Ibid., Art. 72.
50 Ibid., Art. 74.
51 Ibid., Art. 73.
52 Kinship was considered the grassroots social cell in Rwandan politics. It was made up of one isolated family with an autonomous fief or patrimony, or a group of families under a common ascendant, with a common fief or patrimony received by inheritance. See Kagame *Code des institutions*, Art. 1.
53 Kagame, *Code des institutions*, Art. 79.
54 Ibid., Art. 81.
55 Ibid., Art. 84.
56 Kagame, *Code des institutions*, p. 18, footnote 1.
57 Maquet, *Premise of Inequality*, p. 133.
58 Ibid., 130; Donat Murego, "La Revolution Rwandaise 1959–1962," p. 207.
59 Kagame, *Code des institutions*, p. 18, footnote 1.
60 Maquet, *Premise of Inequality*, p. 130.
61 Kagame, *Code des institutions*, Art. 331.
62 Ibid., Art. 332.
63 Bovine Army means all cows owned by the members of a social army. For more information, refer to Kagame, ibid., Art. 198.
64 Ibid., Art. 248.
65 Ibid., Art. 246(a).
66 Ibid., Art. 333.
67 Ibid., Art. 336.
68 Ibid., Art. 337a.
69 Ibid., Art. 370.
70 Maquet, *Premise of Inequality*, p. 102.
71 Kagame, *Code des institutions*, Art. 354.

72 Ibid., Art. 357.
73 Ibid., Art. 361.
74 Ibid., Art. 364.
75 Vanhove, *Essai de Droit Coutumier du Ruanda*, pp. 107–115.
76 Ibid., pp. 107–108.
77 Ibid., pp. 120–121.
78 Charles Ntampaka, "Family Law in Rwanda," in *The International Survey of Family Law*, ed. A. Bainham (The Netherlands: The International Society of Family Law, 1997), 7.
79 Marcel D' Hertefelt, Albert Trouwborst and J.H. Scherer, *Les Anciens royaumes de la zone interlacustre mériodionale (Rwanda, Burundi, Buha)* (London: International African Institute, 1962), 53.
80 Konrad Zweigert and Hein Kötz, *Introduction to Comparative Law*, 2nd ed., Vol. 1 (Oxford: Clarendon Press, 1987), 361 and 370–371.
81 René David and John E.C. Brierley, *Major Legal Systems in the World Today, an Introduction to the Comparative Study of Law*, 2nd ed. (London: Stevens and Sons, 1978), 479 and 500.
82 Jacques, J. Maquet, *The Premise of Inequality in Ruanda: A Study of Political Relations in a Central African Kingdom* (New York: Routledge, 2018), 73.
83 Deo Byanafashye and Paul Rutayisire, *History of Rwanda*, p. 143.
84 Jane F. Gardner, *Women in Roman Law and Society* (London: Routledge, 1986).
85 Mamdani, *Politics and Class*, p. 73; Bgoya and Hyden, "State and the Crisis," pp. 8–10.
86 Deo Byanafashye and Paul Rutayisire, *History of Rwanda*, p. 183.
87 J.M. Kamatali, "Ethnicity and Constitutionalism in Post-Genocide Rwanda," in *Constitutionalism in Africa, Creating Opportunity, Facing Challenges*, ed. J. Oloka-Onyango (Kampala: Fountain Publishers, 2001), 110.
88 Filip Reyntjens, *Pouvoirs et Droit au Rwanda*, p. 38
89 Des Forges, *Defeat is the only Bad News*, p. 89.
90 Filip Reyntjens, *Pouvoirs et Droit au Rwanda*, pp. 30–35.
91 See Convention (IV) respecting the Laws and Customs of War on Land and its annex: Regulations concerning the Laws and Customs of War on Land. The Hague, 18 October 1907. Annex to the Convention: Regulations respecting the laws and customs of war on land- section III: Military authority over the territory of the hostile state: Regulations: Article 43. https://ihl-databases.icrc.org/ihl/WebART/195-200053?OpenDocument.
92 B.O.R.U, 1924, No. 4, pp. 4–5.
93 Filip Reyntjens, *Pouvoirs et Droit au Rwanda*, p. 149.
94 J. Malfeyt, "Note sur le Rapport Politique du Rwanda, 1920–1921," *African Archives* AE/II, no. 1847 (para. 3288).
95 Des Forges, *Defeat is the only Bad News*, p. 142.
96 Malfeyt, "Note sur le Rapport," p. 15; Des Forges, *Defeat is the only Bad News*, p. 159.
97 Des Forges, *Defeat is the only Bad News*, p. 238.
98 Louis De Lacger, *Ruanda*, 2nd ed. (Kabgayi, 1961), 490.
99 Des Forges, *Defeat is the only Bad News*, p. 309.
100 Kagame, *Un abrégé de l'Ethno-Histoire*, pp. 187–188.
101 Filip Reyntjens, *Pouvoirs et Droit au Rwanda*, pp. 115–116.
102 Des Forges, *Defeat is the only Bad News*, p. 158.
103 T. Hyse, *Le Mandat Belge sur le Ruanda-Urundi* (Bruxelles: la Renaissance de l'Occident, 1930), pp. 5–8.
104 The Mandate of Type A concerned those communities that had previously been ruled by the Ottoman Empire, which were considered to have achieved a

certain degree of economic development to the extent that their existence, as independent nations, could have been provisionally recognized. The Mandate of Type C concerned those communities with small population density located far from centers of civilization. Those communities were to be governed as integral parts of countries with a mandate over them. For more information, refer to Filip Reyntjens, *Pouvoirs et Droit au Rwanda*, p. 43.

105 See Loi sur le Gouvernment du Ruanda-Urundi (B.O.R.U. No.1. p. 10/78), in Pierre Leroy and Jacques Westhof, *Legislation du Ruanda-Urundi, Textes Receullis et Annotes*, 2nd ed. (Brussels, 1954), 7.

106 See Arrete Royale of 11 January 1926 en execution de la loi du 21 aout 1925 (B.O.R.U. 3e Annee No.1, pp. 11/179) cited in Pierre Leroy and Jacques Westhof, *Legislation du Ruanda-Urundi*, p. 7.

107 Law of 18 October 1908 on Government of Belgian Congo, Moniteur Belge, 19–20 October 1908, pp. 5887–5894; as revised by the law of 29 March 1911, Bulletin Officiel, 1911, p. 358.

108 Filip Reyntjens, *Pouvoirs et Droit au Rwanda*, p. 50.

109 Rene Lemarchand, *Rwanda and Burundi* (New York: Praeger Publishers, 1970), 67.

110 Ibid.

111 "Du point de vue constitutionnel... des agents administratifs ne controlaient pas seulement l'organization burequcratique, mais, dans une large mesure, ils detenaient egalement les domains de la legislation et de l'administration de la justice." Filip Rentjens, ibid., p. 176 and "La separation des pouvoirs etait quasiment inexistante; les libertes publiques n'etait pas integralment guaranties...les conception de democratie etaine bases sur l'echelle des valeurs a poursuivre" ibid., pp. 176–177. "L'Etat colonial etait etait en some un Etat paternaliste et autoritaire." Ibid., p. 177. "Il y avait peu de contact direct entre le resident et les administrateurs.... L'autonomie des administrateurs du point de vue purement executive etait donc grande... les administrateurs etaient des petits vice-rois, jouissant d'une autonomie considerable" ibid., p. 166.

112 Filip Reyntjens, *Pouvoirs et Droit au Rwanda*, p. 149.

113 Ibid.

114 See Article 6–10 of Ordinance of 5 October 1943 on indigenous courts of Ruanda-Urundi, as modified by the Decree of 5 July 1948 (B.O. p. 841) text available in in Pierre Leroy, *Legislation du Ruanda Urundi.*

115 Filip Reyntjens, No. 182.

116 Juridictions indigenes au Rwanda-Urundi, O.L. no. 348, A.I.M.O.

117 See Decree of 5 July 1948 (.B.O. p. 841) in Pierre Leroy, *Legislation du Ruanda Urundi*, p. 137.

118 Filip Reyntjens, *Pouvoirs et Droit au Rwanda*, p. 149.

119 B.O.R.U. 136. P. 116; Filip Reyntjens and Jan F.J. Gorus, *Codes et lois du Rwanda* (Butare: Université nationale du Rwanda, 1979), 69.

120 Vanhove, *Essai de Droit Coutumier du Ruanda*, p. 4.

121 See Proposed Trusteeship agreement for the mandated Territory of Ruanda-Urundi, submitted by the Belgian Government, A/159/Rev.2 of 12 December 1946, text available in Pierre Leroy, Legislation du Ruanda-Urundi, Textes Receullis et Annotes (Usumbura: Les presses Lavigerie 1949), 8.

122 The United Nations and Decolonization, "International Trusteeship System," under "History," www.un.org/en/decolonization/its.shtml (accessed 13 August 2018).

123 Conseil de Tutelle, P.V. Officiels, 4eme session, suppl. No. 2. Rapport de la mission de visite des Nations Unies dans le Territoire sous tutelle du Ruanda-Urundi sous administration belge, 1948, Doc. T/217, pp. 11–13, and p. 58. Cited in Filip Reyntjens, *Pouvoirs et Droit au Rwanda*, p. 214.

124 Rapport sur le Ruanda-Urundi de la mission de visite des Nations Unies dans les territoires sous tutelle de l'Afrique Orientale, 1951, Doc. T/1031, p. 7.
125 Decree of 5 July 1948 organization judiciaire du Ruanda-Urundi, B.O.1948, text available in Pierre Leroy, *Legislation du Ruanda-Urundi*, 35–42.
126 B.O. 1952.
127 Filip Reyntjens, *Pouvoirs et Droit au Rwanda*, pp. 216–217.
128 See the list of all laws introduced by Belgium in Rwanda in Pierre Leroy and Jacques Westhof, *Legislation du Ruanda-Urundi*, pp. 392–420.
129 The first, but largely ineffective, constitution in post-colonial Rwanda was known as the "constitution of Gitarama" and was adopted by all bourgmestres and conseillers communaux on 28 January 1961. This constitution abolished the monarchy and installed the Republic of Rwanda. However, it had no legal force because it was not legalized by any legislative act and was not formally endorsed by the Rwandan people. Kamatali, "Ethnicity and Constitutionalism," p. 117.
130 Ordonnance-Loi of 12 September 1962. Official Gazette, 1962.
131 Filip Reyntjens, *Pouvoirs et Droit au Rwanda*, pp. 358–364.
132 Ibid., pp. 511–512.
133 Ibid., p. 375.
134 See, for example, law of 15 July 1964, instituting the Civil and Commercial Procedure code (J.O. 1964, p. 275); law of 24 August 1962, instituting the Code of Organization and jurisdiction of Courts (J.O. 1962, p. 307); Law of 23 February 1963 on the Organization of the Supreme Court (J.O. 1963, p. 125); Law of 23 February 1963 instituting the Criminal Procedure Code (J.O.1963); Law of 25 March 1963 on the Status of Magistrates (J.O. 1963, p. 199); Law of 30 July 1964 on the Status of Public Prosecutors officers, J.O. 1964, p. 340); Law of 23 November 1963 on the Organization of Communes (J.O. 1963, p. 507).
135 Filip Reyntjens, *Pouvoirs et Droit au Rwanda*, pp. 402–405.
136 See Amendment constitutionnelle du 18 Mai 1973, J.O., 1973, p. 133.
137 Filip Reyntjens, *Pouvoirs et Droit au Rwanda*, pp. 437–444.
138 Ibid.
139 Rwanda, Constitution de la Republique Rwandaise, adopted on December 20, 1978, J.O. 1978, No. 24bis.
140 Filip Reyntjens and Jan F.J. Gorus, *Codes et lois*, pp. 192–218.
141 Ibid., pp. 69–81.
142 Ibid., pp. 88–109.
143 Ibid., pp. 141–183.
144 Ibid., pp. 82–87.
145 For details on the specific mandate of the commission and its work, see www.rlrc.gov.rw.
146 In the explanatory note of the Bill "repealing all legal instruments brought into force before independence," it was stressed:

> There may be potential gaps in relation with the Law on obligations (Decree of 30 July 1888 establishing Book III of the Civil Code related to contracts and conventional obligations as amended to date). However, it is important to note that a legal void is preferable to archaic laws, especially those inherited from colonization. Moreover, there is already a solution provided for in Rwandan law, where the civil procedure allows judges to legislate in addressing an issue not contemplated by written legislation.
>
> Note received by the author on 21 June 2019 (available in the author's records)

2 Homegrown legal concepts and solutions

Gacaca, *Abunzi*, and *Imihigo*

Introduction

Article 11 of the Rwandan Constitution recognizes that "in order to build the nation, promote national culture, and restore dignity, Rwandans, based on their values, initiate home-grown mechanisms to deal with matters that concern them." The same provision goes on to require laws to "establish different mechanisms for homegrown solutions."

Homegrown solutions are strategies and approaches that draw on local knowledge and focus on what works for indigenous rather than what worked for others. The search for homegrown solutions starts with understanding that the challenges facing a country can be easily identified and solved by those facing them.[1] It is therefore about rejecting the "one-size fits all" approach and prioritizing solutions crafted and implemented with attention to unique, local socioeconomic and cultural imperatives. Often, these solutions are rediscovered from the historical practices and values of the community, then adapted to fit contemporary needs.

By 2018, Rwanda had developed at least 10 key homegrown initiatives: (a) *Gacaca* or community courts, (b) *Abunzi* or community mediators, (c) *Imihigo* or performance contracts, (d) *Girinka* or the One Cow per Poor Family Program, (e) *Itorero* or civic education, (f) *Ingando* or solidarity camp, (g) *Ubudehe* or social categorization for collective action and mutual support, (h) *Umuganda* or community work, (i) *umushyikirano* or National Dialogue Council, and (j) *Umwiherero* or National Leadership Retreat.[2]

Like most homegrown concepts, the aforementioned Rwandan legal solutions are expressed in the language of that home: Kinyarwanda; not because it is fashionable or due to pride in keeping these concepts in their original language, but because concepts are better understood if placed in their cultural and historical context. This context is, unfortunately, often lost or misunderstood when concepts are translated into a foreign language. There is a reason, for example, that the concept of *shoah* is lost when it is translated simply as "genocide," a word that has a powerful meaning but does not convey the particularity of the holocaust. English is full of concepts like *grundrecht*, *cour de cassation*, *jihad*, etc., which are better understood if left in their original historical meanings. Also, it is not surprising that most technical concepts, such as those in medical, legal, and political jargon, are better understood if explained using their Latin or Greek origins. A language does not just express meaning; it expresses the history and philosophy behind the meaning. This is why the homegrown legal concepts and solutions discussed in this chapter will be kept in their original Kinyarwanda forms.

This chapter does not intend to cover all 10 of the aforementioned homegrown initiatives. It will only focus on three: namely (1) *Gacaca*, (2) *Abunzi*, and (3) *Imihigo*, which can be qualified as legal concepts and solutions.

Section 1. *Gacaca* as a homegrown legal concept and solution

Criminal justice should not focus solely on choosing between retribution and forgiveness. The pursuit of retribution and non-retributive methods of justice can coexist and even lead to a more comprehensive and socially forward-looking form of justice. *Gacaca* is an illustration that elements of retribution, truth telling, forgiveness, reconciliation, and rehabilitation can coexist in one form of justice. *Gacaca* seeks to reintegrate wrongdoers into their communities rather than removing them. Instead of making criminal justice an exclusive club for lawyers, justice under *Gacaca* seeks to involve the entire community in a less procedural, participatory structure.

To understand *Gacaca* as a homegrown concept, it is important to approach it from its etymological and customary meaning, *and* from the perspective of its application as a solution to post-genocide challenges in Rwanda.

A. Gacaca*: meaning, origins, and development*

1. The meaning in the word

The concept of *Gacaca* comes from the word *agacaca*, meaning "lawn" or "grass." *Agacaca* is low, spread out, and soft enough for people to sit on. Most publications on *Gacaca* courts have used this to explain their origins and character.[3] However, the concept of *Gacaca* as a court reflects more than the place where that court sits. In some cases, it also denotes the activity that it conducts, which is *Gucoca*, meaning to "flatten" or "deconstruct." People sit on *agacaca* so that they can *Gucoca ibibazo*, meaning "examine, discuss, and analyze the issue in depth," with the goal of finding the truth and a satisfactory resolution to the problem at hand. The use of "*agacaca*" as lawn or grass denotes the informal setting where the talk takes place. It denotes also a relaxed and public place where parties conduct a dialogue on equal footing. However, it also involves the activity that takes place in *agacaca*, which includes deconstructing the facts and discussing them in depth with the goal of finding the truth behind the problem or conflict and solving it.

It is not very certain when or how *Gacaca* entered the traditional Rwandan justice system as a legal concept and practice.[4] Most of what we know about customary justice in Rwanda was written after colonialism, often by colonial authorities. However, the focus of these studies has often been on the formal structure and procedure of the customary justice.[5] *Gacaca*'s being informal, decentralized, and not part of the hierarchy of the official court system[6] makes it difficult to know exactly where it fits into the Rwandan customary justice organization and whether it was formalized and identical nationwide, or different regions, communities, or families practiced it differently.

But the fact that we cannot know for sure when *Gacaca* was introduced in Rwanda, the extent to which it was part of the formal justice system, and whether it was practiced similarly across the country does not deprive it of its value. *Gacaca* was widely practiced in Rwanda. Its decentralized, informal, and flexible nature, as well as its role as a truth-seeking and reconciliation mechanism, have made it more popular and better remembered among modern Rwandans than any other pre-colonial customary justice practice.

The formal *Gacaca*, as it is known in post-genocide Rwanda, has evolved in two key phases: The first phase is the customary *Gacaca* that was practiced in pre-colonial Rwanda, which almost disappeared with the formalization and Westernization of the Rwandan judicial system during and immediately after colonialism; the second phase is the formal *Gacaca* courts that were introduced after 1994 as a judicial solution to the impasse that had been reached in the trials on genocide against the Tutsi. It should be highlighted, however, that an administrative *Gacaca* existed between these two phases in the mid-1970s. This short phase allowed local administrative authorities to solve some small conflicts in their jurisdiction with administrative meetings.[7] Because the *Gacaca* type of conflict resolution was more administrative than legal, it will not be discussed in this chapter.

2. Gacaca *as a traditional legal concept*

As discussed in Chapter 1 on the history of Rwandan law, the traditional judicial system of Rwanda was organized at the micro level, meaning at the family level, and the macro level, meaning from the local village courts to the king's Supreme Court. Therefore, family issues were discussed and addressed at the family level before involving outsiders. Village and broader community issues, such as criminal acts and conflicts involving different families, were addressed at the local level before appealing to the highest level of the king's justice.

In traditional Rwanda, the concept of "family" did not mean the nuclear family consisting of a husband, wife, and children. The Rwandan traditional social structure had at its base the *urugo*, understood as a household nuclear family consisting of a man, his wives, and his children as well as those living in that nuclear family, such as helpers. Several *urugo*[8] constituted what was known as *inzu*: a group of households related by blood and sharing a common patrimony. This category included, for example, the *urugo* of a father and *urugo* of his married sons. The concept of family was understood as extended family, *umulyango*, consisting of several *inzu*.

At the helm of the *umulyango* was the chief of family. He played the role of administrator of the family patrimony, which included the patrimony of all the *inzu* under it. He also defined the rules in the family and acted as the judge and the mediator in conflicts involving its members. He also acted as representative and advocate of the family in its external relations.

In the Rwandan tradition, *urubanza*, meaning a public hearing where a decision on an issue had to be taken, was a family business. It did not focus solely on the individual parties. It involved their entire families or *imilyango*. Under customary law, punishment was collective, affecting both the rule breaker and his property, *and* other members of his *urugo*, *inzu*, and *mulyango*. For this reason, families always made sure that, before an issue was exposed outside the family circle or in any public setting, such as to the administrative chiefs of the village or the king, it was addressed within the family (if it was between members of one family) or between the concerned families (if involving members of different families). The recourse to the public or non-family-based remedies came only if families failed to reach a consensus on their own.

Harmony and social peace within a family or between families was at the foundation of Rwandan culture and values. Families avoided going to a formal court at all costs because of the stigma and consequences that such court could bring upon them. Having *urubanza* between families threatened or broke the ties between them and their members. In *urubanza*, the social harmony between these parties and families was often broken, creating animosity that might last for generations. Opting for a court judgment meant a rejection of reconciliation and restoration of social harmony between the families. Furthermore, its public character constituted a humiliation for the losing family and broke any social ties between the families involved. In a society where social ties and dependence were crucial, making an enemy of a neighboring family meant losing that family's support and always feeling unsafe. *Gacaca* was therefore a mechanism for members of the same family or two neighboring families, under the leadership of their heads or leaders, to deal with their differences and safeguard their social harmony to avoid the consequences of addressing their grievances in a formal, non-family-based hearing.[9]

The ultimate goal of *Gacaca* was not to determine the winner or loser. Although sometimes, it was necessary to determine who was at fault, the goal was to create harmony and social peace between families. *Gacaca* intended to discover the truth, reconcile family members in conflict, and socialize the family member who had broken the family rules or traditions. It involved the concept of "*guhana*." Today, this concept is erroneously translated as "to punish." In the Rwandan tradition, however, the form of accountability imposed in *Gacaca* had little connection to retribution or deterrence. "*Guhana*" meant to warn and advise the wrongdoer about the consequences of his actions and rehabilitate him by reintegrating him into the family or community. This does not mean, however, that retributive and deterring punishments did not exist in Rwanda. They existed, and they were very severe, but their jurisdictions often lay outside or beyond *Gacaca*.

In the absence of a centralized judicial system to protect individual rights, families constituted the only source of individual protection. For this reason, individuals feared disappointing their family or losing the trust of their family leaders as this meant losing their protection and falling on the mercy of outsiders. Although *Gacaca* was not based on any specific rules or procedure, fear of the alternative pushed those involved to take it seriously in finding the truth, reconciling the involved individuals or families, and persuading the wrongdoer to beg for forgiveness and accept socialization back into the family.

Gacaca was a participatory justice system chaired or facilitated by the leaders of the families involved in the conflict, giving a voice to all their members. Each one was allowed to speak and contribute to finding the truth of the issue at hand. *Gacaca* decisions were made spontaneously during or at the end of the process. The person at fault could be identified, and the community could decide the extent to which he should be held accountable, both individually and as a member of the family. If a punishment, restitution, or fine was to be imposed, it was immediately paid, and the person found at fault was expected to offer drinks to all those involved in the *Gacaca* process. If it was not possible for the *Gacaca* decision to be executed immediately, the chief of the family or the chiefs of both families in the conflict were responsible for seeing to its execution.

From the above analysis of the traditional *Gacaca*, one can retain two key characteristics of *Gacaca* sessions: First is the fact that these followed no pre-determined procedures and did not make any clear distinction between the quarrelling parties, witnesses, and audiences; and second is the reality that their main objective was to find the truth and prompt reconciliation between members of the community who, after all, shared common values, rules, and destiny.[10]

B. Gacaca *as a legal solution to post-genocide justice challenges*

As discussed in the chapter on Rwandan and international law, *Gacaca* was not the first choice of the country's government when looking for solutions to the challenges of prosecuting suspects of genocide. *Gacaca* was introduced after the failure of the formal criminal justice system, as an alternative intended to speed up genocide trials while contributing to finding truth and building reconciliation among Rwandans.

In this section, we will discuss (1) the process that led to *Gacaca* courts, (2) the law on *Gacaca* and how it evolved, (3) the achievements of *Gacaca*, and (4) the future of *Gacaca*.

1. *From customary* Gacaca *to* Gacaca *courts for genocide cases*

In 1995, the government of Rwanda held in Kigali a high-level international conference to discuss, among other things, strategies to bring perpetrators of genocide to justice and to organize an effective and efficient judicial system in Rwanda, given the challenges of that time.[11] This conference rejected any possibility for amnesty and suggested that perpetrators of genocide be dealt with in accordance with the rule of law and in appropriate formal courts of law.

The conference did not, however, rule out the options of alternative forms of justice. More specifically, it urged that "in cases not involving crime against the person, customary Rwandan procedures such as the *Agacaca* be used, or adapted, to the extent possible."[12] The conference provided the guiding principles that any alternative form of justice would need to follow, noting that such a form should: (1) not be eligible to everyone; (2) require those eligible to come forward, identify themselves, and provide a full and truthful account of their actions, omitting no material detail; (3) place a time limit on those willing to plead guilty; (4) be public and participatory by making accounts by suspects open to the public and allowing witnesses with knowledge of the individuals' roles in the genocide to come forward and provide additional information on them; and (5) make individuals who would come forward subject to accountability as directed by the appropriate authorities after consultation with the victims or the survivors of deceased victims.[13] The forms of alternative justice recommended by the 1995 Urugwiro Conference included: (a) public acknowledgment of their role in genocide; (b) apologies to the victims of their acts, (c) appropriate financial compensation or reparation to the victims of their acts and/or to the community in which their acts took place, taking into account the resources of perpetrator; (d) appropriate labor or service to the community in which their acts took place; (e) education and training on the subject of human rights; and (f) incarceration not exceeding a defined term of years.[14]

The Government, following the recommendations from the above-mentioned international conference, prepared a bill on the Organization of Prosecution for Offenses Constituting the Crime of Genocide or Crimes against Humanity committed since 1 October 1990 and submitted it to the Parliament. The parliament debates that preceded the adoption of the Organic Law No. 08/96 of 30 August 1996, on the Organization of Prosecution for Offenses Constituting the Crime of Genocide or Crimes against Humanity committed since 1 October 1990, proved to the government, however, that members of parliament were not ready for alternative forms of justice. Many members of the Parliament sought a hardline approach to ending impunity through the strict application of criminal law. They complained about the leniency of the bill, mainly because it allowed the categorization of suspects and allowed them to plead guilty and receive lenient punishments.[15] The Government finally succeeded, however, in persuading the Parliament to adopt the above-mentioned Organic Law No. 08/96 of 30 August 1996, containing some elements of alternative forms of justice.

For the following two years, the government put aside any debate on alternative justice options. Rather, it invested all its efforts into making the 1996 Law work effectively. Due to massive support from foreign donors, the prison capacity was tripled, courtrooms and the offices of prosecutors were renovated, and accelerated training of judges and prosecutors was undertaken.[16] The only law school in the country, which, before 1994, had had fewer than 80 students, suddenly admitted around 600. In 1997, the Rwandan Bar Association opened its doors for the first time, and the shortage of lawyers was filled by paralegals and a limited number of foreign lawyers hired by a Belgian Non-Governmental Organization *Avocats Sans Frontieres*. Despite this government effort, however, it was becoming increasingly evident that the problem was not going to be solved by improving the existing justice system and incorporating some elements of alternative forms of justice into it. No amount of improvement was going make the classical judicial system of retributive justice deal with perpetrators of genocide "in accordance with the rule of law in appropriately formed courts of law." With the realities on the field, the Government of Rwanda and the international community were slowly getting persuaded that classical criminal courts were not fit for mass gross human rights violations like genocide.[17]

Two years after the entry into force of the Organic Law No. 08/96 of 30 August 1996, discussions were turning toward whether or not a better alternative would be a form of justice that incorporated some type of formal retributive justice. Already, Rwandan academicians and NGOs had been exploring the role that *Gacaca* could play in the prosecution of genocide. Although studies conducted by these groups did not advocate *Gacaca* as a solution in genocide trials, they acknowledged its potential role in truth- and fact-finding, and in bringing Rwandans together to talk about post-genocide reconciliation.[18] In 1998, after the government had realized that the ongoing system of classical criminal justice not only decelerated the trial of the 135,000 people in prison at that time but also contributed little to the political need for truth and reconciliation among Rwandans, it reopened its exploration of *Gacaca* as an alternative.[19] In October 1998, the "Urugwiro reflection meetings"[20] created a commission with the mandate to study whether *Gacaca* could be adapted to the requirements of criminal trials.[21] Following the report of this commission and the subsequent debates, a blueprint was adopted to serve as the basis for the government bill on *Gacaca* courts. It tried to merge the benefits of the customary *Gacaca*, particularly those related to truth-seeking and community participation, as well as community harmony and reconciliation, with those related to the formal criminal justice system, particularly those related to the court system, law enforcement, and the principles of legality and fair trial.[22]

2. *The law on* Gacaca *and how it evolved*

After long debates and consultations, Rwanda adopted the Organic Law No. 40/2000 of 26 February 2001, setting up and organizing prosecutions for offences constituting the crime of genocide or crimes against humanity committed between 1 October 1990 and 31 December 1994. After this law underwent a minor amendment in 2001,[23] 250 judges known as *Inyangamugayo*[24] were elected at the cell, sector and district levels- the three layers of the local administrative structure of Rwanda that time. Each of the 9,001 cells elected 19 judges, who, in turn, selected representatives from the country's 1,545 sectors. Those at the sector level elected *inyangamugayo* at their respective district level. In 2002, after the *Inyangamugayo* were trained, a pilot phase of *Gacaca* was launched. The assessment of the pilot phase and training[25] led to the abrogation of the 2001 *Gacaca* Organic Law and the Organic Law no.08/96 of 30 August 1996, organizing proceedings for offences constituting the crime of genocide and crimes against humanity, and replacing them with the 2004 *Gacaca* Organic Law.[26] This law, which underwent some amendments in 2007[27] and 2008,[28] will be the basis of this section.

Through *Gacaca* Organic Law, the government sought to achieve truth, reconciliation, and retribution, and to speed up trials. It also sought citizens' participation in the *Gacaca* criminal trials. This is well reflected in the preamble of the 2004 *Gacaca* Organic Law. This stresses that crimes under this Organic Law "were publicly committed in the eyes of the population, which thus must recount the facts, disclose the truth, and participate in prosecuting and trying the alleged perpetrators." It also insisted that to achieve justice and reconciliation in Rwanda, the culture of impunity must be permanently eradicated through "provisions enabling rapid prosecutions and trials of perpetrators and accomplices of genocide, not only with the aim of providing punishment, but also reconstituting the Rwandan Society." The same preamble also advocated that important penalties under *Gacaca* Organic Law allow "the convicted persons to amend themselves and to favor their reintegration into Rwandan society without jeopardizing the people's normal life."

Gacaca law, as conceived by the government, challenged the two dominant schools in transitional justice of that time. The first school believed that, in order to achieve truth and reconciliation and social harmony, forgiveness and amnesty are the right path,[29] while the second school insisted that the best path is evidence-based retributive criminal justice.[30] Through *Gacaca* courts, Rwanda believed that with the right level of participation by citizens, these two goals, often seen as contradictory, could cohabitate. *Gacaca* also challenged the concept of separation of powers or roles in criminal justice: In *Gacaca*, judges also played the role of investigators and prosecutors.

The *Gacaca* approach could have been seen as a gamble or a risky experiment. But after the failure of the Organic Law No. 08/96 of 30 August 1996 to achieve the goals of either of the above-mentioned schools, no experiment seemed to be off limits. *Gacaca* appeared to be a better solution and achieved greater results than the South African approach that traded impunity for national peace[31] or the international criminal justice system that focuses on the criminal prosecution and punishment of a small number of offenders while leaving many unpunished and caring little about national peace and reconciliation.[32]

The *Gacaca* Organic Law kept the two signature innovations incorporated in the 1996 Organic Law: The confession procedure and the categorization of suspects according to the severity of their crimes. These procedures were very important because penalties were based on categorization, while the guilty plea allowed for lenient sentences. The *Gacaca* Organic Law did, however, revise the 1996 categorization. Article 51 of the *Gacaca* Organic Law No. 40/2000 of 26 February 2001 and that of Organic Law No. 16/2004 of 19 June 2004 maintained the 1996 categorization with minor modifications.[33]

In 2007, however, the above-mentioned Article 51 was revised by the Organic Law 10/2007 to move individuals from the categories of zealous murderers, torturers, and dehumanizers to Category 2.[34] The Organic Law 13/2008 revised Article 51 again and moved a number of defendants initially in Category 1 to Category 2 (suspected of incitement to genocide, alleged supervisors and ringleaders of the genocide, and less senior political officials and perpetrators of sexual offenses).[35] The 2008 version inspired new innovations that included: new ratione materiae jurisdiction (Art. 41–43) and sentence (Art. 72–79)[36] as well as categorization (Art. 51), described in the following table:

Category 1: Tried before ordinary courts

a) Any person who committed or was an accomplice in the commission of an offense that puts him or her in the category of planners or organizers of the genocide or crimes against humanity;
b) Any person who was at a national leadership level and that of the prefecture level – public administration, political parties, army, gendarmerie, religious denominations, or in a militia group – and committed crimes of genocide or crimes against humanity, or encouraged others to participate in such crimes, together with his or her accomplice;
c) Any person who committed or was an accomplice in the commission of an offense that puts him or her among the category of people who incited, supervised, or were ringleaders of the genocide or crimes against humanity;
d) Any person who was at the leadership level at the sub-prefecture and commune – public administration, political parties, army, gendarmerie, communal police, religious denominations, or in a militia – who committed any crimes of genocide or other crimes against humanity, or encouraged others to commit similar offences, together with his or her accomplice;
e) Any person who committed the offence of rape or sexual torture, together with his or her accomplice.

Sentence if guilty with no confession or confession rejected	Sentence if guilty with confession during trial or after appearing on the list of suspects	Sentence if guilty with confession before trial or before appearing on the list of suspects	Sentence if minor (14 to 18 years when offense was committed)

(Continued)

Life imprisonment with special provisions	25–30-year prison term; possibility of commuting half to community service	20–24-year prison term; possibility of commuting half to community service	10–20-year prison term if guilty without confession; 8–9-year prison term following confession during trial or 6.5–7.5-year prison term following confession before trial

Category 2: Trial: Sector trial level; appeals: sector appeal level

a) A notorious murderer who distinguished himself or herself in his or her location or wherever he or she passed due to the zeal and cruelty employed, together with his or her accomplice;
b) Any person who tortured another. even though such torture did not result in death, together with his or her accomplice;
c) Any person who committed a dehumanizing act on a dead body, together with his or her accomplice;
d) Any person who committed or was an accomplice in the commission of an offense that puts him or her on the list of people who killed or attacked others, resulting in death, together with his or her accomplice;
e) Any person who injured or attacked another with the intention to kill, though such intention was not fulfilled, together with his or her accomplice.

Sentence if guilty with no confession or confession rejected	Sentence if guilty with confession during trial or after appearing on the list of suspects	Sentence if guilty with confession before trial or before appearing on the list of suspects	Sentence if minor (14–18 years when offence was committed)
10–15-year prison term	6.5–7.5-year prison term; possibility of commuting half to community service and having one-third suspended	6–7-year prison term; possibility of commuting half to community service and having one-third suspended	10–15-year prison term if guilty without confession; otherwise, half of adult sentence; possibility of commuting half to community service and having one-third suspended, except when no confession is made

Category 2: Trial: Sector trial level; appeals: sector appeal level

f) Any person who committed or aided another to commit an offense against another without intention to kill, together with his or her accomplice.

Sentence if guilty with no confession or confession rejected	Sentence if guilty with confession during trial or after appearing on the list of suspects	Sentence if guilty with confession before trial or before appearing on the list of suspects	Sentence if minor (14–18 years when offense was committed)

5–7-year prison term; possibility of commuting half to community service	3–5-year prison term; possibility of commuting half to community service and having one-third suspended	1–3-year prison term; possibility of commuting half to community service and having one-third suspended	Half of adult sentence; possibility of commuting half to community service
Category 3: tried at cell level; (appeals to sector level)			
A person who only committed an offense related to property.			
Sentence if guilty with no confession or confession rejected	**Sentence if guilty with confession during trial or after appearing on the list of suspects**	**Sentence if guilty with confession before trial or before appearing on the list of suspects**	**Sentence if minor (14–18 years when offense was committed)**
Return or compensation, or equivalent community service	Return or compensation, or equivalent community service	Return or compensation, or equivalent community service	Return or compensation, or equivalent community service

Gacaca jurisdictions were competent to try only those in Categories 2 and 3. Those in Category 1 were tried before ordinary courts.

Gacaca jurisdictions were established at the two different administrative levels of Rwanda: The cell level and the sector level.[37] The *Gacaca* court at the cell level had jurisdiction over offenses in the third category (Art. 41). At the sector level, there were two-level *Gacaca* courts. The first level tried offenses in Category 2 and heard appeals on cases tried by the *Gacaca* at the cell level; the second level, known as the *Gacaca* court of appeals, dealt with appeals formed against decisions from the first level sector *Gacaca* (Art. 42).

Each *Gacaca* jurisdiction was made up of a general assembly, a seat (bench), and a coordinating committee (Art. 5).

The general assembly of the *Gacaca* court of the cell was composed of all the cell's residents aged 18 years and above (Art. 6). This assembly was responsible for (1) electing seat members of the *Gacaca* court of the cell; (2) attending the activities of the *Gacaca* court of the cell; (3) discussing and assisting in the census of victims, suspects, and offenses committed in their cell; as well as (4) submitting evidence and testimonies on all persons suspected of having committed the crimes listed in the above-mentioned categories (Art. 33). The general assembly at the sector level was made of members of the seats (judges) of the *Gacaca* court of the cells constituting that sector as well as seats (judges) of the *Gacaca* court of the sector and the *Gacaca* court of appeals (Art. 7). The general assembly at the sector level was responsible for (1) electing judges at the sector level and (2) supervising the functioning of all *Gacaca* courts in the sector, without meddling in their way of conducting proceedings (Art. 35).

The seat or bench of *Gacaca* judges at each level was made up of 14 people: 9 principals and 5 deputies (Art. 8). This number was revised in 2007 by the Organic Law 10/2007, which brought bench numbers to 9 persons.[38] The seat of the *Gacaca* court at the cell level was responsible for (1) establishing, based on the information and discussions of the general assembly, the list of victims, suspects, and acts committed in that cell; (2) receiving confessions, guilty pleas, repentance, and apologies from the persons who had participated in genocide; (3) receiving and recording evidence and testimonies, and other information concerning how genocide was planned and executed; (4) investigating received testimonies; (5) categorizing the accused as per the provision of the Organic Law; (6) trying cases classified in the third category; and (7) forwarding to the *Gacaca* court of the sector the files of the defendants classified in the second category and to the public prosecutors those classified in the first category (Art. 34). The seat of the *Gacaca* court at the sector level was in charge of (1) making investigations, if necessary, on testimonies given; (2) receiving confessions, guilty pleas, repentance, and apologies from genocide perpetrators; (3) judging cases in Category 2; and (4) examining appeals against judgments passed by *Gacaca* courts at the cell level.

The hearing and judgment procedure before *Gacaca* courts depended on whether the court was dealing with (1) a case of confirmed confession, guilty plea, repentance, and apologies; (2) cases that did not involve confessions, guilty pleas, repentance, or apologies, either because the suspect did not plead them or because their plea was rejected by *Gacaca*; or (3) cases in which the defendant had no address or residence in Rwanda.

In the first situation, the following procedure was followed: (Art. 64) (1) The president of the session calls the case and invites defendants to the bar; (2) each defendant establishes his or her identity; (3) the president of the session requests that the plaintiffs identity themselves; (4) the court secretary makes known to the defendant every charge against him or her and reads the minutes of the defendant's confessions; (5) the president of the session asks each defendant to comment on the accusations; (6) any interested person takes the floor to testify in favor of or against the defendant, and the defendant responds to questions put to him or her; (7) the plaintiff describes all the offenses suffered and how they were committed, if he or she has knowledge of them; (8) if the defendant is present, he or she responds to the plaintiff's declarations; (9) the seat of the *Gacaca* court establishes a list of the victims and offenses that each of them suffered, and the defendant is given the floor to respond; (10) the court secretary reads the statement of the hearing, the court checks the conformity of its content with the declarations, and, if need be, the statement of hearing is corrected; (11) the seat asks the plaintiff and the defendant if they have additional information; (12) the parties to the trial and all the others who took the floor during the hearing, together with members of the seat, put their signatures or fingerprints on the statement hearing containing the defendant's confessions; and (13) the hearing is declared closed, unless the seat deems it necessary to postpone it so as to check certain issues.

For those suspects in the second situation (did not confess or plead guilty), an opportunity was given for them to plead guilty or confess. In case they did, the court followed the above-mentioned procedure of Article 64. If they did not, the following procedure was followed: (Art. 65) (a) The president of the session gives the summary of the nature of the case and reads the provided evidences establishing the defendant's guilt; (b) the president of the session asks each defendant to give his or her defense; (c) the court hears witnesses for or against the prosecuted persons and, if need be, hears evidences from the public prosecution if it is summoned to the trial; (d) the defendant gives his or her defense; (e) any interested person takes the floor, and the defendant answers the questions put to him or her; (f) the seat of the *Gacaca* court establishes a list of the victims and the offenses that each of them suffered, and the defendant is given the floor to respond; (g) the secretary of the court reads the statement of hearing, the court checks the conformity of its content with the declarations, and, if need be, the statement of hearing is corrected; (h) the seat asks the plaintiff and the defendant if they have additional information; (i) the parties to the trial and all others who took the floor during the hearing, together with the members of the seat, put their signatures or fingerprints on the statement of hearing; and (j) the hearing is declared closed.

Suspects with no known address or residence in Rwanda were tried in absentia based on available evidence and witnesses (Art. 66).

As mentioned earlier, *Gacaca* sentences were based on the category of the offenders and whether they did or did not confess to their crimes.[39] The sentence also depended on whether the confession was given before or after a defendant appeared on the list of suspects.

Those who committed offenses against property (Category 4) were only sentenced to the civil reparation for what they damaged (Art. 75).

On top of the penalties mentioned above, convicts could incur a loss of civic rights (Art. 76).

In general, the sentences under *Gacaca* courts were more lenient than those under the Rwandan Penal Code. This may have been because, as stressed in the preamble, these penalties were supposed to allow the convicted persons to correct themselves and to favor their reintegration into Rwandan society. This is mainly reflected in the fact that, in most cases, the convict was given an opportunity to spend half of their term in prison, and the rest could be partly suspended and partly commuted into performing community service. Community service, commonly known in Rwanda as "TIG" or *Travaux d'Intérêt General* in French had a very important role and contribution. It contributed to depopulating prisons, made use of convicts' labor for economic development, and fostered convicts' rehabilitation and reintegration. Because community services often consisted of building victims' houses and infrastructure in their villages, TIG served as some form of compensation.[40]

3. *The achievements of* Gacaca

As stated in the Preamble of *Gacaca* law, *Gacaca* courts had a number of objectives. These included uncovering the truth, encouraging Rwandans to participate in prosecuting and trying the alleged perpetrators, eradicating the culture of impunity, contributing to reconciliation in Rwanda, speeding up prosecution and trials, retribution, reconstituting Rwandan society, acting as a homegrown legal solution to genocide, helping convicted persons to repent, and favoring options in which those convicted reintegrated into Rwandan society without jeopardizing social order and harmony. Some of these goals were direct, while others were indirect; some were short term, while others were intermediate or long term. Still, most of them were very ambitious.

There is no doubt that *Gacaca* courts were a homegrown solution. They were created by a law crafted on the basis of a blueprint developed and improved during the "Urugwiro reflection meetings" on issues affecting the country, including post-genocide justice. The traditional *Gacaca* inspired this blueprint and the debates around it. *Gacaca* courts were unique to Rwanda, and their goal was to solve a unique Rwandan problem: Genocide committed by Rwandans against other Rwandans. Neither the *Gacaca* court system, nor any similar approach, had been tried elsewhere in the world. By adopting it, Rwanda challenged the transitional justice schools of that time that saw the solutions as only retributive justice, on the one hand, and truth, forgiveness, and reconciliation, on the other. The architects of the *Gacaca* courts believed that a combination of all these elements was possible and could be effective if combined with citizens' participation at the local level where crimes were committed and if there was good and well-structured coordination by the government. The Rwandan Government tried to achieve this combination from the day the *Gacaca* courts were launched until the day they were ended.

In the over ten years of *Gacaca* trials, almost every Rwandan adult attended *Gacaca* as either a member of the general assembly, judge (*inyangamugayo*), or witness at the cell or sector level. During the initial stages of *Gacaca*, citizens were sensitized to participate in it. Sometimes, authorities required businesses and schools to close on *Gacaca* days to allow citizens to attend the hearings. As citizen participation increased, and people became aware of the value of *Gacaca*, State power or authority did not have to remain actively involved to guide and stimulate participation in *Gacaca*. Participation and social control grew from within.[41] The participation of citizens was a required ingredient in the success of *Gacaca* courts. The broader public organized in the *Gacaca* body of General Assembly did not attend as passive observers; they were active members contributing to finding truth by either reconstituting the facts, serving as witnesses on both sides of the trial, comforting the survivors, or owning the process. Through this participation, survivors got a chance to tell their stories, be heard, and heal, and the information received from the general assembly and the suspects allowed them to discover where their loved ones had been killed and where they were buried. On the other hand, the truth from the *Gacaca* general assembly contributed to exonerating those wrongly accused and making those who were never tried live a life free from fear of collective guilt that risked to continue hanging over them had there not been justice.

By the end of 2001, *Gacaca* courts counted 254,000 judges elected by the general assemblies.[42] Although this number continued to change, these judges were distributed into 9,013 cell courts, 1,545 sector courts, and 1,545 courts of appeal.[43] The significant number of *Gacaca* courts spread around the country, and the involvement of such a large number of judges helped citizens to feel empowered and to have a sense of ownership of Gacaca justice system. It also contributed to the building of a rule of law from the bottom up. All this contributed in reconstituting the Rwandan society on the basis of civic truth, solidarity, and shared memory.

Although it is not possible to evaluate the quality of justice by the number of cases processed alone, *Gacaca* scored high with regard to the number of cases tried, the extraordinarily short period of time that the completion of these trials took, and the modest budget spent on these trials. In their fewer than ten years of operation, *Gacaca* courts completed 1,958,634 cases involving 1,003,227 people:[44] Of these, 60,552 or 3% were in Category 1, 577,528 or 30% were in Category 2, and 1320,554 or 67% were in Category 3. All these cases were completed with an estimated budget total cost of US$46–US$65 million.[45] Comparing the numbers above with those of the International Criminal Tribunal for Rwanda (ICTR) makes the achievements of *Gacaca* stand out even more. In December 2015, when ICTR closed its doors after ten years of operation, it had only concluded proceedings for 80 accused,[46] and during this period had spent more than US$1 billion.[47]

Gacaca also served its retributive purpose. Out of the 318,788 people found guilty under Categories 1 and 2 of the *Gacaca* courts, 92.93% served a prison term sentence, with only 4.84% serving a life sentence. Among those in Category 1, around 17% received a life sentence, around 25% received a prison term between 25 and 30 years, and around 19% received 10–14 years. Among those in Category 2, 2% received life sentences, around 32% received 10–14 years, and around 23% received 15–19 years.[48] On average, 88% of those in Category 1 and 63% of those in

Category 2 were found guilty. All had to serve some form of sentence.[49] As such, *Gacaca* courts did not only achieve their retributive purpose but also contributed to ending the culture of impunity.

However, the retributive nature of *Gacaca* was balanced with some elements of leniency, especially for those who pleaded guilty. The law on *Gacaca* allowed those who pleaded guilty to have part of their sentence commuted and/or suspended: Those in Category 1 who were found guilty following a confession made before trial had to served 20–24-year prison term with the possibility of commuting half to community service, while those found guilty after confession submitted during trial had to serve 25–30 years with the possibility of commuting half to community services. Those in Category 2 (a–e) who were found guilty following a confession submitted before trial faced 6–7 years in prison with the possibility of commuting half to community service and having one-third suspended, while those found guilty after a confession submitted during trial faced 5.5–7.5 years in prison with the possibility of commuting half to community service and having one-third suspended. Those in Category 2(f) found guilty following a confession submitted before trial faced a 1–3 year prison term with the possibility of commuting half to community service and having one-third suspended, while those found guilty after a confession submitted during trial faced a 3–5 years prison term with the possibility of commuting half to community service and having one-third suspended.

It is worth highlighting that in reality most people served less time than that Gacaca had condemned them for. This is due to the following reasons: First, although most of those in Categories both 1 and 2, were condemned of 10 and 14 years in prison, more than one-third of them were able to lessen their time in prison by doing community service[50]; second, those found guilty following a guilty plea benefited of one-third suspension of their sentence; third, the fact that most of those tried in *Gacaca* had been arrested between 1994 and 1999, by the time *Gacaca* courts found them guilty, they had already served more than five years in prison. This period before trial was deducted from the term they were supposed to serve. Commuting and suspending *Gacaca* prison sentences contributed to depopulating Rwandan prisons, improving living conditions in them, saving government resources,[51] and helping the convicted reintegrate sooner into their communities. In 2008, the number of prisoners in genocide-related cases had fallen to 36,987 from 135,000 in 1998.[52]

Gacaca as a restorative justice had also a positive economic impact. Long prison sentences and a high prison population can affect not only the government that had to feed prisoners but also the families of the prisoners and the country's economy in general. While the guilty people are in prison, their families are often deprived of the additional manpower to cultivate and accomplish other income-generating activities. TIG allowed the country to develop a manpower capacity of 91,556 persons[53] who contributed to its economic development[54] but also to helping improve the lives of the victims' communities.[55] Because TIG was organized to allow convicts to divide their time between TIG and working for their families, the latter also benefited. The community service sentence also allowed convicts to improve their communities while gradually reintegrating them and their families.

Gacaca courts, like many court systems and procedures, cannot claim to be a perfect system. The critics of *Gacaca* accused it of not meeting the highest standards regarding the right to counsel, the presumption of innocence, the right to be informed of the case and to have time to prepare a defense, the right to present a defense, the right to testify in one's defense, the right against self-incrimination, protection from double jeopardy, the right to be present at one's own trial, the right not to be arbitrarily detained, the qualification of judges, the burden and standard of proof, and sentencing.[56] It is true that the above standards are the international ideals that every criminal justice system should aim toward achieving. These are, however, standards for ordinary courts and for ordinary offenses in ordinary times. Even in ordinary situations, no criminal justice system can claim to have achieved them all, all the time and in all cases.[57]

Gacaca courts were extraordinary courts, trying extraordinary cases, in an extraordinary period and in an extraordinary situation. They were developed after ordinary criminal justice had proven to be inadequate to deal with the specific problems of genocide. Therefore, *Gacaca* should not be measured on the basis of international standards set for ordinary courts on ordinary cases. Instead, it should be evaluated on the basis of goals set by the law that created it. On this basis, *Gacaca* courts achieved extraordinary results. As Jean de Dieu Mucyo, one of the key architects of *Gacaca*, and the minister of justice during the longest period of its implementation, has said,

> *Gacaca* was not a perfect system, but it was better than the systems that preceded it. It was not the sole and last solution. In case *Gacaca* was to fail, Rwanda was ready to move to the next better solution instead of returning back to the failed solutions.[58]

It may be too early to fully assess the long-term apocalyptic prophecies made by some authors on the impact on *Gacaca*,[59] but more than eight years after the conclusion of *Gacaca* courts, it would be fair to say that their silence proves that the post-*Gacaca* Rwandan society turned out much better than they predicted.

4. *Beyond* Gacaca *courts*

Gacaca courts were ended in 2012 by the Organic Law No. 04/2012/OL of 15 June 2012,[60] which terminated the courts and determined mechanisms for solving issues that were under their jurisdiction.

This Organic Law placed the jurisdiction of trying genocide cases in the hands of ordinary courts (Art. 4 and 5) but placed offenses related to genocide through acts of looting and damaging of property in the hands of the *Abunzi* mediation committees (Art. 6). These committees are not part of Rwanda's formal court system; they are governed by their own laws.[61] The same Organic Law also transferred all documents, audio, videos, and other means used during the *Gacaca* hearings of the *Gacaca* courts to the National Commission to Fight Against Genocide (Art. 19).

The end of the *Gacaca* courts as jurisdictions in charge of trying genocide cases should not mean, however, the end of a tradition and values that have served Rwandans in the pre-colonial era, colonial periods, dictatorship period, and post-genocide Rwanda. *Gacaca* may have ended as courts for genocide cases, but their benefits and success should motivate the government to create a system in which they could be used, if not for situations similar to those in the traditional *Gacaca* then for small cases that require family or community truth, reconciliation, and participation.

Section 2. *Abunzi* as a homegrown legal concept and solution

Like *Gacaca*, the *Abunzi* system finds its origins in Rwandan tradition and values. The *Abunzi* system is now a constitutional organ. Article 141 of the Rwandan Constitution provides that "the *Abunzi* Committee is responsible for conciliating parties in conflict with the aim of consolidating national unity and peaceful coexistence among Rwandans."

In this section, we will discuss "*Abunzi*" in the context of the traditional Rwandan justice system; the rationale behind its reintroduction into the Rwandan justice system; and, finally, how the contemporary *Abunzi* system has evolved within the positive Rwandan law.

A. Abunzi *under the traditional Rwandan legal system*

The term "*Abunzi*" is often translated in English as "mediators."[62] However, this translation misses how etymologically, philosophically, and technically different these two concepts are. The term "mediator" comes from the Latin "mediatorem," which comes from the verb "mediare," meaning "to halve" or "to be in the middle." "Mediator" in Kinyarwanda should be translated as "*umuhuza*." This fits better with its English definition as a person who stands between parties in conflict, not to propose or suggest a solution but to help them find a solution to their dispute by themselves.

Abunzi are more than mediators. They are people who practice the "*kunga*," meaning to rejoin or reconnect something broken. This term finds its origins in the traditional Rwandan medical procedure of "kunga," consisting of rejoining or reconnecting a broken bone. In this traditional medical profession, *Abunzi* were the traditional healers specialized in the technique of "*kunga*". By borrowing this term from medical practice and applying it in the area of conflict resolution, Rwandans seemed to approach a conflict as a broken bone that needed to be reconnected, using, as is done in medicine, metal screws, pins, rods, and plates to hold the bone in place until it can heal and become whole again.

In terms of modern conflict resolution techniques, this approach is much closer to the conflict transformation theories championed by John Paul Lederach in the sense that traditionally, "kunga" focused not only on the issue or the immediate cause of the conflict but also on transforming the relational and structural causes behind the conflict.[63] In this sense, the closest meaning to *Abunzi* could be "conciliators"[64] in the sense that both *Abunzi* and conciliators go beyond the issue or problem at hand to address the relationship between those involved.[65] Like the traditional healer *Abunzi*, whose success was measured by whether the broken bone healed, the conciliator *Abunzi*'s success required more than reconciliation; it required healing the relationship between the parties in conflict. In other words, *Abunzi* did not seek "minimal reconciliation" but rather a "maximal reconciliation" or total transformation.[66] Borrowing from the three paradoxes articulated by John Paul Lederach,[67] *Abunzi*, as maximalist conciliators, first "promote an encounter between the open expression of the painful past, on the one hand, and the search for the articulation of a long-term, interdependent future, on the other hand." Second, they "provide a place for truth and mercy to meet, where concerns for exposing what has happened and for letting go in favor of renewed relationship are validated and embraced." Third, they "organize the need to give time and place to both justice and peace, where redressing the wrong is held together with the envisioning of a common, connected future." It is within the above philosophy and techniques that the system of *Abunzi* in Rwandan tradition should be understood.

In this tradition, the procedure of *Abunzi* was called upon whenever *Gacaca* failed to solve the problem between families in conflict. In other words, the failure of *Gacaca* meant that if a family (in cases where the issue was within one family) or families (in cases where the issue was between members of different families) could not resolve the conflict, the problem was deeper, and it had already affected the family members or families' relationships. It therefore threatened the broader community subsystem or even the system itself, and justified the intervention of the village chief who, through the process of *kunga* undertook to rejoin or reconnect the broken relationship between the concerned families and thus help them heal. In other words, before going to the formal court system, where the hearing would be held before the administrative officials, whose goal would be to preserve the broader community subsystem or system structure, parties still had the opportunity to deal with their conflict informally through the *Abunzi*. *Abunzi* were the last chance for families to salvage their relationships and avoid a potentially harsh and merciless trial, and possible punishment by the formal system on both the individual parties in conflict and their respective families.

Often, the *Abunzi*'s conclusion resulted in the parties' reconciling. In cases where the *Abunzi* failed to lead the concerned parties to reconciliation, two consequences resulted: First, the family or families could consider the recalcitrant party who had refused or resisted the *Gacaca* and thereafter the *Abunzi* solutions as an outcast, uniting against him and giving up on him, letting him face alone the consequences of formal justice. Alternately, the family or families would be further divided based on the position of each elder involved in the *Abunzi* process. In this case, each side would accompany and support before the formal court the party they believed was right, well aware that by acting and speaking on behalf of the party they believed deserved their support, they also exposed themselves, either directly or indirectly, to punishment their client had to face from the formal court.

Just like other traditional institutions, the system of *Abunzi* lost its significance under colonization. It became more and more informal and slowly died a natural death as colonialists and then post-independent dictatorial political systems degraded the values of the traditional Rwandan society.

B. *From the traditional* Abunzi *to the* Abunzi *Committee as a constitutional organ*

As discussed in the section on *Gacaca*, between May 1998 and March 1999, high-level meetings were held every Saturday in the Office of the President of the Republic of Rwanda in *Urugwiro* to reflect on issues affecting the country during that difficult period. It was in these meetings that the resolution to revive and revise the traditional *Gacaca* to deal with genocide cases was taken. These meetings looked, however, beyond the issue of justice for genocide cases. In this regard, participants regretted that the Rwandan legal and justice system, which was mostly borrowed from abroad, focused more on punishing than on correcting and reconciling people. It was observed, for example, that the formal trial system that existed in Rwanda was leading to division and hatred between individuals or families and was less concerned with reconciliation and agreement between parties.[68] It was therefore recommended that Rwanda reexamines this problem and determine how its law could be based on "the Rwandan culture and value of equity and morality."[69]

The need for a justice system focusing on reconciliation and agreement between parties was met in the 2003 Rwanda Constitution. Article 159 stated, "There is hereby established in each Sector an *Abunzi* Committee responsible for mediating between parties for certain disputes involving matters determined by law prior to the filing of a case with the court of first instance." The language of this Article, together with the fact that it was included in the section of the Constitution related to the judiciary, gave the impression that the Constitution intended *Abunzi* to be part of the Judiciary. The *Abunzi* Committees were intended to be a community mediation and dispute determination service. Their goal was to resolve conflicts and improve relationships, something the more formal court system was less suited to. Although described as "mediation" committees, *Abunzi* were empowered to make legal determinations when they were unable to facilitate a settlement between the parties.[70] The 2015 Constitution, however, moved the organ of the *Abunzi* from the Judiciary to the Executive.[71] This change was aimed at correcting the perception *Abunzi* had developed in the early days of their job, when they acted more as judges than as conciliators. By removing them from the Judiciary, the Constitution seemed to emphasize that their role was first and foremost as conciliators more than judges, and was intended to unite involved parties rather than stigmatize them as guilty or innocent.

Following the 2003 Constitutional decision to create the *Abunzi* Committees, in 2004, the parliament adopted the Organic Law Determining the Organization, Jurisdiction, Competence, and Functioning of *Abunzi* Committees.[72] Article 2 of this Organic Law defined *Abunzi* as an "organ meant for providing a framework for mandatory mediation prior to filing cases in courts hearing at first instance cases related to matters listed ... in Articles 7 and 8 of this organic law." Article 7 listed minor civil issues such as cases related to land, cattle, and breach of contract not exceeding the value of 3 million Rwandan francs (3,000,000 RWF) as well as cases related to family and succession. Meanwhile, Article 8 listed minor criminal matters, such as insults, removing or displacing boundaries of land and plots, harmful accusations, stealing crops, etc.

The 2004 *Abunzi* Organic Law placed *Abunzi* Committees at the sector level only. This was revised in 2006, moving the jurisdiction of the *Abunzi* to the cell level.[73] In 2010, it was further realized that moving *Abunzi* Committees at the cell level was not enough; a new Organic Law established them at both the Cell and Sector levels. The latter served as the appeal level for the Cell level *Abunzi* decisions.[74] These two-level *Abunzi* Committees were maintained and built upon by the 2015 Organic Law, modifying and complementing the 2010 *Abunzi* Organic Law,[75] and again in 2016, when a new law determining the organization, jurisdiction, competence, and functioning of the *Abunzi* Committee[76] was adopted.

The development and improvement of the *Abunzi* Committees through the 2006, 2010, and 2016 laws affected more than their territorial jurisdiction. Since its incorporation into the Rwandan legal system in 2004, the legislation determining the organization, jurisdiction, competence, and functioning of the *Abunzi* Committee has been updated and improved as needs required. For example, labor contracts were first excluded in the *Abunzi* Organic Law of 2004, then included in the 2006 *Abunzi* Organic Law before being removed again in the 2016 Law. The 2004 *Abunzi* Organic Law, as revised and modified until 2016, had placed some minor criminal offenses under the *Abunzi* jurisdiction. However, the 2016 *Abunzi* excluded all criminal matters from *Abunzi* jurisdictions, leaving them only civil matters. Also, while the 2004 Organic Law required *Abunzi* to submit their conclusions/briefs within ten days of their hearing, this number was increased to thirty days in the 2006 Organic Law before being reduced again to ten days in the 2010 Organic Law.

As said earlier, the *Abunzi* Organic Law underwent a number of modifications and improvements, mainly in 2006, 2010, 2015, and 2016. The 2016 Law will be discussed in the next section. It is worth highlighting here, however, that the goal in modifying the 2015 Organic Law was mainly to correct the problems left unsolved by the 2010 Organic Law and to bring it into compliance with the Organic Law No. 04/2012 OL of 15/06/2012, terminating *Gacaca* Courts and determining mechanisms for solving issues that were under their jurisdiction. (Article 6 of this 2012 Organic Law had placed offences related to looting and the damaging of property and offences that were within the jurisdiction of *Gacaca* Courts under the *Abunzi* Committee.) Article 4 (17) of the 2015 Organic Law provided that Mediation Committees at the Cell level would have jurisdiction to determine cases relating to "acts of looting or damaging of property which are not adjudicated by *Gacaca* Courts, committed between October 1, 1990 and December 31, 1994 irrespective of the value of the property looted, whether they were committed by civilians, gendarmes, or soldiers." The 2015 modified Organic Law had also increased further the criminal jurisdiction of the *Abunzi* Committee.[77]

It appears that, as in the case of *Gacaca*, the translation of the traditional practice of *Abunzi* into a modern law was not an easy process. The practice of "kunga" was not an invention of the 2003 Constitution. The former reflected a practice that already existed informally in the Rwandan tradition. However, its formalization into the positive Rwandan law needed to be handled with care, especially making sure that the philosophical and cultural meaning of "kunga" was well reflected in the legal terminology and system of Rwanda's positive law. The effort made to reach this perfection is reflected in the number of times *Abunzi* law was drafted, redrafted, amended, and updated. As said earlier, the idea was incorporated in the 2003 Constitution, and its implementing legislation was immediately adopted in 2004. This law underwent some extensive and minor changes, in 2006 and 2010, when a new law on *Abunzi* was adopted. The 2010 Law was again modified, amended, and complemented in 2015. In 2016, a new *Abunzi* law was adopted, abrogating the 2010 Law, as amended so far. This is the law that will be discussed in the following section.

C. *Organization, jurisdiction, and functioning of the* Abunzi *Committee*

The *Abunzi* system in Rwanda is currently regulated by the Law N° 37/2016 of 08/09/2016 Determining Organization, Jurisdiction, Competence, and Functioning of an *Abunzi* Committee.[78] This defines an *Abunzi*

Committee as an organ responsible for conciliating parties involved in disputes under its jurisdiction (Art. 4) It establishes *Abunzi* Committees at the Cell level, with jurisdiction over the Cell, and *Abunzi* Committees at the sector level. The latter have the jurisdiction to hear appeals on decisions by *Abunzi* of the cell level (Art. 2) The *Abunzi* are not paid; they perform their responsibilities on a voluntary and non-remunerative basis (Art. 4).

1. *The organization of the* Abunzi *Committee*

At the cell and sector levels, an *Abunzi* Committee comprises seven (7) persons, who must be people of integrity,[79] residents of the cell or the sector where they running to be elected as *Abunzi*, and well known for their conciliation skills. The cell council or the sector council elects members of the *Abunzi* Committee for a renewable term of five (5) years. A person cannot be elected if they are a high official, a cabinet member, a parliamentarian, a member of the judiciary, security services, a local administration organ, or performing any other duties that the law considers incompatible with the *Abunzi*'s role. The law requires that at least thirty percent (30%) of members of the *Abunzi* Committees be women (Art. 6–7). *Abunzi* must take an oath of office before starting their function (Art. 8).

After their election at the cell or sector level, each *Abunzi* Committee elects its bureau, composed of a chairperson and a vice chairperson. The bureau's responsibility is to supervise and coordinate the activities of the committee as well as the conduct of its members. The conduct of *Abunzi* is guided by a code of conduct determined by the Minister of Justice (Art. 31). The responsibility of the bureau to give instruction and necessary advice to its members does not involve or mean giving instruction to the *Abunzi* panels on how to settle a dispute referred to it (Art. 9). *Abunzi* panels are required to be guided by the law, facts, and their conscience when making their decision on the cases before them.

2. *The jurisdiction of the* Abunzi *Committee*

The 2016 *Abunzi* law removed all criminal matters from *Abunzi* jurisdiction. These cases are now under the jurisdiction of ordinary courts. With regard to civil matters, the law gives the *Abunzi* Committee at the cell level jurisdiction over:

1 Movable and immovable assets, and succession thereto, where their value does not exceed 3 million Rwandan francs (Frw 3,000,000);
2 A breach of contract between individuals, if its value does not exceed 3 million Rwandan francs (Frw 3,000,000); and
3 Family issues, other than those requiring rendering a decision on civil status. (Art. 10)

In cases involving territorial conflict of jurisdiction, the determination is decided based on any of the following criteria: (1) The *Abunzi* Committee in the territorial jurisdiction of the subject matter, (2) the *Abunzi* Committee of the respondent's place of residence if the subject matter is movable property, or (3) the *Abunzi* Committee of the applicant's place of residence through mutual agreement with the respondent. However, where the summoned person has no known identification or place of domicile or residence in Rwanda, the dispute is referred to the relevant court. In no way may disputes involving the State, its organs, or associations and companies with legal personality, whether private or public, be referred to an *Abunzi* Committee (Art. 11).

With regard to disputes involving land property located in different territorial jurisdictions, the competent *Abunzi* Committee is determined as follows: (1) The *Abunzi* Committee that has jurisdiction over the location of the portion of land and in which both parties reside is competent to settle the dispute. However, (2) when both parties do not reside in the same jurisdiction, the *Abunzi* Committee that has jurisdiction over the location of the portion of land in which one of the parties resides is competent to settle the dispute. Finally, (3) when both parties do not reside in the same jurisdiction where the land is located, the *Abunzi* Committee having jurisdiction over the location of the bigger portion of the land is competent to settle the dispute (Art. 12).

3. *The procedure for selecting the* Abunzi *bench, hearing the dispute, and conciliating the parties*

Parties do not refer their dispute directly to *Abunzi*; their disputes must be submitted, either verbally or in writing, to the executive secretary of the cell or sector, who registers them before submitting them to the *Abunzi* Committee. This is the extent to which the executive secretary of the cell or sector is involved in the work of the *Abunzi* Committee. In no case does the Secretary get involved in the hearing or any other decisions of the *Abunzi* Committee. It is the responsibility of the *Abunzi* Committee to summon the parties; to decide on the venue, day, and time of consideration of the dispute; and to hear the case, free from any administrative or judicial interference (Art. 13).

The law requires that a summoned person appearing before *Abunzi* be given a period of at least seven (7) days and that the summons briefly describe the dispute, venue, date, and time of the hearing (Art. 14).

Although the *Abunzi* Committee is made up of seven people, they are not all involved in the bench hearing a specific dispute. Also, the bench is not predetermined before the hearing. On the day of the first hearing, parties are invited to agree on three *Abunzi*, out of the seven members of the Committee, to whom they want to refer their dispute. In case the parties fail to agree on the three *Abunzi*, the two opposing parties are invited to choose one *Umwunzi*[80] each. The two selected *Abunzi* choose the third. In cases where parties agree on only one *Umwunzi,* the latter chooses the other two from the Committee. Parties have no right to refuse the *Umwunzi* or *Abunzi* chosen following this procedure. The *Abunzi* bench chooses from among its members a chairperson and a rapporteur. The latter must, of course, be literate (Art. 15).

The *Abunzi* session is public. It can, however, be held behind closed doors, as decided by the *Abunzi* on their own initiative or upon request, based on the nature of the dispute. Members of the *Abunzi* Committee that are not chosen to examine the dispute may participate in any conciliation session without the right to vote.

During the conciliation process, *Abunzi* hear from each party and from witnesses when available. *Abunzi* may also seek advice from any other person who is aware of the dispute or issue under consideration. Parties may be assisted by lawyers, but they cannot be represented or pleaded for. During the conciliation session, the *Abunzi* help both parties reach a compromise. When parties fail to do so, the *Abunzi* are required to render their decision in accordance with the law, the culture of the place where the dispute is being settled, and their own conscience, provided the decision is not contrary to written law. (Art. 17) The *Abunzi* decision is made by consensus or, where there is no such consensus, an absolute majority of votes (Art. 20). The *Abunzi* bench must settle the dispute within one month of the day the dispute is registered on the list of disputes of the *Abunzi* Committee (Art. 17). The concerned parties must be informed of the verdict of the *Abunzi* within five days of the day on which it was made.

The Verdict agreed upon by all parties becomes binding between the parties but cannot be enforceable against a third party (Art. 22). Any party that is not satisfied with the verdict of the *Abunzi* Committee at the Cell level may appeal it before the Sector level within 30 days of the day of its notification. The *Abunzi* Committee at the Sector level shall examine only the points challenged by the applicant that the appellant did not accept before the *Abunzi* Committee at the Cell level (Art. 25).

Any party that is not satisfied with the verdict of the *Abunzi* Committee at the Sector level may refer the matter to a competent primary court. This Court shall consider only those points of the verdict challenged by the applicant and to which the applicant raised objections before the *Abunzi* Committee (Art. 28).

4. *The effectiveness and impact of the* Abunzi *Committee*

The *Abunzi* Committee may be providing justice, but it is not part of the judiciary. Article 33 of the 2016 *Abunzi* law places their activities under the executive branch and, more specifically, under the supervision of the Ministry of Justice. It is this Ministry, through its access to justice Department, that supports the *Abunzi* in the performance of their duties through trainings and by supplying them with equipment, and which, in collaboration with the Ministry in charge of local government, monitors their activities.

In 2018, the country counted 171,941 individual *Abunzi*, grouped into 2,563 *Abunzi* Committees: 2,147 Committees at the cell level and 416 at the sector level.[81] The gender representation in the *Abunzi* Committee was 55.7% men and 44.3% women.[82] The number of cases brought before the *Abunzi* has been significantly increasing. During the fiscal year 2014/2015, *Abunzi* Committees received 40,111 cases; in 2015/2016, they received 47,960 cases. In 2016/2017, they received 51,016 cases, including 45,503 civil cases and 5,513 criminal cases. In these 3 years, the number of cases increased by 27%.[83] Of the 51,016 cases received in 2016/2017, the *Abunzi* Committee completed 49,138 (96.3%), representing 38,777 (76%) cases at the cell level and 10,361(20.3%) at the sector level.[84]

Critics may question why the Constitution has placed the "*Abunzi* Committee" organ under the executive branch rather than under the judiciary branch: Because this is an independent organ, like courts or because it is a semi-independent organ, like the Office of the Ombudsman, the National Unity and Reconciliation Commission, etc., all of which also operate under the executive power. This criticism may be relevant, but it should be examined together with other factors. After all, even if *Abunzi* Committees could be considered as courts, they would not be the first courts in the world to be under the Executive Branch and still maintain their independence.[85]

The job performance of *Abunzi* is highly ranked by the Rwandan population. A study conducted in 2012 by the Rwanda Governance Board (RGB) found that public confidence in *Abunzi* is overall at 75%, with 77.4% at the sector level and 74% at the cell level.[86] The same study found that citizens ranked *Abunzi* Committees higher than ordinary courts on the following criteria: (1) reduction of time spent in settling cases, (2) their cost-effectiveness, (3) their capacity to mitigate conflicts between parties, (4) their participatory approach, and (5) the freedom for parties to choose their mediators.[87] The 2018 Report Card[88] found that 80% of the population was satisfied with the *Abunzi* Committees' performance.[89]

Section 3. *Imihigo* as a homegrown legal concept and solution

In 2007, the Rwandan Government reintroduced and modernized "*imihigo*" as a management tool for economic development and poverty reduction.[90] It was defined as a "performance contract." The legal concept of *Imihigo*, like *Gacaca* and *Abunzi*, however, is hard to box into existing English legal terminology. Translating *Imigiho* as performance contract does not capture its entire and original meaning; instead, it limits the meaning of *Imihigo* to the context or activity it was applied to when the government reintroduced this old Rwandan traditional legal concept. Yet *Imihigo* is a much broader concept that goes beyond its recent publicized application in the political and economic fields.

Imihigo (or *umuhigo* in the singular) derives from the verb "*guhiga*," meaning "to challenge a competitor for better performance and results." Understanding the *Imihigo* as a legal concept requires one to first examine its etymological meaning in the Rwandan tradition, and then analyze it using theories of contract law, before applying it in practice to different fields, such as political, economic, and even social aspects of the national, family, and individual life of Rwandans.

A. *Imihigo as a traditional Rwandan Concept*

The definition and scope of what constituted a traditional *Imihigo* varies: As one study has recently concluded, while for some suggest that *Imihigo* was simply a public vow; others argue that it has a basis in war, where warriors would throw a spear into the ground and publicly proclaim the feats they would accomplish in battle.[91] Both meanings should, however, be understood as complementary rather than contradictory or conflicting.

To understand the concept of *Imihigo* in the traditional historical context of Rwanda, one has to appreciate the concept and importance of its pre-colonial social army structure. As discussed in the chapter on the history of Rwandan law, each Rwandan, whatever his or her social or economic condition, had to belong to an army. The rights and duties of each individual, family, and patrilineage depended on their membership and position in the army. However, this role was not limited to combat. It was a corporation whose members could be mobilized not only for military duties but also for economic and social duties. It was a social army. *Imihigo* was introduced around the sixteenth century as a traditional practice of social army leaders making public pledges to the King to engage in specific challenges, mainly military-based.[92] One of the events or practices of social armies was organizing "*inkera z'imihigo*" or vigil of *Imihigo*.[93] The most well-known vigils were organized on the eve of an important army expedition, when each combatant, starting with the head of the unit, reiterated his past prowess and how bravely he and his troops would perform in the upcoming battle publicly, in front of the king, his commanders, and the whole army or militia. As such, he not only challenged himself but also affirmed the courage and commitment of the warriors of his militias. *Imihigo* were not just empty shows of promises; they were founded on past experiences and expertise, and were not only ambitious but also realistic.

The traditional meaning of the concept of *Imihigo* could also be understood in terms of how it was adopted by a number of social army militias to describe themselves. Alexis Kagame, who documented pre-colonial militias in Rwanda,[94] has tried to translate *Imihigo* into French as "*hauts faits,*" meaning great achievements. For example, the *Ingangurarugo* social army created by King Kigeli IV Rwabugiri in 1854 had a Unit named *inshoza-mihigo*, translated as "instigators of great achievements."[95] The *Abashakamba* social army created by Yuhi IV Gahindiro in 1746 had a Unit named *imbungira-mihigo* or "the seekers of the great achievements."[96] There was even a complete social army named *imbanza-mihigo* or "the inaugurators of great achievements." This army was created by Chief Ntizimira under the reign of Kigeli IV Rwabugiri.[97] Other social armies or Units include "*abakera-mihigo*" or "those radiant to the announcement of great achievements."

The meaning of the concept of *Imihigo* could also be understood not from the act itself but from those conducting it. Using again the concept of social armies, Alexis Kagame has defined *Abahizi* or those involved in *Imihigo* as challengers or antagonists. This expression was, for example, used in translating the social army, created in 1675 by King Cyilima II Rujugiro, named *Rwasababizi*. "*Rwasa*" comes from the verb "*kwasa*," meaning "chopping into pieces," or "strike" and "*abahizi*," which is derived from "*guhiga*," meaning "antagonists or challenger."[98] The social army named *Intaganzwa* (undefeatable) created during the reign of King Yuhi IV Gahidniro (1746-?) had a Unit named *Imbabaza-bahizi* or "those who hurt rivals." King Yuhi V Musinga (1897–1931) created a militia named *Incogoza-bahizi*, meaning "those who demoralize rivals."[99] It should also be noted that the last king of Rwanda, Mutara (1931–1959), had a last name, Rudahigwa (which has as rood "*guhiga*"), meaning "the one with no rival."

From the above historical context the concept of "Imigiho" seems to be understood as "great achievements," and its action verb, "*guhiga*," seems to be understood as "compete" or "rivalry." *Imihigo* could therefore mean competitions between rivals to score the greatest achievements possible.

B. Imigiho *as a contract and a covenant*

Black's *Law Dictionary* defines a contract as "an agreement between two or more parties creating obligations that are enforceable or otherwise recognizable at law." William Anson defines contract as three different things, one of which is "a series of operative acts by the parties resulting in new legal relations."[100] Rwandan contract law, which is inspired by the civil law legal system, defines contract as a convention by which one or several persons commit to one or several others to give, to do, or not to do something (Art. 1).[101] It also creates key characteristics to use when categorizing contracts. Contracts can be unilateral, synallagmatic, or bilateral (Art. 2 and 3); they can be commutative or aleatory; (Art. 4) and they can be charitable and onerous (Art. 5 and Art. 6).

Imihigo meets some key characteristics of contracts, as broadly defined by the above three sources, in the sense that it is an act by parties that results in legal relations. Also, *Imihigo* may have some elements of each of the six categories of contracts under Rwandan law, but it is hard to box it into just one of them. An *Imihigo* contract borrows some elements of a unilateral contract in the sense that it commits only the party who sets the goal but also presents some elements of a synallagmatic contract in the sense that it involves many parties. It is also commutative in the sense that some of its elements are certain but also aleatory in the sense that they are uncertain. It has charitable elements in the sense that the performer does not necessarily expect payment, but it also contains some onerous elements in the sense that the winner of *Imihigo* usually gets some kind of reward.

The concept of *Imihigo* can be understood more as a covenant than as a contract in the sense that the setting of challenging targets and the vow to achieve them engages the one or the team who made them, independently of whether other parties or potential parties perform their part or not. *Imihigo* is undertaken as a test of one's bravery and in a competitive spirit. It is like a solemn public vow by a team captain at the beginning of a season to perform not only better than they did in the last season but also better than their rivals in the competition. Because *Imihigo* is not just rhetoric, it involves not only an obligation of means but also the obligation of result. Parties in *Imihigo*, therefore, not only have the duty to prove that they have a specific goal, a strategy, and monitoring and evaluation tools; they also have the obligation to deliver the result they promised. *Imihigo* is both a contract of performance and a contract of result.

In Ancient Rwanda, *Imihigo* consisted of publicly setting challenging targets and committing oneself or one's team to their achievement. The contractual obligation therefrom found its binding source not just in the consent or declaration of the parties involved in the challenge but from the setting in which this declaration or consent was expressed: In front of the public, wise elders, family, community, or one's peers. The fear of shame or losing the trust of the public, the elders, and one's family and community was the force behind everyone's motivation to live up to their declared goal. As one's individual honor is connected to that of his family, community, and peers, fighting for it was akin to fighting for one's family's, community's, and kin's honor. An individual reward was the reward of his entire community, while an individual defeat was a shame of his entire community. In modern society, the public declarations of *Imihigo* are not enough; *Imihigo* are evidenced in signed documents by those involved in their performance. It should be underlined, however, that just as in a marriage, the signing of a marriage contract is not what makes a marriage, the signing of an *Imihigo* contract is not what makes *Imihigo*. In both cases, the contract is not a commitment but an evidence of one.

C. *From the traditional to the contemporary* Imihigo *practices*

The idea of reintroducing the concept of the *Imihigo* contract developed from the evaluation of the first phase of Rwanda's Poverty Reduction Strategy (PRSP: 2003–2005). This evaluation revealed that targets for poverty reduction were not well set; activities were not well prioritized;

and sequenced and policy coordination, monitoring, and evaluation were weak.[102] In 2006, consultations were conducted on how to improve the performance-management system, planning tools, and oversight mechanism for the new Economic Development and Poverty Reduction Strategy (EDPRS: 2008–2012).[103]

The reintroduction of the traditional *Imihigo* was identified as a solution to improve economic development and poverty-reduction strategies. The idea was inspired by a spontaneous exchange that took place in March 2006, when newly elected district mayors gathered around the President of the Republic to discuss how their work in their district fit into the government's national development plans. During this session, one mayor, high-spirited and boasting of his success and that of his district during his term in office, vowed that his district would be the best-performing district in the country. Another mayor quickly countered him in a challenge that he would outperform everyone.[104] One elder in the group reminded everyone that this exchange reminded him of the *Imihigo* exchange of traditional Rwanda. President Kagame, who was chairing the meeting, took this opportunity to challenge all the mayors present to come up with an *Imihigo* for their districts that he could follow up on to evaluate whether the claimed targets were achieved.[105] *Imihigo* were hence introduced as a contract between district mayors and the president of the Republic.[106] The idea was later generalized, expanding *Imihigo* contracts between the public and the government, and linking the allocation of public expenditure to published targets, with the aim of delivering modern, responsive public service. All line ministries and public agencies were then required to sign a formal *Imihigo* agreement based on EDPRS sector priorities, stating the time-bound outputs that would be delivered in return for their budgetary allocation. Progress toward these targets was to be monitored annually through progressive assessment, analysis, and feedback.[107]

Although the reintroduction of *Imihigo* began with mayors and was later extended to all public sectors, its philosophy and guiding principles expanded beyond the public sector. Today, private sectors, communities, families, and individuals adopt the *Imihigo* approach in setting challenging targets and vowing to achieve them, outperforming their own previous targets as well as those of their competitors. The sense of competitiveness imbedded in *Imihigo* helps organizations to drive up the performance levels of managers and team leaders. It not only focuses on achieving the promised outcome but incorporates elements similar to those of the Human and Institutional Capacity Development (HICD) championed by USAID in the sense that it (1) considers the institutional context and requires the agreement of stakeholders; (2) defines desired performance in measurable terms; (3) assesses and deals with the root causes of performance gap; and (4) selects, implements, monitors, and evaluates performance solutions.[108]Also, as the success of HICD requires a change champion,[109] the leader making the *Imihigo* pledge becomes the champion of the change or the action they promised. Unlike HICD, however, under *Imihigo*, the champion is often the team leader or captain, and the performance is not only measured against the goals set by the team involved but also, in a competitive spirit, against the performances and goals set by other teams in the same league.

Today, *Imihigo* covenants are becoming part of the modern Rwandan legal system, borrowing from both modern contract law and the traditional Rwandan legal philosophy, creating a unique type of contract or better, a covenant. With this development, it is high time that law schools start teaching *Imihigo* as part of their courses on contracts.

Notes

1 Chukwumerije Okereke and Patricia Agupusi, *Homegrown Development in Africa: Reality of Illusion?* (London: Routledge, 2015), 3.
2 Rwanda Governance Board, 2017, "Homegrown Initiatives," Rwanda Governance Board, www.rgb.rw/index.php?id=134 (accessed January 15, 2019).
3 *Dictionary of Genocide* (London: Greenwood Press, 2008), s.v. "gacaca?"
4 But see also "Rwaciriwe I Mutakara, ubutabera bubereye u Rwanda Twifuza," a white paper developed by the Rwandan Justice Sector, September 2017. Unpublished. Hereinafter "Rwaciriwe I mutakara." This paper argues that the traditional justice principle of Gacaca and Abunzi were introduced under King Cyilima Rugwe, who reigned in Rwanda between 1345 and 1378.
5 For example, see J. Vanhove's *Essai de Droit Coutumier du Rwanda, Memoire couronne au Councours Annuel de 1940* (Brussels: Library Falk fils, 1941).
6 Vanhove, *Essai de Droit Coutumier du Ruanda*, 115–122; Charles Ntampaka, "Le Retour à la tradition dans le jugement du génocide rwandais: Le Gacaca, justice participative," *Bulletin des Séances de l'Académie Royale des Sciences d'Outre-Mer*, no. 48 (2002): 425–426.
7 Filip Reyntjens, "Le gacaca ou la justice du gazon au Rwanda," *Politique Africaine*, no. 40 (1990): 30–41.
8 The plural or *urugo* in Kinyarwanda is *ingo*. This book will use many *urugo* for the consistency of language, but the correct formulation should be many *ingo*.
9 Rwaciriwe I Mutakara, supra. 7.
10 Stef Vandeginste, "Rwanda: Dealing with Genocide and Crimes Against Humanity in the Context of Armed Conflict and Failed Political transition," in *Burying the Past: Making Peace and Doing Justice after Civil Conflict*, ed. Nigel Biggar (Washington, DC: Georgetown University Press, 2001), 239.
11 Republic of Rwanda: Office of the President, "Recommendations of the Conference held in Kigali From November 1st to 5th, 1995 on: Genocide, Impunity and Accountability: Dialogue for a National and International Response," (December 1995): 16.
12 Ibid., 23.
13 Ibid.
14 Ibid., 24.
15 Francoise Digneffe and Jacques Fierens, ed., *Justice et Gacaca, l'experience rwandaise et le genocide* (Namur: Press universitaires de Namur, 2003), 53–63.
16 Paul Christoph Bornkamm, *Rwanda's Gacaca Court: Between Retribution and Reparation* (Oxford; New York: Oxford University Press, 2012), 23.

17 When you consider the number of people whose trials have been complete since the beginning of trials of the genocide and massacres and compare it with the number of people who are in prison because they are prosecuted for that crime, you find that it would take about 200 years to try all of them.

Republic of Rwanda, *Report on the reflection meetings held in the Office of the President of the Republic from May 1998 to March 1999* (Kigali: Office of the President of the Republic, August 1999), 51 (Hereafter Urugwiro Report)

18 See OHCHR, Gacaca: Le droit coutumier au Rwanda: Rapport final de la première phase d'enquête sur le terrain (1996); Rapport Final de la deuxième phase sur le terrain (1996)

19 The offences of genocide and massacres are not ordinary offences. It is not astonishing that classical justice have difficulties with ordinary offences, and problems resulting from such offences. It is necessary to look for and try justice which is not classical and which would help the Country to come out of the deadlock.

Urugwiro Report. *Supra* p. 51

20 The Urugwiro reflection meetings were a series of informal meetings of leading figures in Rwanda that took place between May 1998 and March 1999 in the office of the president of the Republic of Rwanda to discuss serious problems facing the country. See Urugwiro Report, supra.
21 Ibid., 57.
22 Ibid., 59–67.
23 Organic Law No. 33/2001 of 2001 Modifying and Completing Organic Law No. 40/2000 of 26 January 2001 Setting Up "Gacaca Jurisdictions" and Organising Prosecutions for Offences Constituting the Crime of Genocide or Crimes Against Humanity, Committed Between October 1, 1990 and December 31, 1994.
24 *Inyangamugayo*, is the Kinyarwanda term that means "the one with integrity" or the "one who does not disappoint those who put trust in them."
25 See National Services of Gacaca Courts, Gacaca Courts in Rwanda, Kigali, Report, June 2012, 59.
26 See Article 105 of the Organic Law No. 16/2004 of 19 June 2004, establishing the organization, competence, and functioning of the Gacaca Courts charged with prosecuting and trying the perpetrators of the crime of genocide and other crimes against humanity committed between October 1st, 1990, and December 31, 1994.
27 See Organic Law No. 10/2007 of March 1st, 2007 Amending the 2004 Gacaca Organic Law.
28 See Organic Law No. 213/2008 of 19/05/2008 modifying and complementing Organic Law no. 16/2004 of 19/06/2004.
29 Desmond Tutu, *No Future without Forgiveness* 1st ed. (New York: Doubleday, 1999), 257; Jeremy Sarkin, "The Tension between Justice and Reconciliation in Rwanda: Politics, Human Rights, Due Process and the Role of Gacaca Courts in Dealing with the Genocide," *Journal of African Law* 45, no. 2 (2001): 167.
30 Payam Akhavan, "Justice in the Hague, Peace in the Former Yugoslavia- A Commentary on the United Nations War Crimes Tribunal," *Human Rights Quarterly* 20, no. 2 (1998): 737.
31 Mahmood Mamdani, "Amnesty or Impunity? A Preliminary Critique of the Report of the Truth and Reconciliation Commission of South Africa (TRC)," *Diacritics* 32, no. 3/4 (2002): 32–59.

32 Antonio Cassesse, Reflections on International Criminal Justice, 61 Mod. L.Rev.1 (1998); Jean-Marie Kamatali, "The Challenge of Linking International Criminal Justice and National Reconciliation: The Case of the ICTR," *Leiden Journal of International Law*, 16 (2003):133.

33 Article 51 of the Gacaca organic law No. 16/2004 of 19 June 2004: **First Category**: (1) The person whose criminal acts or criminal participation place among planners, organizers, imitators, supervisors and ringleaders of the genocide or crimes against humanity, together with his or her accomplices; (2) The person who, at that time, was in the organs of leadership, at the national level, at the level of Prefecture, Sub-prefecture, Commune, in political parties, army, gendarmerie, communal police, religious denominations or in militia, has committed these offences or encouraged other people to commit them, together with his or her accomplices; (3) The well-known murderer who distinguished himself or herself in the location where he or she lived or wherever he or she passed, because of the zeal which characterized him or her in killings or excessive wickedness with which they were carried out, together with his or her accomplices; (4) The person who committed acts of torture against others, even though they did not result into death, together with his or her accomplices; (5) The person who committed acts of rape or acts of torture against sexual organs, together with his or her accomplices; (6) The person who committed dehumanizing acts on the dead body, together with his or her accomplices.

2nd Category: 1 The person whose criminal acts or criminal participation place among killers or who commit acts of serious attacks against others, causing death, together with his or her accomplices; 2° The person who injured or committed other acts of serious attacks with the intention to kill them, but who did not attain his or her objective, together with his or her accomplices; 3° The person who committed or aided to commit other offences against persons, without the intention to kill them, together with his or her accomplices.

3rd Category: The person who only committed offences against property.

34 Gacaca Law as modified by Art. 1 of Organic Law No. 10/2007.

35 See Art. 2 of the Gacaca Law as modified by Article 1 of the Organic Law No.13/2008, and Article 51, category 1(3), (4), and (5) of the Gacaca Law as modified by article 9 of the Organic Law No.13/2008.

36 Gacaca Law (Modified 2008), Article 9.

37 The Rwandan administrative structure was made up of (1) cells at the lowest level, (2) sectors made of a number of cells, (3) a district that was made of a number of sectors, and (4) provinces that were made of a number of districts.

38 Seven persons of integrity and two substitutes, see Art. 8 of the Gacaca Law, "modified by" art. 1 of Organic Law No. 10/2007.

39 See supra Category tables.

40 Bornkamm, *Rwanda's Gacaca Court*, 81.

41 Bert Ingelaere, *Inside Rwanda's Gacaca Courts: Seeking Justice after Genocide* (Madison: University of Wisconsin Press, 2016), 104.

42 Usta Kaitesi and Roelof Haveman, "Prosecution of Genocidal Rape and Sexual Torture before the Gacaca Tribunals in Rwanda," in *Victimological approaches to international crimes: Africa*, ed. Rianne Letschert et al. (Cambridge: Intersentia, 2011), 394.

43 See National Services of Gacaca Courts, Supra., 86.

44 Gacaca Report Summary, "Summary of the Report Presented at the closing of Gacaca Court Activities: National Service of Gacaca Jurisdictions" (Kigali, 2012) cited in Anne-Marie de Brouwer and Etienne Ruvebana, "The Legacy of the Gacaca Courts in Rwanda: Survivors' Views," *International Criminal Law Review* 13, no. 5 (2013): 950.

45 Ibid.
46 United Nations: International Residual Mechanisms for Criminal Tribunals, "Key Figures of Cases," under "The Cases," http://unictr.irmct.org/en/cases/key-figures-cases (accessed September 11, 2018).
47 ICTR had an average annual budget of US$ 140 million. See Leila Nadya Sadat, "The Contribution of ICTR to the Rule of Law," in *Promoting Accountability under International Law for Gross Human Rights Violations in Africa: Essays in Honour of Prosecutor Hassan Bubacar Jallow*, ed. Charles C. Jalloh and Alhagi B.M. Marong (Leiden: Nijhoff, 2015): 121.
48 Hollie Nyseth Brehm, Christopher Uggen, and Jean-Damascene Gasanabo, "Genocide, Justice and Rwanda's Gacaca Courts," *Journal of Contemporary Criminal Justice* 30, no. 3 (August 2014): 343.
49 Ibid., 340.
50 Ibid., 344.
51 Phil Clark, "The Gacaca Courts and Abbreviated Criminal Procedure for Genocide Crimes in Rwanda," in *Abbreviated Criminal Procedures for Core International Crimes*, ed. Morten Bergsmo (Brussels: Torkel Opsahl Academic Publisher, 2017), 202.
52 World Prison Brief, "Rwanda," International Center for Prison Studies, www.prisonstudies.org/country/rwanda (accessed September 11, 2018).
53 Brehm, Uggen, and Gasanabo, "Genocide," 343.
54 Convicts built new roads totaling 300 kilometers in Rulindo, their work on one bridge in the district lowered its cost to Rwf 30 million when it was supposed to cost more than Rwf50 million, and they built a dormitory for students at Tumba High School at a cost of Rwf 20 million instead of more than Rwf70 million.

See Jean de la Croix Tabaro, "Over Rwf 40 billion saved through TIG," *The New Times* (March 23, 2013), www.newtimes.co.rw/section/read/90986 (accessed on September 21, 2018)

55 Bornkamm, *Rwanda's Gacaca Court*, 81–83. "Apart from terracing some 7,000 hectares of land and their activities to build roads ... TIG has built 743 rooms for the nine-year basic education in different parts of the country ... they built 4,0000 houses for the homeless ... that included genocide survivors." See also De la Croix Tabaro, "Over Rwf 40 billion."
56 Human Rights Watch, "Justice Compromised: The Legacy of Rwanda's Community-Based Gacaca Courts," *Human Rights Watch* (May 2011): 27–80, www.hrw.org/report/2011/05/31/justice-compromised/legacy-rwandas-community-based-gacaca-courts (accessed September 11, 2018).
57 The experience of Guantanamo Detention is a clear illustration that even countries that champion human rights, with the financial means and a judicial system that is experienced and effective (unlike the one in Rwanda in 1994, which was completely devastated) can score very low on these human rights standards when faced with suis generis crimes and a large number of suspects. On this see the following Human Rights Reports: Getting Away with Torture The Bush Administration and Mistreatment of Detainees, Human Rights Watch Report, July 2011. www.hrw.org/sites/default/files/reports/us0711webwcover_1.pdf accessed on August 5th, 2019; Fighting Terrorism Fairly and Effectively, Recommendations for President-Elect Barack Obama, Human Rights Watch Report, November 16th, 2008; www.hrw.org/sites/default/files/reports/us1108webwcover.pdf accessed on August 5th, 2019; see also Laura Pitter, After 16 Years, End Injustice at Guantanamo, Human Rights

Watch, January 10, 2018, Accessible at www.hrw.org/news/2018/01/10/after-16-years-end-injustice-guantanamo, accessed on August 5th, 2019.
58 Interview with the late Jean de Dieu Mucyo, May 2016.
59 For more details on these authors, and their conclusions, see Gerald Gahima, Transitional Justice in Rwanda, Accountability for Atrocity (London: Routledge 2013). (This author largely agrees with them.) 176–186.
60 Official Gazette n° Special of 15/06/2012.
61 See next section.
62 Ruben De Winne and Anne-Ael Pohu, *Mediation in Rwanda, Conceptions and Realities of Abunzi Justice (2011–2014)*, 1st ed. (Belgium: RCN Justice & Democratie, 2015), 11; Rwanda Women's Network, *Experience of Women in Asserting their Land Rights: The Case of Bugesera District* (Rwanda: Rwanda Women's Network, 2011), 9; Art. 2 Organic Law n° 02/2010/OL of 09/06/2010 on organisation, jurisdiction, competence, and functioning of the Mediation Committee.
63 John Paul Lederach, *Building Peace: Sustainable Reconciliation in Divided Societies* (Washington DC: United States Institution for Peace Press, 1997), 37; Martha Mutisi, "Local Conflict resolution in Rwanda: The case of Abunzi mediators," *Integrating Traditional and Modern Conflict Resolution: Experiences from selected cases in Eastern and the Horn of Africa*, ed. Martha Mutisi and Kwesi Sansculotte-Greenidge (Umhlanga Rocks: ACCORD, 2012), 50–54.
64 The law No. 37/2016 of 08/09/2016, determining organization, jurisdiction, competence, and functioning of Abunzi Committee, moved away from translating the term *Abunzi* as mediators and instead used the term *Abunzi*; where it uses the term *kunga*, it translates it as "conciliation."
65 Dugan developed what she calls a "nested paradigm" as a mechanism that looks at a conflict as having four elements: Issue, relationship, subsystem, and system. She argues that a narrower aspect of conflict resolution would be to resolve the issue that sparked the conflict, but a broader, more preferred aspect looks at the conflict as a broken relationship that needs to be restored as part of the solution. See Marie Dugan, "A Nested Theory of Conflict," *Women in Leadership* 1, no. 1 (Summer 1996): 14–15.
66 Mark R. Amstutz, *The Healing of Nations: The Promise and Limits of Political Forgiveness* (Lanham: Rowman and Littlefield Publishers, 2005), 99.
67 Lederach, *Building Peace*, 31.
68 Urugwiro Meeting, Supra. 68.
69 Ibid., 73.
70 European Union's Lot No 7 Programme, Mid-term Evaluation of Rwanda Justice, Reconciliation, Law and Order Sector's Strategy and Formulation of a New Strategy for the Period 2013/14–2018, Draft Strategy March 2012, 33.
71 Unlike the 2003 Constitution, the 2015 Constitution placed Article 141 defining Abunzi under its Executive branch section.
72 Loi Organic No. 17/2004 du 20/06/2004 Portant Organization, Competence et Fonctionnement du Comité de Conciliateurs.
73 Organic Law N° 31/2006 of 14/08/2006 on Organization, jurisdiction, competence and function of the Mediation Committee (Art. 2: The jurisdiction of the Mediation Committee is the Cell."
74 See Article 2 of the Organic Law N° 02/2010/OL of 09/06/2010 on Organization, Jurisdiction, Competence and Functioning of the Mediation Committee.
75 See Organic Law N° 02/2015/OL. Of 16/07/2015 Modifying and Complementing Organic Law N° 02/2010/OL of 09/06/2010 on Organization, Jurisdiction, Competence and Functioning of the Mediation Committee.

76 See Article 2 Organic Law N° 37/2016 of 08/09/2016 Determining Organization, Jurisdiction, Competence and Functioning of an Abunzi Committee.
77 For example, fraud (included in 2004 but withdrawn from the 2006 organic law), making off without payment, night disturbance, and blackmail were included or reintroduced into the law.
78 This law was published in the Official Gazette N° 37bis of 12/09/2016.
79 A person of integrity, or in Kinyarwanda *inyangamugayo*, means "a person the public or people in the community find honest, credible, and who demonstrates that he cares about his integrity in his community."
80 Umwunzi is the singular of *Abunzi.*
81 Republic of Rwanda Ministry of Justice, *Annual Report of Activities 2016/2017* (Kigali, November 2017), 20.
82 Republic of Rwanda Ministry of Justice, "Rwanda Home Grown Solution Mediation Committee (Abunzi)," under "Abunzi Achievements," Republic of Rwanda Ministry of Justice, www.minijust.gov.rw/index.php?id=141 (accessed November 11, 2018).
83 Ministry of Justice, *Annual Report*, 21.
84 Ibid.
85 In the US, Administrative Courts and Immigration Courts are under the executive branch but still maintain their independence as courts.
86 Rwanda Governance Board, "Documenting Home-grown initiatives: Assessing Performance of Mediation Committees," *Rwanda Governance Review* II, Special Issue (December 2012): 71.
87 Ibid.
88 The Citizen Report Card (CRC) is an annual publication of RGB, which is produced to ascertain the levels of community satisfaction with regard to services rendered. Its purpose is to provide public agencies and policy makers with feedback from users on the quality and adequacy of public services delivered at the grassroots level. This mainly primary-data survey involves the usage of questionnaires to interview individual heads of households as well as conduct community focus group discussions of the service beneficiaries and service providers on each service sector; see www.rgb.rw/index.php?id=45.
89 Rwanda Governance Board, *Citizen Report Card: CRC 2018, Ishusho y'uko abaturage babona imiyoborere n'imitangire ya serivisi mu nzego zibegereye* (Rwanda Governance Board, October 2018), 85.
90 Republic of Rwanda, *Economic Development and Poverty Reduction Strategy, 2008–2012* (Kigali, September 2007), x.
91 Daniel Scher and Christine Macaulay, "How Tradition Remade Rwanda: The secret ingredient in Rwanda's effort to rebuild its nation after the violence of genocide," *Foreign Policy* (January 2014).
92 David Booth and Diana Cammack, *Governance for Development in Africa, Solving Collective Action Problems* (London: Zed Books Ltd, 2013), 65.
93 Deo Byanafashye and Paul Rutayisire, *Histoire du Rwanda, Des origins a la fin du XXe siècle* (Huye: Universite Nationale du Rwanda, 2011), 122.
94 Alexis Kagame, *Les milices du Rwanda precolonial* (Bruxelles, 1963).
95 Ibid., 165.
96 Ibid., 133.
97 Ibid., 170.
98 Ibid., 99.
99 Ibid., 176.
100 William R. Anson, *Principles of the Law of Contracts: With a Chapter on the Law of Agency*, ed. Arthur L. Corbin, 3rd Am. ed. (New York: Banks Law Publishing Co., 1919), 156.

101 Reyntjens and Gorus, *Codes et lois*, 89.
102 African Development Bank: Rwanda Field Office, *Performance Contracts and Social Service Delivery-Lessons from Rwanda* (RWFO Policy Brief, March 2012), 6.
103 Ibid., 7.
104 D. Scher and C. Macaulay, "How Tradition Remade Rwanda," Foreign Policy, January 28th, 2014. https://foreignpolicy.com/2014/01/28/how-tradition-remade-rwanda/.
105 Ibid.
106 Republic of Rwanda, *Economic Development*, 114.
107 Ibid., 114 and 141.
108 Malik Khalid Mohmood, *Human and Institutional Capacity Development Handbook, a USAID Model for Sustainable Performance Improvement* (Washington, DC: USAID, October 2010), 8.
109 Susanne Bond Hinsz, Julian Glucroft, Molly Hageboeck, and Eric Hyman, *E3 Bureau Capacity Development Assessment: From Capacity Development to Sustainable Development* (Washington DC: USAID, June 2017), 75.

3 Rwandan constitutional law

Section 1. Introduction

A constitution is the fundamental and organic law of a nation or state that establishes the institution and apparatus of government, defines the scope of governmental sovereign powers, and guarantees individual rights and liberties.[1] It is both the system and the document in which this system is recorded. It can be written or unwritten. In the case of Rwanda, the country acquired its first written constitution immediately after its independence in 1962. Before that, it had been governed by an unwritten constitution.

This chapter investigates post-independence Rwandan constitutional law and therefore covers only the period in which the Rwandan written constitution was in use. It is divided into two key parts: The first part discusses the historical development of Rwandan constitutional law from independence to 2003 when the current constitution was adopted; the second part studies the 2003 Constitution and its subsequent amendments and revisions until 2015.

Section 2. History of Rwandan constitutional law

The development of Rwandan constitutional law has been influenced by three key constitutional moments[2] that shaped the present-day country. The first is the independence of Rwanda in 1962, the second is the creation of the one-party system in 1975, and the third includes the 1990 war and the 1994 genocide against the Tutsi. The constitutions that resulted from or legitimized these key moments are studied in the following sections.

A. Post-independence Rwandan constitution

The first formal constitution of the Republic of Rwanda was adopted on 24 November 1962. This was not, however, the first written constitution of post-colonial Rwanda. Here, we will discuss the first constitution of autonomous Rwanda, known as the "Constitution of Gitarama," adopted on 1 February 1961, before studying the first constitution of independent Rwanda.

1. *The Constitution of Gitarama*

Following the jacquerie of 1959,[3] the June–July 1960 elections of local authorities (Bourgmestres and Counsellors),[4] and the creation of the transitional government,[5] Belgium conferred internal autonomy to Rwanda in early January 1961.[6] On 28 January 1961, the transitional government, with the help of the Belgian colonial authorities, called all the local authorities elected the year before for a gathering in Gitarama, currently known as Muhanga. This gathering led to what came to be dubbed the "Coup of Gitarama," in which the following important resolutions were made: (1) The abolition of the monarchy system and its symbols as well as the adoption of a republican system with the red, yellow, and green flag as its symbol; (2) the creation of republican institutions – namely, the legislative assembly, the Supreme Court, and the government – and the nomination of their leaders; and finally, (3) the adoption of the constitution known as the "Constitution of Gitarama."

The legitimacy of this constitution has remained controversial for the following four reasons:[7] First, although Belgium, which had received the trusteeship of Rwanda from the United Nations (UN), recognized the republican institutions and the leaders that resulted from the gathering of Gitarama, it never formally recognized this constitution.[8] As a matter of fact, Belgium made it clear in one of the early sessions of Rwanda's Legislative Assembly that, as far as its trusteeship mandate was concerned, the Constitution of Gitarama had no legal binding force.[9] Second, even after the adoption of this constitution, the elected Rwandan authorities continued to recognize the authority of Belgium to exercise trusteeship on Rwanda[10] and to accept and apply legislative measures adopted by Belgian authorities on Rwanda.[11] Third, the fact that the Constitution of Gitarama was not published in the Official Gazette or any official legal publication deprived it of its general, public, and legal character. Fourth, the Constitutive Assembly created to put together the first post-independence Rwandan constitution operated *de novo* in full ignorance of the Constitution of Gitarama. All of these factors prove that the legitimacy of this constitution was questionable.

Because of the above reasons we will not discussed all the 80 articles of the Constitution of Gitarama. It is, however, worth highlighting two of its key characteristics: First, in drafting it, its framers were inspired by the French constitution as well as constitutions from former French colonies; second, it left unchanged most of the administrative structure introduced by the Belgian colonial power.[12] The fact that the legitimacy of this constitution is questionable does not make it irrelevant. As will be detailed in the following section, discussing the 1962 constitution, a number of provisions of the Constitution of Gitarama were reproduced in the new constitution.

2. *The 1962 constitution*

Following the failure of the Constitution of Gitarama, the very first Rwandan Legislative Assembly met as the Constitutional Assembly on 4 October 1961. Its main agenda was to receive and discuss the draft constitution submitted by a number of Assembly members.[13] This draft was adopted on 24 November 1962, and its text was promulgated in the Official Gazette on 1 December 1962.[14]

As in most constitutions, the framers of the 1962 Constitution highlighted in its preamble their background, justification, and vision. They stressed first that their Constitutional Assembly was invested with national sovereign powers to abrogate the UN trusteeship treaty and declare independence, and, second, that this independence found its legitimacy in the 25 September 1961 Referendum that, by an overwhelming vote of 79.80%, definitively abolished the monarchy and established a republican democratic regime.

The 1962 constitution was made up of 111 articles, distributed into 11 parts. The first part, entitled "the republic" and inspired by the "Constitution of Gitarama," consisted of 11 articles. It declared Rwanda as a democratic, social, and sovereign republic (Art. 1); that the monarchy had been abolished and could never be reestablished; and that Kigeli V, the last king of Rwanda, and his dynasty were hereby dethroned and their privileges revoked (Art. 2). It adopted the national flag as red, yellow, and green, with the letter "R" in black in the middle (Art. 4). It also recognized the multiparty system and a "constructive opposition" that rejected "destructive agitation" (Art. 10). It left, however, the determination of the national anthem, the capital of Rwanda, rules on Rwandan nationality, and naturalization to ordinary law.

The second part of this constitution was regarding "Public Liberties." It was made of five chapters. The first chapter, consisting of 13 articles, protected the human person. It guaranteed all fundamental freedom included in the Universal Declaration of Human Rights (UDHR) (Art. 13). Among the rights specifically included were: Equality (Art. 16), the right to life (Art. 12), freedom of expression (Art. 18), freedom of association (Art. 19), freedom of movement (Art. 22), property (Art. 23), domicile (Art. 24), and private correspondence (Art. 21). Other guarantees included the principle of legality and prohibition of double jeopardy (Art. 15) as well as the rights of the accused (Art. 15). This chapter also contained an important article that abolished caste privileges and permanently forbade their reestablishment in any shape or form (Art. 16). The second chapter, made up of six articles, protected the family as the foundation of Rwandan society (Art. 26). It guaranteed equality between spouses (Art. 30) and their rights to raise their children (Art. 27). It consecrated monogamous marriage as the only recognized type in Rwanda (Art. 28) and prohibited polygamy (Art. 29). Despite its recognition of equality between husband and wife, it stressed that the husband was the natural head of the household (Art. 30). Chapter 2 also guaranteed the right to education. It declared primary education as obligatory (Art. 34), recognized both public and private education (Art. 32), and abolished privileges in the field of education[15] (Art. 33). The same chapter also stated that military service was obligatory for every male citizen of 18 years of age or older and that this service should mainly focus on physical, moral, and civic training for youth (Art. 35). Chapter 4 of this part, made up of 3 articles, guaranteed the freedom of religion (Art. 37) and the autonomy of religious institutions, as long as they did not encroach on the State's prerogatives and did not interfere in politics (Art. 38). The same chapter also forbade any communist activity or propaganda (Art. 39). The last chapter included five articles guaranteeing and organizing the right to work. Although it saw work as both a right and a duty (Art. 41), it abolished forced and extrajudicial labor (Art. 40). It also guaranteed the right to join labor organizations and to strike (Art. 42), except in the case of civil servants, who were forbidden from striking (Art. 43).

The 1962 Constitution has been criticized for its approach to have a generic provision that guarantees all rights contained in the UDHR (Art. 13) and still duplicate some rights of the Declaration as specific constitutional provisions (Art. 14–43) and for its failure to specify the fate of those rights of the UDHR it left out (right to social security, unemployment, motherhood, and childhood assistance, etc.)[16]

Part 3 of the constitution defined, in its three articles, the high institutions of the republic. The three recognized institutions were the president of the Republic and the government, the National Assembly, and the Supreme Court (Art. 46). This part guaranteed the principle of separation and collaboration of powers (Art. 45), and required every top official in these institutions to make an oath that they would maintain the republican regime (Art. 47).

Part 4, made up of three chapters, covered executive power. Chapter 1 discussed the president of the republic. It stated that this Supreme Head of State (Art. 51) would be elected by universal suffrage by a simple majority. He would nominate a vice president, after approval from the National Assembly, who would assist him with his responsibilities (Art. 52). The presidential term would last for four years, renewable only 3 times (Art. 53). To be eligible, the president had to be between 35 and 60 years old (Art. 54). His powers included nominating and revoking members of his government, negotiating and concluding treaties, declaring war, and promulgating laws. He also had a veto right. In cases where he vetoed a bill, he had to send it back to the Parliament for reexamination; he could not veto a reexamined bill unless it was unconstitutional (Art. 56). The president also enjoyed immunity. The National Assembly could lift this immunity, however, by a vote of 3/4 if it accused him of an offense (Art. 61). Also, in cases in which the National Assembly found by a majority of 4/5 of votes that the president had committed an act of indignity, the Supreme Court could depose him (Art. 61).

Chapter 2 of this part, consisting of six articles, discussed the government. This was made up of the president and his ministers (Art. 62). Ministers were responsible for their ministerial departments, but they also countersigned presidential acts in their areas (Art. 62 and 63). Ministers and Secretaries of State could sit in Parliament in the same quality as elected members (Art. 67). Chapter 3 devotes five articles on the responsibilities of the government. It provided that the president was responsible before the National Assembly. The vice president and ministers reported to him, not the Parliament (Art. 69). The National Assembly could call for and question the president or his government by a vote of no confidence on his general policies, but only the president could be called to question. He could, however, be represented by a member of his cabinet (Art. 69). The resignation of the president ignited the resignation of the entire cabinet (Art. 71).

Part 5, made up of 16 articles, discussed the legislative power. It placed this in the hands of both the National Assembly and the president of the Republic. Members of the National Assembly were elected for four years by universal and direct suffrage. To be eligible, a member of the National Assembly had to be a Rwandan of at least 21 years of age (Art. 73). The president of the Republic exercised legislative power through decrees at times when it was impossible for the National Assembly to meet. In emergency cases, however, the president could act by legislative ordinance. These ordinances were valid only for 6 months unless confirmed by the National Assembly (Art. 75). The constitution also required that every law be published in the Official Gazette of the Republic of Rwanda within 15 days of its signature. It stated that laws had to be entered into force only ten days after their publication (Art. 77).

Part 6 contained nine articles regulating the relationship between the legislative and the executive powers. One of the most important was Article 97, which said that, if two ministerial crises occurred within three consecutive years because of a motion of censure or a vote of no confidence, the National Assembly would automatically be dissolved. It could also be dissolved by a simple majority vote by the National Congress.[17] This dissolution would automatically result in the resignation of the president of the Republic. In this case, elections had to be held between 20 and 40 days after the dissolution. They would be organized by the college of secretary generals of different ministerial departments under the supervision of the *Conseil d'État* and the Supreme Court.

Part seven of the constitution contained eight articles dealing with the judiciary. It provided that this was independent from the legislative and the executive (Art. 98), and that it was the guardian of individual liberty (Art. 101). It created the canton tribunal, the tribunal of the first instance, the court of appeals, and the Supreme Court as ordinary courts of the nation (Art. 99). The Supreme Court, which acted as the guardian of the constitutionality of laws (Art. 102), was comprised of five sections: the Department of Courts and Tribunals, the Court of Cassation, the Constitutional Court, the *Conseil d'État*, and the Court of Auditors (Art. 103). The president of the Supreme Court, as well as his vice presidents, who acted as the presidents of the five sections, were nominated by the president of the Republic from a list established by a joint session of the Parliament and the government (Art. 104).

This constitution was credited for taking its inspiration from progressive constitutions and stable democracies of that time, including those of France, Guinea, Mauritania, Senegal, and Madagascar.[18] However, its lack of strong constitutionalism, particularly with regard mechanisms to enforce constitutional limits, and checks and balance[19] led it to failure. The good principles it had incorporated did not take long to become empty promises. By placing political interests above the law, post-independence leaders failed to plant the seeds of a sustainable society based on a rule of law. As Locke has suggested, holding power, however it was achieved, affects not only a person's opportunity but also his motivation. According to Locke, public officials, even those who are democratically elected, often come to have interests that are distinct from or contrary to those of their community, society and government.[20] Motivated by these interests, government officials begin ignoring constitutional provisions on checks and balances, and power limitations, then move on to poking holes in these institutions, removing them one by one before arriving at the final stage: Removing completely from the constitution provisions that place checks and balances on their power. This seems to have been the process followed by the post-independence leaders of Rwanda.

Due to their popularity after independence, the leaders of the ruling party, MDR-Parmehutu, moved to assimilate the party leadership with that of the State. First, they crushed any political opposition that threatened their monopoly; then, they moved to silence and purge dissenting voices, even within their own party.[21] The last assault to the constitutionalism of the 1962 Constitution was made on 18 May 1973, when twelve of its articles were revised.[22] The four-year presidential term, renewable only three times, was extended to a five-year term, renewable indefinitely. Article 54, which placed the age limit to run for president at 60 years old, was also removed. Even though at this point, it had become symbolic, the position of vice president of the republic was also removed. Additionally, Article 44 was revised, placing the country under a "democratic socialist" system.

The new revisions did not last long because, on 5 July 1973, fewer than two months after their adoption, a military coup took place. Although the 5 July 1973 Proclamation did not specifically suspend the constitution, some of its provisions made parts of it inapplicable. For example, the 1973 Proclamation prohibited all political activity in the territory of the Republic and suspended all political parties. It removed the government and dissolved the National Assembly. It placed all power in the hands of the "Peace and

National Unity Committee."[23] Following these steps, the country fell under a military rule, picking and choosing which legal provisions benefited its agenda and applying them while ignoring the rest.

B. The one-party system constitution of 1978

Following the 5 July 1973 military coup by Major General Juvenal Habyarimana, the elected president was removed, the Parliament was dissolved, and the government was temporarily replaced by a committee made up of 11 top military officers.[24] Although only 31 articles of the constitution, mainly those related to the three branches of government, were suspended, the country effectively lost its formal constitution.[25] This constitutional vacuum lasted until 20 December 1978, when a new constitution was adopted, not to create a new regime but to legalize the military regime and the one-party system already in place.

The path leading to and the philosophy behind the 1978 Constitution were developed on 5 July 1975, when President Habyarimana created the National Revolutionary Movement for development or *Mouvement Revolutionnaire Nationale pour le Developpement* (MRND) in French. The MRND Manifesto clearly defined the dictatorial vision of the group that took power in 1973. Its preamble reads:

> Our movement is a popular movement, and it requires unconditional adhesion. In other words, the People and the Society as a whole speak with one voice [...] No individual or group can escape the control of the "Social Body" in motion, meaning the People, in search for a better social, economic, political, intellectual, and moral life.[26]

The Political Committee of the MRND charged in 1977 with drafting the 1978 constitution was animated by the above philosophy. This committee initially copied the constitution of Zaire that dedicated the ruling party as the sole institution of the Republic.[27] Despite some improvements of this draft, the final result maintained the same spirit. The 1978 Constitution was adopted by referendum on 17 December 1978[28] and was made of 98 articles. Its foundation, stressed in the preamble, stood on three key constitutional moments: The 1959 Revolution, the 1962 independence, and the 1973 military coup. These events were presented as if they followed each other naturally.

The framers of the 1978 Constitution justified it based on the need to safeguard the 1959 revolution; adapt the principles of the 1962 Constitution to new national realities; and pursue renovations introduced after 5 July 1973, particularly with regard to peace and national unity. This preamble also introduced two key innovations as constitutional realities: The MRND one-party system and the concept that the country had to first utilize its own resources before calling for outside help.

Title one of the constitution, made up of eleven articles, declared Rwanda as a democratic, social, and sovereign Republic (Art. 1). Like the Constitution of Gitarama and that of 1962, it abolished the monarchy and kept the Rwandan flag red, yellow, and green, with the letter "R" in the center (Art. 2 and 3). The most innovative provision in this first title is Article 7, which created a one-party system, clearly constitutionalizing the dictatorship. It provided that the Rwandan people must be politically organized within the National Revolutionary Movement for Development (MRND), the unique political framework outside of which no political activity was allowed. No political opposition or dissent was allowed. The same article stressed that "every Rwandan is automatically member of the National Revolutionary Movement for Development"; therefore, every Rwandan was, by birth, a member of the one-party system. No consent was required to join, and there was no option to leave. Finally, Article 7 shielded the top leadership of the movement from the jurisdiction of ordinary courts in criminal matters.

Title two, consisting of 22 articles, contained public liberties. It included almost all freedoms recognized in the UDHR, such as equality, religion, association, assembly, etc. Like its predecessor, it outlawed all forms of slavery and serfdom (Art. 17) as well as non-sentenced forced labor (Art. 29). The same title guaranteed the right to asylum (Art. 15). It also recognized monogamy as the only legal marriage type in Rwanda (Art. 25), and imposed on the State the duty to protect the family as the natural foundation of Rwandan society (Art. 24). Unlike its 1962 predecessor, this constitution also protected the freedom of assembly (Art. 22), the right to leave and return to one's country (Art. 21), and the right to privacy (Art. 22).

Title three discussed separation and collaboration between the three branches of government. This was the longest title in this constitution. It was made up of 57 articles, divided into four chapters. With sixteen articles, Chapter 1 discussed the executive power. It illustrated not only a strong executive power exercised by the president of the Republic but also the significant role the one-party system had to play. It placed the executive powers in the hands of the president of the Republic, assisted by a cabinet appointed by him (Art. 35). According to Article 40 of this constitution, only the president of the MRND was allowed to run as candidate for president of the Republic. He was elected by direct universal suffrage by a majority of votes cast. If he did not get this majority, the one-party MRND would reelect a new president and submit this person as the new candidate for the president of the Republic. Unlike the 1962 Constitution, which allowed only male citizens to run for president, the 1978 Constitution did not make any such discrimination. It provided, however, that the candidate must be at least 35 years old. The presidential term was set to five years, renewable indefinitely (Art. 40).

Although not formally part of any of the three branches of government, the secretary general of the MRND was given significant constitutional powers. He was first in line to replace the president of the Republic in case of impediment or incapacitation (Art. 42), followed by the president of the Parliament (Art. 43). He was also allowed to participate in cabinet meetings with a consultative voice (Art. 48).

With 23 articles, Chapter 2 of title three organized the legislative powers. It provided that the legislative power was collectively exercised by both the president of the Republic and the Parliament, known in French as *Conseil National de Development* (CND). To be elected as a member of the CND, one had to be at least 21 years old. Members were elected for a five-year term (Art. 52). Although the power to initiate laws was granted to both the executive and members of CND, they were limited with regard to the latter. For example, Article 66 provided that any proposition or amendment submitted by a member of CND could not be admitted in cases where its adoption might have as a consequence the decrease of public resources or the creation of new public charges. The only chance such an initiative had of being admitted was when it also defined financial sources to cover its financial costs (Art. 66).

In case of emergency, or when it was impossible for the CND to meet, the president could legislate by way of decree adopted by the cabinet (Art. 64). The Constitutional Court was responsible for reviewing every law or decree to determine its constitutionality. If it was found to be unconstitutional, the court had to return it to the Parliament or to the president for reexamination (Art. 69). The authentic interpretation of laws was laid in the hands of the legislative power (Art. 73).

Chapter 3 of this title was related to the relationship between the CND and the government. It allowed the cabinet ministers to sit in Parliamentary sessions and have a voice, though without voting powers (Art. 74). It also gave the president the power to dissolve the CND. However, he could only exercise this power once per term without any consequences because the dissolution of CND by the president twice in the same term automatically resulted in his own resignation (Art. 79).

With only ten articles, Chapter 4, dealing with the judiciary, was the shortest in the title. It declared the judiciary independent from the executive and legislative powers but made the president of the Republic the guardian of the judiciary (Art. 81). Unlike the 1962 Constitution, which involved the legislative in the appointment of members of the judiciary, the 1978 Constitution placed this power solely in the hands of the president of the Republic. The only requirement was that the minister of justice selects these members and that this proposition receives the assent of the High Council of the Magistrates (Art. 82). Unlike the 1962 Constitution, the 1978 Constitution did not include the Supreme Court. It created two kinds of courts: Ordinary courts and extraordinary courts. Ordinary courts included: The Tribunal of Canton, the Tribunal of First Instances, the Court of Appeals, and the Court of Cassation (Art. 83). Extraordinary courts included: The *Conseil d'État* and the Constitutional Court. The *Conseil d'État* dealt with administrative cases (Art. 84). The Constitutional Court, composed of the court of cassation and the *Conseil d'État*, was in charge of checking the constitutionality of laws and decrees as well declaring, when conditions were met, the resignation of the president (Art. 85).

Title four of the constitution, made up of just one article, organized the conditions for revising the constitution. It forbade any revision aimed at altering the republican form of the State, the territorial integrity of the country, or its republican democratic principles (Art. 91).

The last part of the constitution, title five, dealt with transitional issues related to its entry into force.

C. The 1991 war constitution and the post-1994 genocide constitution

1. The 1991 Constitution

With the end of Cold War and the fall of the Berlin Wall in November 1989, African dictatorship regimes were swept up by the wind of change that prompted citizens to request more freedoms and democracy. In Rwanda, this was first felt on 1 October 1990, following the attack of the Rwandese Patriotic Front (RPF). Just one month after this attack, President Habyarimana, who had resisted the idea for a long time, gave in and allowed the multiparty system.[29] A constitutional amendment to the 1978 Constitution was initiated, pursuant to its Article 91, and on 21 April 1991, the proposed changes were submitted to the CND, which adopted them on 30 May 1991. Following this adoption, the amendment was promulgated on 10 June 1991.

The preamble of the 1991 Constitution reiterated most of the beliefs and values underlined in the 1962 and 1978 Constitutions, especially with regard to the 1959 social revolution, the 1962 independence, and the 1973 coup. In reiterating these values and principles, the constitution ignored the divisiveness that the RPF had started the war to correct. The same preamble highlighted its own particularity when its framers stressed that they "are concerned about defending the republican form of government." If one reads this paragraph in light of the government's use of political rhetoric to define the 1990 RPF's attack as motivated by the need to bring back the monarchy, the Preamble of this constitution better fits the divisive policy of the regime than the creation of national unity. It is therefore not surprising that the 1994 genocide against the Tutsi happened under the watch of this constitution.

As said earlier, the 1991 Constitution was more an amendment of the 1978 Constitution than an entirely new document. Of its 102 articles, only five are worth highlighting here because they constitute key amendments. The most important amendment is Article 7, which ended the one-party system of the MRND. The new article provided that

> political parties fulfilling the legal requirements can concur to the expression of suffrage. They shall be formed and shall exercise their

> activities freely, provided that they respect democratic principles and do not infringe upon the republican form of government, national territorial integrity, and the security of the State.

The second key change was Article 35, which created the post of prime minister. Article 51 gave the prime minister some specific powers, particularly those related to directing government action and determining the assignments of members of the cabinet, which had been under the president's control. The newly amended Article 40 (4) provided that the president of the Republic could be reelected but could not exercise more than two successive terms. Also, unlike Article 42 of the 1978 Constitution, which provided that, in case of impediment, incapacity, resignation, or death, the president would be replaced by the secretary general of MRND, the amended Article 42 provided that in those situations, the president of the Republic would be replaced by the president of the National Assembly.

This revised constitution was criticized for creating a stronger presidential system that gave President Habyarimana "crushing powers" and for escaping the Constitutional Court's scrutiny, which other acts of the Parliament had had to go through.[30]

2. *The 1995 fundamental law*

To end the war that started on 1 October 1990 between the government forces under President Habyarimana's regime and the RPF the two parties entered into negotiations not only to end the war but also to set new foundations for a democratic and non-discriminatory regime. The conclusion was the signature of a comprehensive peace accord known as the Arusha Peace Agreement of 4 August 1993 and its six protocols. The six protocols are:

1. The N'sele Ceasefire Agreement of 29 March 1991 between the government of the Republic of Rwanda and the Rwandese Patriotic Front, as amended in Gbadolite on 16 September 1991 and at Arusha on 12 July 1992. This agreement focused mostly on creating a cease-fire environment and setting up verification and control mechanisms through an international observation mission to allow the two parties to negotiate.
2. The protocol of agreement between the government of the Republic of Rwanda and the Rwandese Patriotic Front on the rule of law, signed at Arusha on 18 September 1992. This protocol set key rule of law principles that were intended to serve as the foundation of the country moving forward. These principles included national unity, democracy, pluralism, and respect of human rights.
3. The protocols of agreement between the government of the Republic of Rwanda and the Rwandese Patriotic Front on power-sharing within the framework of a broad-based transitional government, signed at Arusha,

respectively, on 30 October 1992 and 9 January 1993. These two protocols defined the transitional institutions: Namely, the presidency of the Republic, the broad-based transitional government, the transitional National Assembly, and the judiciary. While allowing President Habyarimana to remain in power during the transition, they shifted most of the president's powers to the hands of the prime minister and the broad-based transitional government. The same protocols also defined the ministerial portfolios and the transitional National Assembly's seats assigned to each political party recognized in Rwanda. With regard to the judiciary, these protocols created the Supreme Court, made up of the Department of Courts and Tribunals, the court of cassation, the Constitutional Court, the *Conseil d'État*, and the Public Account Court. Although these protocols declared the judiciary independent from the legislative and the executive, they also allowed the executive to appoint delegates and commissioners to the Supreme Court, with the power to participate in the court's deliberations.

4 The protocol of agreement between the government of the Republic of Rwanda and the Rwandese Patriotic Front on the repatriation of refugees and the resettlement of displaced persons, signed at Arusha on 9 June 1993. This protocol dealt mainly with policies related to the fate of the property of refugees who fled Rwanda after 1959 and how to resettle them upon their return.

5 The protocol agreement between the government of the Republic of Rwanda and the Rwandese Patriotic Front on the integration of the armed forces of the two parties, signed at Arusha on 3 August 1993. This protocol set the policies to follow in integrating members of the Rwandese Patriotic Army into the national army.

6 The protocol of agreement between the government of the Republic of Rwanda and the Rwandese Patriotic Front on miscellaneous issues and final provisions signed at Arusha on 3 August 1993. This protocol dealt mainly with issues related to state security services and other miscellaneous issues, such as the oath of public officials, resignation of public officials, deletion of references to ethnic groups in official documents, authentic interpretation of the peace agreement, and duration of the transitional period.

The Arusha Peace Agreement, which was an umbrella document that tied together the above six protocols, consisted of 11 articles. Article 1 declared the end of the war between the government and the RPF. Article 2 listed the above protocols as integral parts of the peace agreement. Article 3 stated that the documents that would constitute the fundamental law to govern the transitional period were the Constitution of 10 June 1991 and the Arusha Peace Agreement. The same article provided, however, that Articles 34, 35, 38, 39, 40, 41, 42, 43, 44, 45, 46, 47, 48, 49, 50, 51, 52, 54, 55, 56, 57, 58,

59, 60, 63, 65, 66, 67, 68, 70, 71, 73, 74, 75 paragraph 2, 77 paragraphs 3 and 4, 81, 82, 83, 84, 85, 86, 87, 88 paragraph 1, 90, 96, 99, and 101 of the 1991 Constitution would be replaced by the provisions of the peace agreement relating to the same matters. Most of these provisions were related to the executive powers, legislative powers, and the judiciary. Although the repealed provisions were clearly mentioned, their replacements were not specific. This created some confusion in the identification and application of the constitutional provisions into force.

Article 3 also provided that, in case of conflict between the provisions of the constitution and those of the peace agreement, the provisions of the peace agreement would prevail. Article 4 provided that, in case of conflict between the provisions of the fundamental law and those of other laws and regulations, the provisions of the fundamental law would prevail. The remaining articles were related to the nomination of the prime minister, the period within which transitional institutions had to be set up, and the fate of the government and Parliament in place at the time of the signature of the agreement.

But the fundamental law as described in the Arusha Peace Accord did not last long because their entry into force was interrupted by the genocide that started in April 1994 and ended when the RPF took power in July 1994. After the RPF took over the country, it issued on July 17 a nine-point declaration in which it reaffirmed that, subject to amendments made necessary by the tragic situation in the country, the constitution of 10 June 1991 and the Arusha Peace Agreement would constitute the fundamental law.[31] Two key questions resulted, however, from this declaration. First, the declaration did not specify which provisions of the Arusha Peace Agreement were subjected "to amendments made necessary by the tragic situation in the country." Second, although the declaration contained some provisions of value and significance, it failed to declare them part of the fundamental law. For example, it created the position of the vice president of the Republic[32] (Point 2) and banned MRND and CDR, the two parties that had been in power during the 1994 genocide, and other political parties that may have been in coalition or solidarity with them from joining the government or Parliament, as had been agreed upon in the Arusha Peace Agreement. Also, the declaration awarded to RPF all the executive or legislatives posts that the Arusha Peace Agreement had given to the banned parties.

The RPF declaration of 17 July 1994 was endorsed in a protocol of Agreement signed on 24 November 1994 by representations of eight Rwandan political parties. This protocol also redistributed the seats in the Transitional National Assembly according to political affiliation.[33]

Although the RPF Declaration of 17 July 1994 had made constitutional changes to the fundamental law, its legal significance and authority remained unclear. Could a constitution or a fundamental law be amended by a declaration? The answer to this question was retroactively addressed by the transitional National Assembly, meeting on 5 May 1995 to adopt the fundamental law to govern the transitional period of the Republic of Rwanda.[34] Their resultant act was made up of only three articles. Article 1 provided that

> the Fundamental Law of the Republic of Rwanda consists indissolubly of the Constitution of June 10, 1991, the Arusha Peace Accord, the RPF Declaration of July 17, 1994 concerning the Establishment of Institutions, the Protocol of Agreement between Political Forces RPF, MDR, PDC, PDI, PL, PSD, PSR, and UDPR on the Establishment of National Institutions, signed on November 24, 1994.

Aware of possible conflict and contradictions that could result from the application of these four documents' making up the fundamental law, Article 2 tried to set the rules on how to resolve potential conflicts. It provided that

> in case of conflict between the provisions of the Peace Agreement and those of the RPF Declaration of July 17, 1994 concerning the establishment of institutions, the latter shall prevail. Similarly, in case of conflict between the RPF Declaration of July 17, 1997 concerning the Establishment of Institutions and those of the Protocol of Agreement between the Political Forces RPF, MDR, PDC, PDI, PL, PSD, PSR and UDPR on the Establishment of National Institutions, signed on November 24, 1994, the latter shall prevail.

To give legitimacy to all acts adopted or performed under the regime of the 17 July 1994 RPF Declaration that had narrowed the documents constituting the fundamental law, and to give this RPF declaration retroactive fundamental value, Article 3 provided that "the present Fundamental Law shall enter into force as of July 17, 1994."

The effectiveness of the conflict resolution mechanism provided in Article 2 of the above Act of the Transitional National Assembly was tested on 23 March 2000, when President Bizimungu, who, according to point 9 of the RPF Declaration of July 17, 1994, "by consensus of the Political Bureau of the RPF, assumed the function of president of the Republic," resigned for "personal reasons." At this point, a constitutional question was raised with regard to who should assume the interim power until the election of the new president.

The difficulty in answering the above question resulted from the conflict between Article 48 of the Arusha Peace Agreement, protocol on power-sharing within the framework of a broad-based transitional government, and point 2 of the RPF declaration of 17 July 1994, creating the post of vice president of the Republic. Article 48 of the above-mentioned protocol provided that "in the event of resignation or death, permanent impediment, or incapacitation of the President of the Republic: [...] (2) the interim Presidency shall be assumed by the Speaker of the Transitional National Assembly." On the other hand, there was an understanding that the RPF Declaration, in creating the post of vice president, intended that, in case of resignation or death of the president of the Republic, the vice president would assume power in the interim. Therefore, as in in the hierarchy of fundamental texts, since the RPF declaration was superior to the Arusha Peace Agreement, the former had to prevail.

The conflict between the president of the transitional assembly and the vice-president of the Republic of Rwanda on who, constitutionally, should be the interim president, could have been easy to solve, had the RPF Declaration been clear about the responsibilities of the vice president and had it specified that the latter would become acting president in case of resignation of the president. Unfortunately, this declaration was silent on these two issues. To resolve the conflict between the intent of the RPF declaration and the terms of Article 48 of the protocol on power-sharing, the government seized the Supreme Court for their interpretation.[35]

In its ruling, the Supreme Court, while acknowledging that there was a conflict between the provisions of Article 48 of the protocol on power-sharing and those of point 2 of the RFP declaration, concluded that the interim duties of the president of the Republic should be carried out by the vice president of the Republic until the appointment of a new president.[36] This conclusion was based on two key factors: First, the court argued that it was self-evident that "the substance of the function of the Vice-President of the Republic consists mainly in assisting the President of the Republic and replacing him in case of resignation, death, inability, or unforeseen circumstances."[37] By defining the responsibility of the vice president as including replacing the president in case of resignation, the Supreme Court interpreted point 2 of the RPF declaration as in conflict with Article 48 of the protocol on power-sharing. It then proceeded to solve this conflict by applying Article 2 of the fundamental law, which stipulated that "in case of inconsistency between the Peace Agreement provisions and those of the RPF Declaration of 17 July 1994 relating to setting up institutions, the latter prevails."[38]

While praising the soundness and practicality of the above decision, however, one author has questioned (1) whether, in creating the post of the vice president, the RPF declaration intended the vice president, not the president of the transitional National Assembly, to replace the president of the Republic in case of resignation, and (2) whether it was the responsibility of the Supreme Court to interpret the intent of the RPF Declaration in the first place.[39]

The system of a fundamental law made up of scattered documents ended in 2003 when a new constitution was adopted.

Section 3. Contemporary Rwandan constitutional law

A. The making of the 2003 Constitution

Pursuant to Article 24 of the Arusha Peace Agreement, protocol on power-sharing within the framework of a broad-based transitional government, the Legal and Constitutional Commission was established by Law No. 23/99 on 24 December 1999. This commission was tasked with (1) drafting a list of adaptations of national legislation to the provisions of the Peace Agreement, in particular, those provisions relating to the rule of law, and (2) preparing a preliminary draft of the constitution that would govern the country following the transitional period.[40] It comprised twelve commissioners, eight of whom represented political parties officially registered in Rwanda, one representing the army and national police, two representing the civil society, and one representing the private sector.

Article 2 of the above-mentioned Law 23/99 detailed the task of this commission as follows: (a) Prepare the draft-bill of the constitution; (b) search for, receive, and collect thoughts given by the population, (c) get inspirations from constitutions of other countries; (d) explain to the population what the constitution is and the main ideas that it is comprised of; (e) prepare the draft-bills of laws that govern the last transition period; and (f) put together all the laws that must be modified for the purpose of adapting them to the constitution.

The drafting and adoption of the new constitution followed a participatory approach. To achieve its tasks, the Commission elaborated a three-year strategic action plan divided into six phases: (1) Training and sensitization of the population regarding the constitution; (2) consultation of the population on the contents of the constitution; (3) writing and validation of the draft text of the constitution; (4) referendum on the text of the constitution, as approved by the Parliament; (5) management of the last period of transition; and (6) harmonization between the laws and the new constitution.[41]

The preparations for the new constitution followed the above-mentioned phases.[42] After they were acquainted with their duties and responsibilities, the commissioners began by training and sensitizing the population regarding the constitution and the major ideas making up its core parts. Different categories of grassroots leaders were briefed, and they, in turn, briefed the population. The key groups briefed included secondary schools and university students, and the government and private sector workforce. It is estimated that between 2001 and 2002, a civic education campaign of almost 600 meetings was run to increase popular awareness of the constitutional reform and request their inputs.[43]

The Commission even traveled outside the country to brief and collect ideas from the Rwandan diaspora. Members of the commission traveled to the United States and Canada, and organized several international seminars in Rwanda to hear from other experts in constitution drafting.[44]

After the sensitization phase, the commission began collecting ideas and contributions from the Rwandan citizenry on what their constitution should look like. Ideas were either contributed immediately after the explanatory briefings or forwarded to the commission in special pouches or via the Internet. These ideas, which came in form of answers to a questionnaire, were pooled together and sorted according to their pertinence. Every answer was graded according to pertinence and where it came from (an individual person, a group of persons, an expert in a specific area, an institution, or a department survey).[45] Answers were then bound together in book form and returned to the people who had contributed them for the purpose of crosschecking.

After the phases of sensitization and consultation, and the collection of contributions, the Commission went on to write in a consultative process[46] the first draft of the constitution. This was followed by several sessions of validation of the draft text of the constitution.

The validated constitutional draft was then presented to the government, then to the National Assembly, for approval. The last phase was the adoption of the proposed constitution in a referendum. This referendum was held on 26 May 2003, and its confirmation by the Supreme Court took place on 2 June 2003.[47]

The 2003 constitution was based on the following seven principles: (1) Transparent power-sharing, (2) building the rule of law and a democratic government that is open to different thoughts and ideas, (3) combating genocide and all its ramifications, (4) eradicating ethnic and regional factors of disunity while promoting the unity of Rwandans, (5) equality among Rwandans in general and between men and women in particular, (6) putting into place a government that is committed to securing the welfare of the people and to offering equal opportunities to all and sundry, and (7) debating problems facing the country with a view toward reaching a consensus.[48]

The contents of the 2003 Constitution[49] is discussed in the following section together with its subsequent amendments until 2015.[50]

B. The 2003 Constitution, as revised in 2015

The constitution in force in Rwanda at the time of this publication is that of 2003, as revised in 2015. Made up of 177 articles divided into 12 chapters, the revised constitution was passed by referendum on 18 December 2015 and came into force on 24 December 2015.[51]

The following section discusses the revised version but, wherever necessary, goes back to the 2003 Constitution and its subsequent amendments to show the development or modifications of some of its provisions. Key Supreme Court cases challenging or explaining some of these provisions will also be discussed.

1. *The preamble*

To comprehend what people care about when drafting a constitution and to decipher the real constitution behind the formal constitutional text, one has to understand the preamble of the constitution under study. This understanding should focus not only on the words of the preamble but also on its tone and timing. This is true whether we are studying the preamble of the Constitution of Gitarama; the 1962 Constitution; the 1978 Constitution and its 1991 amendment; or the 2003 Constitution, as amended in 2015.

It is clear that the preambles of the 2003 and 2015 Constitutions sound more unifying and less revolutionary than those that came before. Both the 2003 and the 2015 constitutional texts highlight the consciousness of the people of their country's tragic history, particularly of the genocide committed against the Tutsi, which decimated more than a million sons and daughters of Rwanda; they also emphasize the commitment of the Rwandan people to preventing and punishing genocide, and to fighting its negationism and revisionism while eradicating its ideology and all its manifestations, particularly those related to divisionism and discrimination based on ethnicity, region, or any other grounds.

Both texts emphasize the privilege Rwandans have in common language; common culture; and common heroes who sacrificed themselves to found the country and struggle for the security, justice, freedom, tranquility, dignity, and pride of its people; they also stress the people's commitment to upholding Rwandan values based on family, morality, and patriotism, and ensuring that all State entities serve everyone's common interest.

Furthermore, both texts stress the Rwandan peoples' commitment to peace, unity, security, and reconciliation, particularly their vow to build a state based on the rule of law, respect of human rights, and principles of equality, and a government based on consensus and pluralistic democracy, and power-sharing.

While the 2003 preamble sounded more backward-looking because of its emphasis on the responsibility of previous regimes in the tragic history of Rwanda, its 2015 amended version appears more forward-looking. In other words, the 2015 preamble shows a society that is seeking to heal from the past while building the future.

2. *Sovereignty, supremacy, republic, and homegrown solutions*

Chapter 1 (Art. 1–3) of the constitution relates to the sovereignty of Rwandans and the supremacy of the constitution. It stresses that the authority of the nation comes from Rwandans, that all Rwandans have the right to vote and be elected, and that suffrage is universal. It sets the constitution as the supreme law of the country and declares null and void any law, decision, or acts contrary to the constitution.

Chapter 2 (Art. 4–9) focuses on Rwanda as a republic and all of its national symbols. It declares the country to be an independent, sovereign, social, and secular republic founded on the principle of "Government of Rwandans, by Rwandans and for Rwandans." All of the land, rivers, and airspace within its borders are its territory. International treaties defining its boundaries that have been ratified by Rwanda are considered in the determination of its territory. This territory is divided into administrative entities. Decentralization occurs at the local level. Rwanda's capital is Kigali. Although there are three official languages – *Kinyarwanda*, English, and French – the national language is *Kinyarwanda.* Official documents can be written in any or all of the official languages. The flag, motto of the Republic, seal of the Republic, and national anthem are the country's national symbols. The flag has blue, yellow, and green stripes. There is a yellow sun inside the blue stripe. The motto of Rwanda is *Ubumwe Umurimo, Gukunda Igihugu*. Its seal includes the motto and the phrase *Repubulika Y'u Rwanda* at the top. The seal also includes the sun, with rays, sorghum and coffee tree, a basket, a blue wheel with teeth, and two shields. The national anthem is *Rwanda Nziza*.

Chapter 3 discusses the fundamental principles and homegrown solutions (Art. 10–11). The first part highlights the following principles, which the State of Rwanda is committed to upholding: preventing and punishing the crime of genocide, fighting against genocide denial and revisionism, eradicating the genocide ideology, ending discrimination and division, fair power-sharing, having a state governed by the rule of law, having a pluralistic democratic government, equality of all Rwandans (demonstrated by at least 30% of positions in decision-making bodies' being held by women), creating a State that promotes social welfare and mechanisms for equal opportunity, and always looking for solutions through dialogue and consensus. The second part of the chapter stresses that Rwandans should initiate homegrown solutions to build the nation, promote national culture, and restore dignity.

3. *Rights and duties*

Chapter 4 (Art. 12–43) emphasizes the key human rights and freedoms, which include the following:

1 Everyone has the right to life and physical and mental integrity. A human being is sacred, and the State is obligated to respect, protect, and defend human beings. Torture; physical abuse; and cruel, inhuman, or degrading treatment are prohibited. Experimentation is prohibited without consent.
2 Everyone is born equal, remains equal, and is entitled to equal protection under the law. Discrimination based on, *inter alia*, ethnic origin, family or ancestry, clan, skin color or race, sex, region, economic

categories, religion or faith, opinion, fortune, cultural differences, language, economic status, and physical or mental disability is prohibited and punishable by law. While the right to marry and have a family is guaranteed by law, the only recognized marriage is a civil monogamous marriage between a man and a woman. Marriage requires consent. Legal marriages performed in other countries are recognized. Spouses are entitled to equal rights throughout the marriage and at the time of divorce. Children are entitled to protection by their family, other Rwandans, and the State.

3 The right to education and the freedom of learning and teaching are guaranteed. Primary education is free and compulsory. Everyone has the right to good health and the right to live in a clean and healthy environment. All individuals have the right to privacy of self, family, home, and correspondence. Only with consent or by law can there be a search or entry of a private home.

4 The State guarantees a person's liberty and security. Someone can only be prosecuted, arrested, detained, or punished under a law that has been enacted at the time of the offense. Security measures are only necessary when the law provides or in relation to public order or State security.

5 The right to a country and nationality is recognized to all Rwandans. Banishment of Rwandans is prohibited. Dual nationality is permitted, and anyone of Rwandan origin or descent is entitled to Rwandan nationality. Every Rwandan can move freely within and out of Rwanda. This right is only restricted for public order, national security, to avoid a public threat, or for protection. The right to seek asylum is determined by the law.

6 Everyone has a right to due process. This includes: The right to be informed of the charges; the right to legal representation and defense; presumption of innocence until proven guilt; the right to appear before a court; no retroactive prosecution, arrest, detention, or punishment for an act that was not an offense under national or international law at the time the conduct occurred; no liability for an act that an individual did not commit; and no punishment harsher than was required at the time of the offense. The inability to fulfill a contractual obligation does not result in imprisonment. There is no statute of limitations for the crimes of genocide, crimes against humanity, or war crimes. Foreigners can be extradited, but Rwandans cannot be extradited to other countries.

7 Everyone has the right to employment and to equal pay for equal work. Trade unions are allowed, and every worker has the right to join trade associations and use a trade union to defend his or her rights. Collective bargaining is allowed. Workers have the right to strike lawfully as long as this does not infringe on another's rights.

8 Everyone has the right to private property. The State grants private ownership of land and the concession, transfer, and use of land, as determined by law.

9. The State guarantees freedom of thought, conscience, religion, and worship. Ethnic, regional, and racial discrimination or division is illegal. There is freedom of press, expression, and access to information as long as it does not disrupt public order, good morals, or the protection of youth and children, or infringe on citizens' rights to honor and dignity or on individuals' privacy. Peaceful and unarmed assembly is a right and does not require prior authorization, except when required by law.

The constitution recognizes that individual rights and freedoms may be limited by law when there is a need for recognition and respect for the rights of others, public morals, public order, and social welfare. However, individuals have the right to challenge such a law before the judiciary, which has the responsibility to protect their rights and freedoms in accordance with the constitution and other laws.

Chapter 5 (Art. 44–53) contains the duties of the State and its citizens. It stresses that State property, including both private and public property of the State, government entities, and public legal institutions, must be respected. The State must promote good health through various activities and Rwandans have the responsibility to participate in these activities. The chapter also states that every Rwandan is required to respect others; refrain from discrimination; and promote respect, solidarity, and tolerance. The State has a duty to preserve and promote national values related to cultural traditions and practices, unless this affects human rights but also Rwandans must respect the constitution and laws. However, they can refuse to obey superior orders if they are blatant violations of human rights and freedoms. Other duties included in this chapter are the State's obligation to take special measures, including education and welfare, for people with disabilities, and the State duty for the welfare of vulnerable populations, including the elderly and indigent. They also include everyone's responsibility, including the State's, to preserve and protect memorial sites of the genocide against the Tutsi and to protect the environment.

4. *Political organizations*

Chapter 6 (Art. 54–60) not only guarantees but also regulates political organizations. Rwanda has a multiparty system in which political organizations can be formed and operate freely as long as they comply with conditions set by the law. Duly registered political organizations receive State grants. Every Rwandan can join a political organization without discrimination, and everyone is protected against any discrimination based on their political organization membership or lack thereof. However, judges, prosecutors, soldiers, police officers, and members of the National Intelligence and Security Services cannot be members of political organizations.

Political organizations must always reflect the unity of Rwandans and promote the equality of men and women through their recruitment processes, their leadership, and their activities. They are forbidden from organizing based on race, ethnic group, tribe, lineage, region, sex, religion, or any other division that could lead to discrimination.

The 2003 Constitution required the leadership structures of political organizations to maintain offices only at the national, provincial, and Kigali city levels.[52] This provision was amended in 2005 to require offices only at the national level, leaving the organic law the power to determine the administrative levels where such organizations could place their other offices.[53] The 2015 revised constitution removed the limitations that the 2003 and 2005 had placed on where political organizations could place their offices, leaving this issue to be regulated by the law on political parties.

Political organizations that violate these constitutional requirements can face punishment by the Senate. This may include warnings; suspension of activities for no more than two years or the entire Parliamentary term; or cancellation of the certificate of registration, if the political organization grossly violates the fundamental principles of the constitution, are discriminatory, or violate other constitutional obligations imposed upon them. If the political organization is canceled, individuals representing this organization in the Chamber of Deputies lose their Parliamentary seats.

The constitution created a National Consultative Forum of Political Organizations to bring organizations together for dialogue, national consensus, and cohesion. While the 2003 Constitution seemed to require all political organizations officially recognized in Rwanda to join the forum,[54] the 2015 amended constitution is silent on whether membership is obligatory or optional. However, the organic law governing political organizations and politicians[55] provides that a political organization enrolls in the forum voluntarily. Interested parties must submit their application to join, and the decision to grant admission is made by the forum. In 2019, the forum consisted of 11 political organizations: (1) Rwandese Patriotic Front – RPF *INKOTANYI*, (2) Liberal Party – PL, (3) Democratic Union of Rwandese People – UDPR, (4) Ideal Democratic Party – PDI, (5) Social Democratic Party – PSD, (6) Party for Progress and Concord – PPC, (7) Centrist Democratic Party – PDC, (8) Rwandese Socialist Labor Party – PSR., (9) Party for Solidarity and Progress – PSP, (10) Social Party *Imberakuri* – PS *Imberakuri*, and (11) Democratic Green Party of Rwanda – DGPR.[56]

5. *The legislative power*

Chapter 7 covers the branches of government. Section 2 of this chapter (Art. 64–96) covers the legislative power, which is vested in the Parliament. There are two chambers of Parliament: The Chamber of Deputies and the Senate. The Parliament makes and passes laws, legislates, and has control over the executive. Members of Parliament represent the entire nation. Before they begin their duties, members of Parliament take an oath before the president. If the president is absent, they take the oath before the president of the Supreme Court. The first sitting of each chamber at the beginning of each Parliamentary term is held to elect the bureau composed of the speaker and deputy speakers of the Chamber of Deputies, and the president and vice presidents of the Senate. The president of Rwanda convenes and presides over the sitting. This sitting must be held within 15 days of the election results. The president of the Senate and speaker of the Chamber of Deputies must be of Rwandan nationality by origin and must not hold any other nationality. An oath of office is required. Nobody can be a member of the Chamber of Deputies and the Senate at the same time. Nor can a deputy or a senator also be a cabinet member.

Members of Parliament have special immunity rights. They cannot be prosecuted, pursued, arrested, detained, or judged for an opinion or a vote that was held during their duties. Members suspected of a felony or misdemeanor cannot be prosecuted or arrested unless this is authorized by the chamber they belong to. For this to happen, there must be a two-thirds majority vote of the members present, unless the member was caught performing an illegal act. An extraordinary session can be convened if Parliament is in recess. If a member of Parliament is convicted of a felony or misdemeanor, they lose the Parliamentary office. Laws provide for the ways in which members of chambers can be removed. In these cases, there needs to be a three-fifths majority vote of the concerned chamber.

The Chambers of Parliament hold public sittings in the capital. In the event that something occurs to prevent them from holding a sitting in the designated location, the president of Rwanda decides where it will be held. To count as a sitting for each chamber, a meeting must be held at the designated building and have an official invitation and agenda, and at least three-fifths of its members must be present. If a sitting is held in a place that does not meet these standards, it is not effective. While the Parliamentary sittings are public, the meetings can be held in private if the president of the Republic, the president of Senate, the speaker of the Chamber of Deputies, one-quarter of the members of the concerned chamber, or the prime minister requests this. The decision to seat in camera must be approved by the absolute majority vote of the members present.

The chambers of Parliament cannot meet jointly unless required to do so by the constitution or another law, a national ceremony, or the president of the Republic (after consultation with the speaker of the Chamber of Deputies or president of the Senate in the speaker's absence) establishing matters that need to be considered jointly.

There are sittings for both ordinary and extraordinary sessions. Ordinary sessions are held on the same day and are the same length for both chambers of Parliament. The president of the Senate or the speaker of the Chamber of Deputies convenes the ordinary sessions. Both extraordinary sessions and extraordinary joint sessions occur after members of the concerned bureau are consulted or at the request of the president of the Republic (after a proposal by the cabinet or one-quarter of the members of the chamber of Parliament concerned). An extraordinary session lasts no more than 15 days and is limited to considering only the matters for which it was convened. Each chamber of Parliament is financially and administratively autonomous.

There are 80 deputies in the Chamber of deputies. Each serves a five-year term and can be re-elected. Fifty-three are elected from a list of names that political organizations propose or independent candidates elected based on proportional representation. Twenty-four women are elected. The National Youth Council elects 2 Deputies. The National Council of Persons with Disabilities elects 1 Deputy. At least 30% of the Deputies must be women.

Deputies can vacate their office through resignation from the chamber, expulsion from the chamber, resignation from their political organization, expulsion from their political organization, revocation of the certificate of registration of the political organization that seconded them, joining another political organization, death, or some permanent impediment to fulfilling their duties. After a Deputy resigns, they are replaced according to the election laws. The president of the Republic can dissolve the Chamber of Deputies for election purposes. This can only happen at least 30 days, but no more than 60 days, before the end of the Parliamentary term. Elections are held during this time.

There are 26 senators who comprise the Senate; 12 are elected through the electoral college. The president of Rwanda appoints eight, and the National Consultative Forum of Political Organizations designates four. There is one academic or researcher from a public university or institution, and one academic or researcher from a private university. Both individuals must be at least an associate professor and must be elected by the academic and research staff of the universities or institutions. Former heads of state can become members of the Senate after submitting a request to the president of the Senate and receiving approval within 30 days from the bureau of the Senate. Senators that the president appoints do not have to be approved by the Supreme Court. Women must comprise at least 30% of the elected and appointed senators. Senators serve a five-year term, renewable once, unless they were a former head of State – in which case there is no term limit. They can vacate their seats in several ways: resignation, death, removal by a court decision, or some permanent impediment to fulfilling their responsibilities. Election laws govern how the vacating senator is replaced. If an appointed senator leaves office unexpectedly, the appointing authority chooses the replacement. The elected or appointed replacement will complete the term of the vacating senator but is eligible for another term.

The Senate monitors the application of the principles in Article 10 (fundamental principles), provisions of Articles 56 (obligations of political organizations), and Provisions of Article 57 (prohibitions for political organizations) of the constitution. It can vote to revise or amend the constitution, organic laws, laws approving international treaties and agreements on armistice, peace, accession to international organizations, modification of national laws, or those approving international treaties and agreements relating to the status of persons, laws relating to defense, and national security. Also, the Senate approves the appointments of the following: President; vice president; judges of the Supreme Court; the president and vice president of the high court and the commercial high court; the prosecutor general and the deputy prosecutor general; the chairpersons, vice chairpersons, and other commissioners of national commissions; the ombudsman and their deputies; the auditor general of the state finances and his or her deputy; ambassadors and permanent representatives to international organizations; provincial governors and heads of public institutions; and parastatals with legal personality.

Deputies or the government, acting through the cabinet, can initiate and amend laws. If a draft law can affect the national budget through reduction of government revenue or an increasing of State expenditures, the initiator must indicate how the State will make up for lost revenues and increased spending. Prior to consideration and adoption in a plenary sitting, the appropriate Parliamentary committee will review the draft laws. The chamber of Parliament can choose to adopt the draft law in the plenary sitting without examination by the Parliamentary committee. There must be an absolute majority vote of present deputies or senators to pass ordinary laws. Organic laws are passed by three-fifths of eligible deputies or senators present. If Parliament cannot sit, the president of the Republic can pass decree-laws approved by the cabinet. These laws have the same force as ordinary laws. If not adopted by Parliament in its next session, they lose their legal effect. Through the petition of the appropriate chamber of Parliament, members of Parliament or the government can request urgent consideration of a draft law or any other matter. After the petition, the chamber will decide on the urgency. After submission to the government, the draft law will be granted if there are reasonable grounds for it. If it is determined to be urgent, it is considered first. Draft laws, which the Senate must examine, are submitted to them once adopted by the Chamber of Deputies. If the Senate rejects the draft law or the Chamber of Deputies does not accept the proposed amendments, a joint committee made up of an equal number of deputies and senators is established. A joint committee of Parliament can also be established to decide on any matter relevant to the law adopted as long as there is a three-fifths majority vote of the plenary assembly of each chamber of Parliament, and the law itself has not been formally declared. If either chamber fails to reach an agreement, then the draft law is returned to the initiator.

The hierarchy of laws from highest to lowest is as follows: The constitution, organic law, international treaties and agreements ratified by Rwanda, ordinary law, and orders. A lower law cannot contradict a higher law.

This hierarchy did not exist in the 2003 Constitution version. Also unlike this constitution, which placed the power for authentic interpretation of laws in the hands of the Parliament,[57] the 2015 amendment moved this power into the hands of the Supreme Court.[58] The cabinet or The bar association can request the interpretation of laws,[59] and individuals can go through the bar association to request the same. In 2015, the Supreme Court ruled that because the constitution is silent on which court has the jurisdiction to hear cases related to the interpretation of the constitution, and given the fact that a court cannot refuse to decide on a case for lack of law or regulation on the issue at hand, this power should be lodged with the Supreme Court.[60]

6. *Executive power*

Section 3 of Chapter 7 of the Constitution covers the Executive power (Art. 97–125) that is placed in the hands of the president and the cabinet.

The president of the Republic is the head of state, the defender of the constitution, and the guarantor of national unity. He or she ensures that the State continues, the country remains independent and sovereign, and international treaties are respected. To be a candidate for president of the Republic, one must be of Rwandan nationality by origin, not hold any other nationality, be irreproachable in his or her conduct and social relations, not have been sentenced to six months or more imprisonment, not have been deprived of civil or political rights by a court decision, be at least 35 years old at the time of candidacy, and live in Rwanda at the time of candidacy. Under the 2003 Constitution, a candidate had to have at least one parent of Rwandan nationality by origin.[61] This requirement was removed in the 2015 constitutional amendment.

Elections for the president of Rwanda are held at least 30 days, but no more than 60 days, before the end of the incumbent president's term. An organic law that determines the procedures involved in the election helps ensure that it is free and fair. The 2003 Constitution provided that the president of the Republic was to be elected for a term of seven years, renewable only once.[62] The 2015 Constitution shortened this to a five-year term, renewable only once.

Article 172 of the 2015 Revised Constitution provides however that

> without Prejudice to Article 101 of this Constitution, considering the petitions submitted by Rwandans that preceded the coming into force of this revised constitution, which were informed by the particular challenges of Rwanda's tragic history and the choice made to overcome them, the progress so far achieved and the desire to lay a firm foundation for sustainable development, a seven year presidential term of office is established and shall follow the completion of the term of office referred to in the first paragraph of this Article.

The above provision was however found controversial by a number of donors and journalists,[63] and political organizations because although it stands with the principle that the presidential term is five years renewable only once; it delayed the enforcement of this presidential term to allow the president who was on power during its adoption, to finish his term and run for another seven-year term. This meant that the five-year presidential term is to be effective only after 2024. One of the opposition parties in Rwanda, the Democratic Green Party of Rwanda, challenged the above constitutional provision before the Supreme Court, arguing that Article 101 of the 2003 Constitution states that "the President of the Republic is elected for a term of seven years renewable only once," and this forbids any change of term limit. According to the Green Party, the president in power in 2015 was given an opportunity to run for more terms than what the 2003 Constitution had provided. The Supreme Court did, however, dismiss the Green Party's argument and ruled that there was no violation of the 2003 Constitution because changes in the 2015 Amended Constitution had been democratically adopted by a legal process of referendum, and therefore, the will of the people had to be respected.[64]

Before assuming office and within 30 days of the election, the president swears a specific oath before the president of the Supreme Court. The president cannot hold any other job or profession. The incumbent president stays in office until the president-elect assumes office. During this time, the incumbent president cannot declare war, declare a state of siege or state of emergency, call a referendum, or grant mercy to people sentenced. The constitution cannot be amended during this time. If the president-elect dies, is unable to assume office permanently, or decides not to take office, new elections are held. If the president is convicted of treason or another serious constitutional violation, he or she no longer holds office, and the president of the Supreme Court declares the office of president vacant. The president can be charged in the Supreme Court if there is a two-thirds majority vote of each chamber of Parliament or a joint sitting. The prosecutor general, the deputy prosecutor general, or both prosecute the president. If the office of the president is officially declared vacant, the President is replaced by the president of the Senate; in his or her absence, the President is replaced by the speaker of the Chamber of Deputies; and in the absence of both, the President is replaced by the prime minister. The replacement acts as president but cannot appoint public officials, call a referendum, initiate an amendment to the constitution, exercise the prerogative of mercy, or declare war. Elections to replace the president must be organized within 90 days of the vacancy. The successor is elected for a five-year, once renewable term. If the president is temporarily unable to perform his or her duties, the prime minister serves in an acting capacity.

The president of the Republic promulgates laws within 30 days of receipt. Prior to promulgating a law, he or she can request a second reading by Parliament. After the second reading, Parliament adopts the law, either by two-thirds majority for ordinary laws or three-quarters for organic laws. The president can call a referendum after consulting with the Supreme Court. It can be on the following: An issue of national interest, a constitution or draft constitution, or a law or draft law, in accordance with the provisions of the constitution or any other law. If passed by referendum, the president has eight days to proclaim the results.

The president is the commander-in-chief of the defense force. He or she has the power to declare war, sign armistice and peace agreements, declare a state of siege or state of emergency, grant pardons, and issue national currency. He or she represents Rwanda in foreign relations and appoints ambassadors and envoys to foreign countries. The president can enact presidential orders. Those that are approved by the cabinet include: The implementation of laws that fall within his or her responsibility; the establishment and determination of the service responsibilities of the office of the president, the Senate, the Chamber of Deputies, and the Supreme Court; the coordination of activities and collaboration among security and national defense institutions; and the ability to appoint or dismiss judges, prosecutors, and other officials. These officials include: The president, vice president, and judges of the Supreme Court; the president and vice president of the high court; the president and vice president of the commercial high court; the prosecutor general and deputy prosecutor general; the director of the cabinet in the office of the president of the republic; chairpersons, vice chairpersons, and other commissioners of national commissions; heads and deputy heads of government-specialized organs and public institutions, and parastatals with legal personality; heads and deputy heads of public universities and institutions of higher learning; the principal private secretary to the president of the republic; advisers in the office of the president; heads of services in the office of the president; clerks of Parliament and their deputies; secretary general of the Supreme Court; secretary general of the National Public Prosecution Authority; permanent secretaries in ministries and secretary generals of other public institutions; other heads of public institutions as the law decides; and members of boards of directors of public institutions and government representatives in the enterprises in which the government is a shareholder. The President also has the authority to delegate some of these powers.

An organic law determines the benefits that the current president and former presidents will receive. If a president has been convicted of treason or a serious intentional violation of the constitution, he or she does not receive benefits. A former president cannot be tried for treason or a serious and deliberate violation of the constitution if no charges were brought while he or she was in office. The protection of a former president for treason was not included in the 2003 Constitution; it was incorporated in the 2008 Constitutional Amendment[65] and was maintained in the 2015 Amendment.

The prime minister, ministers, state ministers, and other members determined by the president of the Republic compose the cabinet. The president selects, appoints, and dismisses the prime minister. After the president is sworn in, he or she appoints the prime minister within 15 days. Unlike the 2003 Constitution, which provided that other members of the cabinet are appointed and removed from office by the president of the Republic upon proposal by the prime minister,[66] the 2015 Amended Constitution replaced the term "upon proposal" with "after consultation." This means that the proposal no longer comes from the prime minister; instead, he or she is only consulted. However, the 2015 amended Constitution did maintain the principle of power-sharing at the executive level. It provides that cabinet members must be selected from political organizations on the basis of the seats they hold in the Chamber of Deputies. However, the majority cannot have more than 50% cabinet members.

The cabinet implements national policies and is accountable to the president and Parliament. The constitution determines the president and Parliament's oversight of the cabinet. All cabinet members, including the prime minister, ministers, and state ministers, must publicly swear an oath before the president of the Republic. The cabinet works together. During meetings, it deliberates on draft laws and draft decree laws; drafts of presidential orders; prime minister's orders; orders issued by ministers, state ministers, and other cabinet members; and other matters. The cabinet and its functioning is established through a presidential order. Orders issued by ministers, state ministers, and other cabinet members are determined by a presidential order, and adopted without the cabinet's consideration. Cabinet members cannot be members of Parliament or any other paid activity. The law on leadership code of conduct determines other duties that are forbidden.

The prime minister has specific responsibilities and powers. These include leading the functioning of government and ensuring the implementation of laws; formulating government programs with other cabinet members; introducing government programs to Parliament within 30 days of taking office; assigning duties to cabinet members, ministers, and state ministers; convening and preparing the agenda for cabinet meetings; chairing the cabinet meetings (unless the president of the Republic is in attendance, in which case the president chairs); signing orders establishing public institutions; and signing orders to appoint or dismiss the following positions: Director of cabinet in the office of the prime minister; executive secretaries of national commissions; advisors and heads of service in the office of the prime minister; other senior officials of public institutions not otherwise specified; director generals and directors in Parliament, the Supreme Court, the office of the prime minister, the National Public Prosecution Authority, ministries, and other public institutions; national, intermediate, and primary level prosecutors; and civil servants. The prime minister countersigns laws that Parliament has adopted, and decree laws and orders that the president has signed. Ministers, state ministers, and other cabinet members countersign orders of the prime minister.

If the prime minister resigns or leaves office, all of the members of the cabinet also resign. The prime minister gives the president of the Republic the resignation of the cabinet. The outgoing cabinet only does routine business until the appointment of the new cabinet by the president.

Any minister, state minister, or other cabinet member can resign by giving his or her resignation to the president of the Republic through the prime minister. If the resignation is not withdrawn within five days, it becomes effective if the president agrees to it.

7. Collaboration between the legislature and the executive (Art. 126–138)

The branches of the government are separate and independent of each other. The constitution defines the responsibilities, organization, and functioning of each branch. The State has to ensure that the people in each branch are competent and have integrity. The principle of power-sharing in State institutions must be respected at all times. The president of the republic and the speaker of the Chamber of Deputies cannot belong to the same political organization.

The Chambers of Parliament give the president and prime minister the agenda of plenary sittings and Parliamentary committees. The prime minister and other cabinet members can attend and take the floor during sittings. They can also bring technical advisers, who are only allowed to take the floor during the committee meetings.

The prime minister can request that a vote of no confidence be passed by the Chamber of Deputies for approval of government programs or adoption of a draft law. Three days must pass before the debate can occur. A no-confidence vote can pass if voted on by a two-thirds majority of the Chamber of Deputies. If the prime minster loses a vote of no confidence, they must resign within 24 hours.

To gather information and supervise government activities, the Chamber of Deputies uses methods such as oral and written questions, hearings, commissions of inquiry, and interpellation. It can question the performance of the cabinet or its members through a vote of no confidence. When the motion is against one member, only interpellation and one-fifth of the Chamber of Deputies signatures are needed for it to be accepted. When it concerns the entire cabinet, there need to be signatures by at least one-third chamber of deputies. There can only be a vote after 48 hours have passed from the initial request. The motion must be voted on through secret ballot with two-third members of the Chamber of Deputies voting in favor. Sessions are closed during this time.

A cabinet member who has had a vote of no confidence passed against him must resign. If the no-confidence vote is against all of the cabinet, then the entire cabinet must resign. If the no-confidence motion is rejected, the signatories of the motion cannot reintroduce the motion during the same session.

To supervise government activities, the Senate can present questions concerning the entire cabinet or several ministries to the prime minister. It can also create commissions of inquiry to overlook cabinet activities. It is not allowed to initiate a motion of no confidence or conduct interpellation.

Once in a Parliamentary session, the prime minister informs both chambers about the activities of the government. Some sittings are devoted to questions and answers between Parliamentary members and the cabinet. The cabinet provides the Parliament with explanations and the management of activities.

When the president of the Republic declares war, he or she must inform the Parliament within seven days. A simple majority is needed by each chamber to adopt the vote.

The president addresses either or both chambers in person or via a written letter. There is no debate on the communication. If Parliament is not in session, the chambers convene specifically to hear the communication. The president of the Republic can dissolve the Chamber of Deputies when there is a serious matter of national importance. However, this can be done no more than once during his or her term. There must be elections of new members within 90 days of dissolution. The Senate cannot be dissolved.

The president can declare a state of siege or a state of emergency with cabinet approval. It must be justified, specify the area it applies to and its potential consequences, and it must indicate the rights, freedoms, and guarantees that are provided by law and will be suspended during the state of siege or emergency. It cannot exceed 15 days, unless approved by a two-thirds majority vote of each Parliamentary chamber. If there is a war, laws can be enacted to set the state of siege or emergency to a longer period. This period should not, however, exceed the time necessary to return the situation to normal.

A declaration of siege or emergency must not violate the right to life and physical integrity of individuals or the rights given to people in relation to their status, capacity, and nationality. It cannot violate the principle of non-retroactivity of criminal law or the right to defense and freedom of conscience and religion. The declaration of the state of siege or emergency cannot affect the president's power or the power of the Parliament and Supreme Court. It cannot change the principles set out in the constitution regarding the responsibilities of the State and its public officials. There can be no elections during a siege or a state of emergency, or for 30 days after. A state of siege can only be declared if there is a threat or aggression from a foreign state, or any other serious threat or a danger to the constitutional order. A state of emergency is declared when there is a public disaster or constitutional crisis that does not warrant a declaration of a state of siege. The Chamber of Deputies cannot be dissolved during a state of siege or a state of emergency. Both chambers are recalled if they are in recess. If the Chamber of Deputies has been dissolved, or its term of office has ended before the state of siege or emergency, the Senate exercises the powers relating to the state of siege or emergency.

8. The judiciary

Section three of Chapter 7 of the constitution covers the judiciary (Art. 148–157), which is composed of ordinary and specialized courts. The High Council of the Judiciary (HCJ) is its highest governing body. The HCJ sets the general guidelines that govern the organization of the judiciary.

The judiciary is independent and has financial and administrative autonomy. According to the principles of the judicial system, justice must prevail in all matters for the people, and nobody can judge their own case; court proceedings are public unless the court decides otherwise; there must be a written explanation delivered in public for every decision; court decisions are binding and cannot be challenged, except through lawful procedures; and judges are independent and are expected to exercise their judicial functions lawfully.

There are ordinary and specialized courts. Ordinary courts include the supreme court, the high court, intermediate courts, and primary courts. Specialized courts include commercial courts and military courts. The constitution allows an organic law to remove or establish an ordinary or a specialized court.[67]

After consultation with the cabinet and the HCJ, and with approval by the Senate, the president of the Republic appoints the president and vice president of the Supreme Court, the president and vice president of the high court, and the president and vice president of the commercial high court. The president of the Supreme Court cannot be of foreign nationality and must be Rwandan by origin. The HCJ appoints the judges in charge of other ordinary courts and commercial courts. With the Senate's approval and after consulting with the cabinet and the HCJ, the president of the Republic appoints the judges of the Supreme Court. Judges of military courts are appointed in accordance with appropriate laws.

All judges take an oath of office. The president, vice president, and judges of the Supreme Court, along with the presidents and vice presidents of the high court and commercial high court, swear an oath of office before the president of the Republic. Other judges swear an oath before the authorities noted in the law governing them. The presidents and vice presidents of the Supreme Court, the high court, and the commercial high court are appointed for five-year terms that are renewable once.

With a three-fifths majority vote of either the Chamber of Deputies or the Senate, and a two-thirds majority vote of each chamber of Parliament, the president, vice president, and judges of the Supreme Court, and the presidents and vice presidents of the high court and the commercial high court can be removed from their positions due to misbehavior, incompetence, or gross professional misconduct. Judges in ordinary and commercial courts can be removed by the HCJ. The laws governing the military court dictate how those judges are removed.

9. *Other state organs*

There are several national commissions, specialized organs, national councils, and public institutions (Art. 139–147). The national commissions include the National Commission for Human Rights, the National Unity and Reconciliation Commission, the National Commission for the Fight against Genocide, the National Electoral Commission, and the National Public Service Commission. The specialized organs include the Office of the Ombudsman, the Office of the Auditor General of State Finances, the Gender Monitoring Office, the Chancellery for Heroes, the National Orders and Decorations of Honor, and the Rwanda Academy of Language and Culture. The national councils include the National Women Council, the National Youth Council, and the National Council of Persons with Disabilities. Other national commissions, specialized organs, and national councils can be established or removed by law.

In addition to listing key commissions, organs, and councils, the constitution elaborates further on three organs: The National *Umushyikirano* Council, the *Abunzi* Committee, and the National Public Prosecution Authority.

The National *Umushyikirano* Council is a meeting between the president of the Republic and representatives of the citizens. The council meets once a year, with the President convening and presiding, and debates issues regarding the nation and national unity. The council sends resolutions to the appropriate institutions for approval.

The *Abunzi* Committee is responsible for pacifying parties in conflict to preserve national unity and promote peaceful co-existence. The committee includes people with integrity and mediating skills.

The National Public Prosecution Authority is a single institution that investigates and prosecutes offenses. It includes the office of the prosecutor general, the prosecution service at the intermediate level, and the public prosecution services at the primary level. The prosecutor general, the deputy prosecutor general, and national prosecutors compose the office of the prosecutor general. With the Senate's approval, the prosecutor general and the deputy prosecutor are appointed by a presidential order for a once-renewable, five-year term. The president nominates a candidate for each position. The prime minister appoints other prosecutors.

The minister in charge of justice supervises the National Public Prosecution Authority and determines the general policy of matters relating to prosecution. The minister can provide written instructions to the prosecutor general or any prosecutor to begin or cease investigation or prosecution. The minister must inform the prosecutor general if such instructions are proposed in the context of general policy, urgency, or public interest.

The High Council of the National Public Prosecution Authority is responsible for creating general policy guidelines and guaranteeing that the prosecution services function effectively.

When jurisdiction falls to the military courts, the military prosecution department is responsible for prosecution. The military prosecutor general heads the department and is assisted by the deputy military prosecutor general.

10. *National defense and security, state finances and taxes, and international treaties and agreements*

Chapter 8 of the constitution covers national defense and security (Art. 158–161). The Rwanda Defense Force, the Rwanda National Police, and the National Intelligence and Security Service are the national defense and security bodies of Rwanda. These organizations work together to coordinate their activities. The Rwanda Defense Force is the national military and provides national defense. The Chief of Defense Staff is in charge of operations and general administration of the force. The government can downsize, discharge, demobilize, or dismiss the force or members of the force. The Rwanda National Police ensures the security of its people and property. The National Intelligence and Security Services is responsible for intelligence, immigration and emigration issues, and the prevention of and protection against national security threats.

Chapter 9 of the constitution covers State finances and taxes (Art. 162–166). It requires the Chamber of Deputies to adopt the State finance law every financial year. (This law determines the State's revenue and expenditure.) The Senate provides the Chamber of Deputies with its opinion on the state budget prior to adoption. If the financial year starts before the State budget is passed, the prime minister provisionally authorizes the budget of an amount that is one-twelfth of the previous year's budget.

Only law can impose, modify, or remove a tax. Also, a tax exemption or reduction can be granted only when authorized by law. The Office of the Auditor General audits state finances and assets. It also submits a complete report on the balance sheet of the previous year's State budget to both Chambers of Parliament. The report includes how the budget was executed, unnecessary or unlawful expenditures, and whether public funds were embezzled or squandered. The president of the Republic, the Cabinet, the President of the Supreme Court, and the Prosecutor General receive a copy of the report. Parliament examines the report and makes a decision within six months. Officials receiving a copy of the report must implement the recommendations in areas where there were irregularities and other shortcomings. At the request of Parliament, the Auditor General can conduct audits of State institutions or the use of State funds.

Chapter 10 of the constitution covers international treaties and agreements (Art. 167–170). The president of the Republic or his delegate can negotiate, sign, and ratify international treaties and agreements. Parliament is notified of these, unless the treaties or agreements concern armistice, peace, commerce, accession to international organizations, commitment of state finances, modification of national legislature, or the status of people. These are ratified after Parliament approval.

If a treaty or agreement involves ceding, exchanging, or adding territory, it requires the consent of Rwandans through referendum before ratification. If a negotiation relates to an international treaty or agreement not subject to presidential ratification, the President and Parliament are still notified. Where an international treaty or agreement has been duly ratified or approved and has been published in the Official Gazette, it is law. International agreements that permit foreign military bases on national territory are prohibited. International agreements permitting the transit or dumping of hazardous waste and materials are prohibited. Where an international treaty or agreement conflicts with the constitution or organic law, it cannot be ratified unless the constitution or organic law is amended.

11. Amendment and revision (Art. 175)

With the approval of the Cabinet or a two-thirds majority vote from each Chamber of Parliament, the president of the Republic can initiate an amendment to the constitution. Approval of the amendment requires a three-fourths majority vote by each Chamber of Parliament. A referendum is required if the amendment is related to the Presidential term of office, the system of democratic government based on political pluralism, the republican form of government, or national sovereignty. Proposals on the amendment of the provision on procedure for amending or revising the constitution are not permitted.

Laws must be published before they are enforced. Ignorance of a published law is not an excuse for not following it. Unwritten customary law remains applicable, as long as it is not inconsistent with the constitution, laws, or orders and does not violate human rights or prejudice public safety or good morals.

Notes

1 *Black's Law*, s.v. "constitution."
2 On the theory of "constitutional moments," see Bruce Ackerman, *We the People* (Cambridge: Belknap Press of Harvard University Press, 1991), 6–7 and 40–57.
3 Rene Lemarchand, *Rwanda and Burundi* (New York: Praeger Publishers, 1970), 159–169.
4 Ibid., 178.
5 Ordinance Legislative no. 221/275 of 18 October 1960, B.O.R.U, 1960, 1780.
6 Ordinance Legislative no. 02/16 of 15 January 1961, B.O.R.U., 1961, 228–243.
7 Filip Reyntjens, *Pouvoirs et Droit au Rwanda: droit public et evolution politique, 1916–1973* (Tervuren: Musée royal de l'Afrique centrale, 1985), 292.

8 Legislative Ordinance no. 02/38 od 6 February 1961 described institutions created by the General Assembly held in Gitarama as including "transitional Government, Council of Rwanda and bourme…." No mention of the Constitution, see UN Doc A/4706/Add.1. See also "note verbale remise a la Commission par le Secretaire General du Rwanda-Urundi," in which Belgium recognized the leaders and institutions created in Gitarama to be "de facto" while waiting for a "de jure" solution to be reached between Rwanda and the UN. F. Nkundabagenzi, ed., *Rwanda Politique 1958–1960* (Bruxelles: The Centre, 1961), 397–399.
9 Assembly Legislative., doc. no.4, sess. of 23 February 1961, 1.
10 See, for example, the position of the legislative assembly on the role of Belgium in Nkundabagenzi, *Rwanda Politique*, 405.
11 For example, the legislative ordinance No 02/38 of 6 February 1961 was adopted a few days after the adoption of the constitution and the elected officials of Rwanda accepted it as binding.
12 Filip Reyntjens, *Pouvoirs et Droit*, *supra.*, 291.
13 Assemblee Legislative, Doc. No. 2 (1961–1962), session of 4 October 1961.
14 J.O., 1962, No 22bis of 1 December 1962.
15 Before independence, some schools were specifically designed to teach the children of chiefs to prepare them to take over from their parents in the administration. It is these privileges that this article is mainly referring to.
16 Rene De Wolf, Apercu de la Constitution Rwandaise, Revue Juridique du Rwanda, Vol. V. No. 1, 1 January 1981, 18.
17 The National Congress is composed by the college of counselors of communes, members of the National Assembly, and members of the Government (Art. 97 of the Constitution).
18 Reyntjens, F. *Povoir et Droit au Rwanda*, 326.
19 Nicholas W. Barber, *The Principles of Constitutionalism* (Oxford: Oxford University Press, 2018), 3.
20 John Locke, *Second Treaties on Civil Government*, ed. Peter Laslett (New York: New American Library, 1965), 410.
21 On how political opposition was crushed by MDR Parmehutu and how after this crush, some of the leaders around its president turned inside the party to silence and purge any dissenting voices. Reyntjens, F. *Pouvoir Droit au Rwanda*, 445 and 473.
22 The text of this amendment was published in Conseil National de Developpement, "Recueil des Textes Relatifs au Pouvoir Legislatif au Rwanda de 1960 a nos Jours," Kigali, August 1989, 55–81.
23 See Military Coup in Rwanda Follows Tribal Dissension, The New York Times, July 6th, 1973, 3.
24 See Proclamation du 5 Juillet 1973 du haut –Commandement de la Garde Nationale See J.O.R.R. No. 13 of 5 July 1973.
25 See Reyntjens, Filip La Nouvelle Constitution du 20 Decembre 1978, Revue Juridique du Rwanda, Vol. IV, No. 2, of April 1st, 1980, 197.
26 M.R.N.D, Manifeste et Statuts, ervice de la documentation et de la propagande à la Présidence de M.R.N.D, Kigali 1985.
27 F. Reyntjens, *La Nouvelle Constitution du 20 Decembre 1978, supra.*, 198.
28 Rene De Wolf, *Apercu de la Constitution Rwandaise, supra.*, 15.
29 Deo Byanafashye and Paul Rutayisire, *Histoire du Rwanda, Des origins a la fin du XXe siècle* (Huye: Universite Nationale du Rwanda, 2011), 489.
30 Bashoga, Bernard, Quelques lacunes de la Constitution de la Republic Rwandaise du 10 Juin 1991, in Revue Jurique du Rwanda, Vol. XVI, No. 1, January 1992, 62–65.
31 "Declaration du FPR Relative a la Mise Place des Institutions," *Official Gazette* year 34, no. 11 (June 1995).

32 The post of Vice-President was awarded to Major-General Paul Kagame, who held it jointly with that of Minister of Defense.
33 "Protocole d'Accord entre les forces politiques FPR, MDR, PDC, PDI, PL, PSD, PSR, et UDPR, sur la mise en place des institutions nationale," *Official Gazette* year 34, no. 11 (June 1995).
34 "Fundamental Law of the Republic of Rwanda," *Official Gazette* year 34, no. 11 (June 1995): 3.
35 The letter from the Prime Minister to the Supreme Court requesting that the latter declare the vacancy of the post of the president of the Republic following the resignation of President Pasteur Bizimungu, on the one hand, and to draw legal consequences resulting from this issue on the other. See letter no. 153/03.4, 24 March 2000.
36 Supreme Court of Rwanda, "Decree No. 1/2000 of March 20, 2000," *Official Gazette of the Republic of Rwanda* (Special Issue March 2000): 6.
37 Ibid., 5.
38 Ibid.
39 On the first question, he argued that this was not the case:

> *Le raisonnement de la Court à l'avantage du réalisme, mains il n'a pas pu réunir toutes les atouts juridique pour être convaincant. Pour faire valoir la clause de l'article 2 de la loi Fondamentale du 26 mai 1995, il aurait fallu que la Déclaration du FPR ait entendu confier au Vice-Président les attributions claires qui pouvaient, comme telles, créer un conflit juridique avec clés du Protocole sur le partage du pouvoir. Or. Ce n'est pas le cas.*

On the second question, he argued that the Fundamental law gives such powers not to the Supreme Court but rather to the Transitional National Assembly, which, in Article 18 of the Protocol on Miscellaneous Issues and Final Provisions, provides that "it shall be the duty of the Transitional National Assembly to make an authentic interpretation of the Peace Agreement." One may, however, question whether this author was right to extend the application of article 18, which specifically applies to the Peace Agreement, to all fundamental law texts, including the RPF declaration. A negative answer would cause his first argument to fall and inevitably his final argument. See Aloys Muberanziza, "Quelques Réflexions sur la Loi fondamentale Actuelle a la Veille de la Mise en Place d'une Nouvelle Constitution au Rwanda," *Revue Scientifique de Droit*, no. 5 (June 2000): 18–29.
40 Republic of Rwanda, *Towards a Constitution for Rwanda: Action Plan 2002–2003* (Kigali: Legal and Constitutional Commission, April 2002), 3.
41 Id.
42 For different phases followed by the commission, from the sensitization to the submission of the draft constitution to referendum, see National Unity and Reconciliation Commission, *Report of the National Unity and Reconciliation Commission* (Kigali: National Unity and Reconciliation Commission, October 2002), 52–56.
43 Ingrid Samset and Orrvar Dalby, *Rwanda: Presidential and Parliamentary Elections 2003* (NORDEM Report, 2003), 9.
44 Republic of Rwanda, *Towards a Constitution for Rwanda*, 10.
45 Id.
46 Samset and Dalby, *Rwanda*, 9.
47 See Supreme Court ruling No. 772/14.06/2003.
48 National Unity and Reconciliation Commission, *Report of the National Unity*, 54.
49 Official Gazette, n° Special 04 June 2003.

50 Official Gazette n° Special of 24 December 2015.
51 Article 177 of the Constitution of the Republic of Rwanda of 2003 Revised in 2015; ibid.
52 Art. 52 "The leadership organs of political organizations shall only maintain offices at the national, provincial and Kigali City levels."
53 Art. 52 "The leadership organs of political organizations shall have offices at the national level."
54 See Art. 56.
55 Organic Law No. 10/2013/OL of 11/07/2013 Governing Political Organizations and Politicians, Official Gazette n° Special of 12/07/2013.
56 National Consultative Forum of Political Organizations, http://forumfp.org.rw/index.php?id=2.
57 "The authentic interpretation of laws shall be done by both Chambers of Parliament acting jointly after the Supreme Court has given an opinion on the matter" Art. 96.
58 "Authentic interpretation of laws is done by the Supreme Court" Art. 96.
59 In the case N° RS/SPEC/00001/2017/SC, the Supreme Court provided the guidelines regarding the application of this provision (para. 25, 26) and ruled that in case the Bar Association receives a request from a citizen to request that the Supreme Court undertake an authentic interpretation of a legal text, the Bar has the power to accept, refuse, or reformulate this request (Para. 28).
60 *Democratic Green Party of Rwanda v. Republic of Rwanda*, RS/SPEC/002/15 (2015).
61 Art. 99.
62 Art. 101.
63 Clement Uwiringiyimana, Rwandans vote on constitution changes to let Kagame extend rule, Reuter December 18, 2015, www.reuters.com/article/us-rwanda-politics/rwandans-vote-on-constitution-changes-to-let-kagame-extend-rule-idUSKBN0U10KQ20151218.
64 *Democratic Green Party of Rwanda v. Government of Rwanda*, para 37.
65 "A former Head of State shall not be prosecuted for any of the preceding crimes when no proceedings in respect to such an offence were brought against him/her during his/her presidency" Article 115 (Amendment n°3 of 13/8/2008, Article 22).
66 See Art. 116 of the 2003 Constitution and Art. 116 of the 2015 Amended Constitution.
67 It is in this regard that the Organic Law No. 002/2018 of 04/04 established the Court of Appeals, a court that was not specifically provided for in the constitution.

4 Rwandan international law

As a State and a member of multiple international organizations, including the United Nations, and party to more than 250 multinational treaties, Rwanda is an active player in international law. As such, it is influenced by but also influences the development of international law. Since the 1990s and due to the tragic 1994 Genocide against the Tutsi, Rwanda's contribution to the development of international criminal law, international humanitarian law and refugee law, and international economic law has been very significant.

This chapter does not intend to cover all the fields in which there is a connection between Rwanda and international law. Instead, it covers three key areas related to the 1990s war and the 1994 genocide: International human rights law, the International Court of Justice, and international criminal law. Before addressing these three key areas, it is important to understand the connection between international law and domestic Rwandan law.

Section 1. Incorporation and position of international law in the Rwandan legal system

A. Sources of Rwandan international law[1]

Unlike national law, international law is not a product of any parliament or legislature. To know whether a rule is part of international law, one has to trace it back to one of its sources, as defined in Article 38 of the Statute of the International Court of Justice (ICJ)[2]: Namely, international conventions, whether general or particular, establishing rules expressly recognized by Rwanda; international custom, as evidence of a general practice accepted as law by Rwanda; and the general principles of law recognized by civilized nations. In addition to these three primary sources, Article 38 contains two secondary sources: Namely, judicial decisions and the teachings of the most highly qualified publicists of the various nations.

There is no hierarchy in the order of the above sources of international law, and therefore, in theory, they should all be considered on equal footing; however, in practice, two sources have remained the most influential: Treaties and international customary law. The discussion of the Rwandan International Law (RIL) in this chapter will primarily focus on treaty law but in some cases focuses on international customary law.

The term "international convention" used in Article 38 of the International Court of Justice (ICJ) is frequently used to mean, among other things, a covenant, agreement, protocol, charter, act, convention, accord, or statute. It is, however, commonly known as a treaty. Article 2 of the 1969 Vienna Convention on the Law of Treaties (VCLT),[3] ratified by Rwanda on 3 January 1980,[4] defines a "treaty" as an "international agreement concluded between states in written form and governed by international law, whether embodied in a single instrument or in two or more related instruments and whatever its particular designation." Treaties are usually compared to domestic contracts. They often appear in written form, are designed for a specific purpose, and require formal consent to be binding. This consent is expressed by ratification. Treaties can be bilateral or multilateral. They can also be lawmaking, establishing legislation-like rules (*Traité-loi*) among nations (for example, the United Nations Convention on the Law of the Sea, etc.), or take the form of a simple contract (*traité contrat*. For example, a bilateral trade agreement).[5]

The principle of *pacta sunt servanda* enshrined in Article 26 of the VCLT provides that "every treaty in force is binding upon the parties to it and must be performed by them in good faith." The VCLT, however, allows countries to formulate reservations when signing, ratifying, accepting, approving, or acceding to a treaty unless

> (a) the reservation is prohibited by the treaty (b) the treaty provides that only specified reservations, which do not include the reservation in question, may be made, or (c) in cases not falling under sub-paragraphs (a) and (b), the reservation is incompatible with the object and purpose of the treaty. (Art. 19)

Art. 38 of the ICJ refers to "international custom, as evidence of a general practice accepted as law." In order for a customary international law to exist, two elements are required: (a) Evidence of a general practice and (2) *opinio juris*. The practice can be evidenced by diplomatic correspondence, policy statements, press releases, the opinion of official legal advisers, comments by the government, state legislation, recitals in treaties and other international instruments, etc. These practices, however, have to be consistent, general, and uniform. Although consistency should not be assessed based on how long the practice has been into existence and the general nature of a practice evaluated on the basis of the number of countries involved, these factors can be used as an important evidence to prove the consistency or generality of a practice.[6] With regard to *opinio juris*, the practice must be "of force, not because it was prescribed by any superior power, but because it has been generally accepted as a rule of conduct."[7] The concept of *opinio juris* was confirmed by the ICJ in the case of *Nicaragua v. United States*, in which the Court ruled that the State undertaking such a practice, or other States in a position to react to it, must have conducted themselves in a way that expresses "evidence of a belief that this practice is rendered obligatory by the existence of a rule of law requiring it."[8]

B. The process of creation and incorporation of international law in the Rwandan legal system

International law from any source listed in Article 38 of the ICJ statute can be directly incorporated and applied in Rwanda. This is illustrated in Article 19 of the Rwandan Constitution, which allows a judge, when examining the rights of a child, to examine not only the treaty law but also customary international, general principles of law and, as secondary sources, "judicial decisions and the teachings of the most highly qualified publicists of the various nations" in assessing "specific mechanisms of protection."

Although the Rwandan Constitution is more specific about the incorporation of treaty law in its legal system, it is silent on how such incorporation happens for other sources of international law. The situation is a bit easier with regard to customary international law, where the judge will need to examine who is involved in the development of a custom, how long it has been in existence, how general the practice is, how consistent and relevant it is, etc.[9] when looking for evidence of Rwanda's practices on the issue in question and whether or not its considers itself to be bound by that practice. It becomes harder when the Rwandan judge applies "general principles of law recognized by civilized nations" or secondary sources provided by Article 38 of the ICJ. In international law, there is no definite answer on what constitutes general principles of law or which judicial decisions and teachings of highly qualified publicists constitute sources of international law.

The Rwandan Constitution grants the power to negotiate and sign international treaties and agreements to the president of the Republic. He or she can, however, delegate this power to the minister of foreign affairs or anybody else (Art. 167). He or she can negotiate and sign any treaty, but the constitution prohibits him or her from negotiating and signing international agreements permitting foreign military bases in Rwandan territory as well as those permitting the transit or dumping on national territory of toxic waste and other hazardous materials likely to cause serious damage to public health and the environment (Art. 169).

The power to ratify treaties is granted to the president, but the conditions under which he or she can exercise these powers depend on the nature of the international treaty or agreement (Art. 167).

The first category concerns treaties and agreements ceding or exchanging Rwandan territory or adding to it the territory of another country. These cannot be ratified without the consent of Rwandans via a referendum.

The second category applies to international treaties and agreements concerning armistice, peace, commerce, accession to international organizations; those that engage state finances, and those requiring modification of national legislation or relating to peoples' status. These can only be ratified after approval by the Parliament.

The third category concerns any international treaty or agreement that does not fit into either of the above two categories; these can be ratified by the president without consulting anyone. The constitution requires only that the Parliament be notified of the treaty and agreement following its conclusion. While an international treaty or agreement contains provisions that conflict with a constitutional or organic law provision, the power to ratify or approve it cannot be exercised until the concerned constitutional or organic law provision is amended (Art. 170). This means that technically, before any ratification, an assessment must be conducted on whether an international treaty or agreement is in conflict with the constitution or organic law provisions. Obviously, this assessment is conducted by the executive, which, once it concludes that such a conflict exists, must request the Parliament to amend the concerned constitutional or organic law provision. Articles 167 and 170 of the Constitution, therefore, grant the Parliament the power of checks and balances over the president's powers to negotiate, sign, and ratify international treaties. If the Parliament opts not to approve the treaty referred to in the above-mentioned category or opts not to change the concerned constitutional or organic law provision, the treaty cannot be ratified. If it is ratified by error or negligence in violation of Articles 167 and 170, although it will remain valid internationally, it cannot be self-executing under domestic law. In practice, the president exercises the power of ratification via a cabinet decision.[10]

C. *Position of international treaties and agreements in the Rwandan legal system*

Upon publication in the official gazette of the Republic of Rwanda, international treaties and agreements that have been duly ratified or approved have the force of law as national legislation (Art. 168). This makes Rwanda a monist country. Unlike the dualist system that sees international law and national law as distinct, each with its own subjects, contents, and authority, the monist system creates a unitary legal system in which both national and international law have identical subjects, sources, and substantive contents.[11] Under monist systems, all activities of the state are regulated by a single legal system that includes both national and international law. International law is ranked in the hierarchal order of laws of the country. This is the case in Rwanda: International law is part of the legal system and hierarchy of the Rwandan positive law.

The Rwandan Constitution positions international treaties and agreements very high in its hierarchy of laws. Article 95 of the Constitution ranks Rwandan laws as follows: The Constitution, then organic laws, then international treaties and agreements ratified by Rwanda in the third position. In the fourth position is ordinary law, while in the last position are orders. The same provision states that "A law cannot contradict another law that is higher in hierarchy." This provision is similar to that of the French Constitution, which, in its Article 55, provides that "treaties or agreements duly ratified or approved shall, upon publication, prevail over acts of parliament, subject to the application of each agreement or treaty by the other party."[12] Similar provisions have been identified in constitutions, such as those of Germany (Art. 25),[13] the Netherlands (Art. 94),[14] and Poland (Art. 91).[15]

Rwanda's judges must apply international law to cases the same way they apply domestic law, subject to the hierarchy defined by the constitution. This means that courts' decisions should not only be in conformity with the Constitution and other domestic laws; they should also apply to and be in conformity with international law in force. Similarly, legislation and administrative decisions should not only conform with the Rwandan Constitution and organic laws; they must also be checked for contradiction with international law. As we will discuss in the next chapter, however, there is still some resistance by national courts to applying international law and, when they apply it, to giving priority to international, self-executing human rights treaties over national ordinary laws.

Section 2. Rwandan international human rights law

A. Key ratified human rights treaties

Of the nine core human rights instruments, Rwanda has ratified eight: (1) The International Convention on the Elimination of All Forms of Racial Discrimination,[16] (2) the International Covenant on Civil and Political Rights,[17] (3) the International Covenant on Economic, Social, and Cultural Rights,[18] (4) the Convention on the Elimination of All Forms of Discrimination against Women,[19] (5) the Convention against Torture and Other Cruel, Inhuman, or Degrading Treatment or Punishment,[20] (6) the Convention on the Rights of the Child,[21] (7) the International Convention on the Protection of the Rights of All Migrant Workers and Members of Their Families,[22] and (8) the Convention on the Rights of Persons with Disabilities.[23] The ninth, still to be ratified, is the International Convention for the Protection of All Persons from Enforced Disappearance.

Rwanda has made no reservations on any of the provisions of human rights treaties mentioned above. In 2008, it removed those that it had placed on the International Covenant on Economic, Social and Cultural Rights,[24] the International Convention on the Elimination of All Forms of Racial Discrimination,[25] and the Convention on the Prevention and Punishment of the Crime of Genocide.[26] In 2010, it removed those that it had placed on the Geneva Convention on Refugees[27] and the Protocol to Geneva Convention Relating to the Status of Refugees.[28]

Rwanda has also accepted individual complaints and procedures contained in the Optional Protocol to the Convention on the Rights of Persons with Disabilities[29] and the Optional Protocol to the Convention on the Elimination of All Forms of Discrimination against Women.[30] By accessing the Optional Protocol to the Convention against Torture and Other Cruel, Inhuman or Degrading Treatment or Punishment, the Optional Protocol to the Convention on the Elimination of All Forms of Discrimination against Women, and the Optional Protocol on the Convention on the Rights of Persons with Disabilities, Rwanda has accepted the inquiry procedures under these protocols.[31]

However, it has not yet accepted the individual complaints provided under the Optional Protocol to the International Covenant on Civil and Political Rights, those under the Optional Protocol to the International Covenant on Economic Social and Cultural Rights, or those from the Optional Protocol to the Convention on the Rights of the Child.

At the regional level, Rwanda has ratified: (1) The African Charter on Human and Peoples' Rights,[32] (2) its Protocol on the Establishment of an African Court on Human and Peoples' Rights,[33] (3) the African Charter on the Rights and Welfare of the Child,[34] and (4) the Protocol to the African Charter on Human and Peoples' Rights on the Rights of Women in Africa.[35]

B. Rwanda and international and regional human rights bodies

1. The human rights council

The United Nations (UN) Human Rights Council was created on 15 March 2006[36] to replace the UN Commission on Human Rights as the UN Charter Human Rights body. It is an inter-governmental body that acts as the subsidiary organ of the General Assembly. It is made up of 47 rotating member states. Seats are distributed as follows among regional groups: Group of African states (13 countries), group of Asian states (13 countries), group of Eastern European states (six countries), group of Latin American and Caribbean states (eight countries), and group of Western European and other states (seven countries). Members are elected for a three year-term. Those elected to the council must uphold the highest standards in the promotion and protection of human rights, fully cooperate with the council, and be reviewed under the universal periodic review (UPR) mechanism during their term of membership.

Rwanda was elected to join the UN Human Rights Council for the first time on 1 January 2017 for a three-year term and served as vice chair of the council in 2018. It was reviewed for the first time under the UPR mechanism in January 2011,[37] and again in November 2015.[38] Rwanda, like other countries, is continuously reviewed every four years. The objectives of the UPR are (a) the improvement of the human rights situation on the ground; (b) the fulfillment of the State's human rights obligations and commitments, and assessment of positive developments and challenges faced by the State; (c) the enhancement of the State's capacity and technical assistance, in consultation with, and with the consent of, the State concerned; (d) the sharing of best practice among States and other stakeholders; (e) support for cooperation in the promotion and protection of human rights; and (f) the encouragement of full cooperation and engagement with the council, other human rights bodies, and the Office of the United Nations High Commissioner for Human Rights.[39] The review is based on human rights contained in: (1) The Charter of the United Nations; (2) the Universal Declaration of Human Rights; (3) human rights instruments to which a State is party; and (4) voluntary pledges and commitments made by States, including those undertaken when presenting their candidatures for election to the Human Rights Council. The review is based on: (a) The national report of the country under review, (b) a compilation prepared by the Office of the High Commissioner for Human Rights, and (c) credible and reliable information provided by other relevant stakeholders.[40]

2. *African commission on human and peoples' rights*

The African Charter on Human and Peoples' Rights was ratified by Rwanda on 15 July 1983.[41] It created an African Commission on Human and People's Rights (Art. 30) with the mission (1) to promote human and peoples' rights; (2) to ensure the protection of human and peoples' rights under the conditions laid down by the charter; (3) to interpret all provisions of the present charter at the request of a state party, an institution of the African Union, or an African organization recognized by the African Union; and (4) to perform any other tasks that may be entrusted to it by the Assembly of Heads of State and Government (Art. 45).

The headquarters of the African Commission is in Banjul, Gambia. The commission consists of 11 members chosen from member countries (Art. 31). Commissioners are elected for a six-year renewable term. They are not paid and do not work full time. This means that they usually hold other positions in their respective states. In 2007, a Rwandan, Zainabo S. Kayitesi, was elected commissioner. Her six-year term was renewed in 2013. Ms. Kayitesi held this position jointly, first with that of chairperson of the Rwanda National Human Rights Commission and later with that of vice president of the Rwandan Supreme Court.

The charter requires its member states to submit a report every two years on legislative or other measures taken, with the intent of putting the rights and freedoms recognized and guaranteed by the charter into practice (Art. 62) By late 2019, a number of states were late in submitting their report under this article: 18 were late by one or two reports, 18 were late by three or more reports, and 29 had not submitted any reports.[42] Rwanda was one of only nine African countries that had submitted all their reports.[43]

The charter allows states to submit communications to the commission in cases in which the concerned state "has good reasons to believe that another State Party to this Charter has violated the provisions of the Charter" (Art. 46). It also allows "communication other than those of State Parties" (Art. 55). By 2018, the commission had received one communication against Rwanda by the Democratic Republic of the Congo (DRC) under Article 46[44] and two under Article 55: one filed by the *Association pour la sauvegarde de la paix au Burundi*[45] and another filed by the *Organisation mondiale contre la torture, Association Internationale des juristes démocrates, Commission internationale des juristes, Union interafricaine des droits de l'Homme.*[46]

3. *The African court on human and people's rights*

The Protocol to the African Charter on Human and Peoples' Rights on the Establishment of an African Court on Human and Peoples' Rights[47] was adopted on 9 June 1998 in Burkina Faso and came into force on 25 January 2004. The court became operational in 2006. Rwanda ratified the protocol on 5 May 2003. By August 2019, only 30 states had ratified it, though 22 had signed but not ratified it. Two states had neither signed nor ratified it.[48]

The African Court on Human and Peoples' Rights complements the protective mandate of the African Commission on Human and Peoples' Rights (Art. 2). The court's jurisdiction extends to all cases and disputes submitted to it concerning the interpretation and application of the African Charter on Human and Peoples' Rights, the protocol on the establishment of this court, and any other relevant human rights instruments ratified by the state concerned (Art. 3). The court can also provide an advisory opinion (Art. 4). In principle, only the commission, state parties, and any African Intergovernmental organization are entitled to submit cases to the court (Art. 5–1). However, the court may also allow Non-Governmental Organizations (NGOs) with observer status, and individuals, to come before the commission when the concerned state, at the time of ratification of this protocol or anytime thereafter, has made a declaration accepting the competence of the court to receive such cases. By September 2019, only nine states had declared their acceptance of the court's receiving cases brought against them by individuals and NGOs.[49] Until 29 February 2016, Rwanda was one of those states.[50] On that date, however, it decided to "withdraw for review its declaration."[51] Later on, this withdrawal became final.[52]

The African Court on Human and Peoples' Rights is headquartered in Arusha, Tanzania. It consists of eleven judges elected in their individual capacity, all of whom are nationals of Member States of the African Union.

By October 2019, the court had two judges of Rwandan origin: Justice Jean Mutsinzi, who was its president between September 2008 and September 2010, and Justice Marie-Therese Mukamulisa, who joined the court in July 2016 for a six-year term.[53]

By October 2019, the court had rendered 12 advisory opinion cases and 70 contentious cases.[54] Among those 82 cases, nine are against Rwanda: Four cases on *Mulindahabi Fidele v. Republic of Rwanda*;[55] two cases on *Rutabingwa Chrysanthe v. Republic of Rwanda*;[56] *Ingabire Victorie Umuhoza v. Republic of Rwanda*;[57] *General Kayumba Nyamwasa and others v. Republic of Rwanda*;[58] and *Faustin Uwintije v. Republic of Rwanda.*[59]

The protocol indicates that state parties must strive to comply with the judgment in any case to which they are parties within the time stipulated by the court and to guarantee its execution (Art. 30). As different reports[60] of the court have stressed, one of the biggest challenges has been bringing countries to comply with the court's judgments.

C. *Application of international human rights in Rwanda's domestic courts*

Article 27 of the 1969 Vienna Convention on the Law of Treaties provides that "a party may not invoke the provisions of its internal law as justification for its failure to perform a treaty." However, the performance referred to in this provision is an international performance. After all, international law is first and foremost the law between states. The problem is, therefore, not a State's performance internationally, because this is regulated by the above-mentioned Vienna Convention, but rather a State's performance domestically with regard to covenants it has taken toward its own citizens.

Ratification, whether in a monist or a dualist system, is the process by which states consent to be bound by international treaties and agreements. However, international law has not yet managed to solve the problem of where a ratified treaty fits within the hierarchy of State law. Neither has it solved the question of whether covenants that countries have taken toward their citizens are self-executing, meaning directly enforceable in domestic court, or not. This is left to the constitution of each state.

As a civil law-system country, Rwanda has, since its independence, presumed to have a monist system.[61] As such, its legal system is considered unitary, combining both national and international law under one legal order and hierarchy. The place of international law in the hierarchy of Rwandan law, and the question of whether its courts can directly apply international covenants, such as the human rights practices that Rwanda has committed itself to, have remained controversial. Until 2003, Rwandan law was silent on these two questions.[62] In 2003, however, the Constitution offered an answer to the hierarchy of international law in the Rwandan legal system. This Constitution placed international treaties and agreements above all laws other than the constitution. Article 190 of this Constitution provided that

> upon their publication in the official gazette, international treaties and agreements which have been conclusively adopted in accordance with the provisions of law shall be more binding than organic laws and ordinary laws, except in the case of non-compliance by one of parties.

The 2015 Constitution, however, moved international treaties down one notch. Its Article 95 places international treaties and agreements ratified by Rwanda in the third position in the hierarchy of laws: Below the constitution and organic law but above ordinary law and orders.

Article 95 did not specifically state that international treaties and agreements are self-executing. However, by positioning them in the hierarchy of laws in Rwanda and specifically stating that "a law cannot contradict another law that is higher in hierarchy," it left no room for the judiciary to avoid applying them. If international law is already part of Rwandan law, and the role of the judge is to interpret the law and administer justice,[63] it is the duty of the judge to apply the law as defined and hierarchized in the constitution. This position seems to be supported by the Government of Rwanda, as it stated in 2009[64] to the UN Human Rights Committee:

> Under Rwanda's monist legal system, a convention or treaty enters into force as soon as it has been ratified. No further procedure is required to incorporate it into domestic law [...] According to the Constitution, therefore, international instruments are directly applicable in Rwanda, provided that they are duly ratified and applied by the other party. As these instruments have primacy over domestic laws, except for the Constitution and referendum laws, the right to invoke them before the domestic courts is guaranteed.[65]

Rwandan courts have ruled that judges should not apply international treaties and agreements that only, they are also called to apply other sources of international law. This was confirmed by the High Court, which ruled:

> International conventions, doctrine, or the jurisprudence from other jurisdictions cannot be applied when they are contrary to Rwandan laws, unless those scholars or courts made those decisions pursuant to the international laws that were ratified by Rwanda and by which it abides.[66]

The challenge is not the commitment of the Rwandan judiciary to accepting international law as part of Rwandan law and applying it. The challenge is, rather, the lack of interest or lack of deep knowledge about international law and its rules of interpretation among Rwandan judges. For example, in the case RADA0037/13/CS,[67] which was related to the firing of Vu, a civil servant, for refusing to perform an oath holding the national flag, the applicant argued that her freedom of religion

> as provided for by the Constitution and International Human Right Conventions is inviolable. Therefore, a decision that is contrary to those principles cannot be made against a person. She finds that an employer should not have dismissed her on the ground of refusing to take the oath because she was already in service.[68]

The Court, however, did not address the question of whether or not the oath requirement met the standards established by International Covenant on Civil and Political Rights (ICCPR) to justify the government's limitation of the freedom of religion.[69] Rather, it ruled that:

> Taking the oath by holding the national flag does not violate [...] Article 18 of International Covenant on Civil and Political Rights of 16/12/1966, article 14, 15 and 19 of the African Charter on Human and Peoples' Rights, which Counsel Nk. relies on, because the common aim of all those provisions is that every person has freedom of belief and religion and also that all people are equal before the law, either in getting employment or ownership of property, while those beliefs should not jeopardize the national laws and none should rely on them to withdraw from legal obligations.[70]

The problem here was not that the freedom of religion could not be limited; it was how the judge treated the international law that guarantees the applicant's freedom of religion as some alien law not part of the Rwandan "national law." In taking this position, they failed to assess whether the national law limiting Vu.' s freedom of religion was "necessary to protect public safety, order, health, or morals or the fundamental rights and freedom of others," where it fits in the general hierarchy of Rwandan laws, and where it finds the power and authority to limit a right guaranteed by the constitution and international human rights treaty.

Section 3. Rwanda and the International Court of Justice (ICJ)

Rwanda's contribution to international law through the ICJ is mainly reflected in the *Democratic Republic of Congo v. Rwanda* case.[71]

On 23 June 1999, the DRC filed before the ICJ a case against Burundi, Uganda, and Rwanda for "acts of armed aggression committed ... in flagrant breach of the United Nations Charter and of the Charter of the

Organization of African Unity." The DRC requested the cessation of the alleged acts as well as reparation for intentional destruction and looting, and restitution of national property and resources appropriated for the benefit of the respective responding states. However, on 15 January 2001, it informed the court of its intention to discontinue the proceedings instituted against Burundi and Rwanda.

On 28 May 2002, the DRC filed again before the ICJ an application instituting proceedings against Rwanda for massive, serious, and flagrant violations of human rights and international humanitarian law, resulting from acts of armed aggression perpetrated by it on the territory of the DRC in breach of its sovereignty and territorial integrity, as guaranteed by the United Nations Charter and the Charter of the Organization of African Unity.

In its submission, the DRC argued that the ICJ's jurisdiction derives from the compromissory clause[72] of the following treaties ratified by Rwanda: The 1948 Convention on the Prevention and Punishment of the Crime of Genocide, the 1965 International Convention on the Elimination of All Forms of Racial Discrimination, the 1979 Convention on the Elimination on All Forms of Discrimination against Women, the Constitution of the World Health Organization (WHO), the Constitution of United Nations Education, Scientific and Cultural Organization (UNESCO), the 1971 Montreal Convention for the Suppression of Unlawful Acts against the Safety of Civil Aviation, and the 1984 New York Convention against Torture and Other Cruel, Inhuman, or Degrading Treatment or Punishment. The DRC also argued that the jurisdiction of the court derived from the supremacy of peremptory norms (*jus cogens*), as reflected in certain international treaties and conventions, in the area of human rights.

With regard to the 1948 Convention on the Prevention and Punishment of the Crime of Genocide, the DRC invoked Article IX, stating that:

> Disputes between the Contracting Parties relating to the interpretation, application, or fulfillment of the present Convention, including those relating to the responsibility of a State for genocide or for any of the other acts enumerated in Article III, shall be submitted to the International Court of Justice at the request of any of the parties to the dispute.

The DRC argued that, although, in ratifying this convention, Rwanda had made a reservation on this article, by its *décret-loi* of 15 February 1995 and a statement of 17 March 2005 by its minister of justice at the sixty-first session of the United Nations Commission on Human Rights, Rwanda has withdrawn its reservation. Article 1 of the above-mentioned *décret-loi* provided that "all reservations entered by the Rwandese Republic in respect of the accession approval and ratification of international instruments are withdrawn." The above-mentioned declaration of the Rwandan minister of justice that the DRC relied on said, "the few [human rights] instruments not yet ratified ... as well as reservations not yet withdrawn, would shortly be ratified ... [or] withdrawn."

The Rwandan government responded that it had never notified withdrawal of its reservation to Article IX of the Genocide Convention to the United Nations Secretary-General, or taken any measure to withdraw it, and that only such formal action on the international plane could constitute the definitive position of a state in regard to its treaty obligations. With regard to the above-mentioned declaration of the minister of justice, Rwanda argued that this was "unspecific" about which reservations, and besides, the statement could not bind it or oblige it to withdraw a particular reservation since it had been made by a minister of justice and not by a foreign minister or head of government.

The court agreed with Rwanda's position that the adoption of a withdrawal *décret-loi* and its publication in the official gazette of the Republic of Rwanda are part of the domestic legal order of Rwanda and have no effect within the international legal order. To have any effect, the withdrawal would have had to be the subject of a notification by Rwanda to the Secretary General of the United Nations. Besides, the ICJ and the DRC should have learned about this withdrawal not from Rwandan domestic law but from the UN Secretary General. With regard to the declaration of the minister of justice, the ICJ rejected Rwanda's argument that the minister of justice cannot bind the Rwandan state because she is not the minister of foreign affairs or head of state; however, it agreed that the withdrawal declaration had not been made in sufficiently specific terms in relation to Article IX of the Genocide Convention and that it therefore could not be considered confirmation by Rwanda that it is withdrawing or has withdrawn said reservation.

Having rejected the DRC argument that Rwanda had withdrawn its reservation, the court examined the argument that Rwanda's reservation to Article IX of the Genocide Convention was invalid. To support its position, the DRC presented three key arguments. First, it argued that the Genocide Convention contains norms of *jus cogens*, and the Rwandan reservation was therefore in violation of Article 53 of the Vienna Convention on Law of Treaties, which forbids treaties that conflict with peremptory norms. Second, the DRC argued that the Rwandan reservation was incompatible with the objective and purpose of the Genocide Convention because it excused Rwanda from preventing and punishing genocide. Third, the DRC argued that such a reservation was in contradiction with the fact that Rwanda had requested that the United Nations create an international criminal tribunal to prosecute genocide.

Rwanda argued that the DRC's arguments were completely different matters that did not affect the country's right to make a reservation on the ICJ jurisdiction. The ICJ agreed with Rwanda: First, that the mere fact that rights and obligations *erga omnes* may be at issue in a dispute, or that a dispute relates to compliance with *jus cogens* norms, does not automatically give the court jurisdiction to entertain that dispute. The jurisdiction of the court is always based on the consent of the parties. Second, the court agreed that the reservations, which were meant to exclude a particular method of settling a dispute, relating to the interpretation, application, or fulfillment of the convention, could not be regarded as incompatible with the object and purpose of the convention. For the Court such reservations bore on the jurisdiction of the court and not on the substantive obligations relating to the acts of genocide themselves under the convention. The court stressed further that there is no peremptory norm of general international law requiring a state to consent to the jurisdiction of the court in order to settle a dispute relating to the Genocide Convention.

With regard to the 1965 International Convention on the Elimination of All Forms of Racial Discrimination, to which Rwanda had also made a reservation regarding the ICJ jurisdiction, the DRC used the same argument: Namely, that Rwanda's reservation was unacceptable because it was incompatible with the object and purpose of the treaty, and because this treaty contained peremptory norms. Again, however, the ICJ sided with Rwanda, concluding first, that the Rwandan reservation was not incompatible with this treaty because two-thirds of the state parties to the Convention had not expressed their objection to it, and that the DRC itself had not raised any objection to the Rwandan reservation when it acceded to the convention.[73] Second, a dispute concerning non-compliance with a peremptory norm of general international law cannot suffice to serve as the ground for the Court's jurisdiction to entertain such a dispute. Besides, the court concluded, there exists no peremptory norm requiring states to consent to such jurisdiction to settle disputes relating to the Convention on Racial Discrimination.

The court also rejected the DRC argument based on the 1979 Convention on the Elimination on All Forms of Discrimination against Women (CEDAW). It concluded that, although Rwanda has not made reservation to Article 29 of CEDAW[74], the DRC had failed to initiate arbitration, as the first act needed in order to meet the cumulative steps required by CEDAW to trigger ICJ jurisdiction. The court also rejected the DRC arguments based on Article 75 of the Constitution of WHO;[75] Article XIV, paragraph 2, of the Constitution of UNESCO;[76] and Article 14, paragraph 1, of the 1971 Montreal Convention for the Suppression of Unlawful Acts against the Safety of Civil Aviation. With regard to the WHO Constitution, the Court concluded that the DRC had failed to make recourse to negotiation before seizing the court. With regard to the UNESCO Constitution, the court found that the DRC had failed to prove that its dispute with Rwanda was related to the interpretation of the UNESCO Constitution. Finally, with regard to the Montreal Convention, the court concluded that the DRC had failed to show that the conditions required in Article 14, paragraph 1, of this convention, requiring the DRC to resort to arbitration before seizing the court, have been fulfilled.

In a nutshell, through the *DRC v. Rwanda* case, the ICJ reiterated two key international law principles. First, that the jurisdiction of the court has been and remains exclusively based on the consent of the parties and, second, that the mere fact that rights and obligations *erga omnes* or peremptory norms of general law (*jus cogens*) are at issue in a dispute, cannot in itself constitute an exception to the principle that its jurisdiction always depends on the consent of the parties.

However, having prevailed in the *DRC v. Rwanda* case put before the ICJ did not embolden Rwanda. On 15 December 2008, it notified the United Nations secretary general that it had decided to withdraw the reservation relating to Article IX of the Genocide Convention[77] and Article 22 of the 1965 International Convention on the Elimination of All Forms of Racial Discrimination.[78] By ending its reservation against the jurisdiction of the ICJ, Rwanda agreed that this court can hear cases related to treaties that recognize it, and to which Rwanda has ratified, without reservation regarding this court jurisdiction.

Rwanda has not yet, however, made a declaration recognizing the jurisdiction of the Court as compulsory, as provided by Article 36, paragraphs 2 and 3, of the ICJ statute. Paragraph 2 of this Article provides that

> the jurisdiction of the Court comprises all cases which the parties refer to it, and all matters specially provided for in the Charter of the United Nations, or in treaties and conventions in force: (a) the interpretation of a treaty, (b) any question of international law, (c) the existence of any fact which, if established, would constitute a breach of an international obligation, and (d) the nature or extent of the reparation to be made for the breach of an international obligation.

Paragraph 3 of the same article provides that "the declarations referred to above may be made unconditionally or on condition of reciprocity on the part of several or certain states, or for a certain time."

By late 2019, only 73 states had deposited with the secretary general of the United Nations their declarations recognizing the jurisdiction of the court as compulsory.[79] Such countries have, in principle, the right to bring one or more other states, which have accepted the same obligation, before the court by filing an application instituting proceedings with the court. Conversely, they also undertake to appear before the court, should proceedings be instituted against them by one or more other states.

Section 4. Rwanda and international criminal law

A. Introduction

International criminal law is a relatively new branch of international law. Until recently, it was made up of a small number of international treaties. These treaties, which were introduced in the late nineteenth century, evolved, expanded, and were updated, leading to the famous four Geneva Conventions in 1949, which are considered today to be the foundation for the punishment of war crimes.[80] The 1946 Statutes of the Nuremberg and the International Military Tribunal introduced us to crimes against humanity and crimes against peace.[81] The world adopted the Genocide Convention in 1948[82] and the Torture Convention in 1984.[83] Obviously, the international instruments on international crimes are not limited to those mentioned above. The list is very long,[84] but those related to war crimes, crimes against humanity, crimes against peace, and torture dominate contemporary international criminal law.

B. International criminal law conventions ratified by Rwanda

Rwanda ratified the four Geneva Conventions in May 1964, both the 1977 Additional Protocols (I and II) to the Geneva Convention in November 1984, the 1972 Convention on the Prohibition of Biological Weapons in May 1964, the 2000 Optional Protocol on the Involvement of Children in armed conflict in April 2002, the 1993 Convention Prohibiting Chemical Weapons in March 2004, the 1997 Anti-Personnel Mine Ban Convention in June 2000, the 2008 Convention on Cluster Munitions in August 2015, the 1954 Hague Convention for the Protection of Cultural Property in December 2000, the 1968 Convention on Statutory Limitation to War Crimes in April 1975, the 1948 Convention on the Prevention and Punishment of Genocide in April 1975, the 1977 Organization of African Unity (OAU) Convention on Mercenaries in June 1979, the 2013 Arms Trade Treaty in June 2013, and the 1984 Convention against Torture and Other Cruel, Inhuman, or Degrading Treatment or Punishment in December 2008.[85]

In ratifying the above treaties, Rwanda, like many other countries that did the same, hoped that there would never be a situation or time when they would be called to enforce them. The fear of self-fulfilling prophecies kept many countries, including Rwanda, from doing much to develop mechanisms of prevention and prosecution of crimes such as genocide and other international gross human rights violations. When in 1990s the horrors of war crimes, crimes against humanity, and genocide swiped Rwanda, Former Yugoslavia, and Sierra Leone, these countries were not the only ones unprepared: The international community as a whole did not either have sufficient legal and institutional framework to deal with these crimes.

It appears, therefore, that the post-Nuremberg international criminal law that we know today developed mainly following the horrific international crimes committed in 1990s.

The contribution of Rwanda to contemporary international criminal law is reflected in both the work of the International Criminal Tribunal for Rwanda (ICTR) and the domestic prosecution by both Rwandan and foreign courts for war crimes, crimes against humanity, and genocide committed in Rwanda.

C. International criminal tribunal for Rwanda (ICTR)

If not for the genocide against the Tutsi, ICTR would not have existed. Its creation was on Rwanda's request and insistence. On 28 September 1994, the representative of Rwanda at the United Nations sent a letter to the president of the Security Council,[86] expressing the country's frustration as a result of the "evident reluctance by the international community to set up an international tribunal to expose and punish the criminals who are still at large." The same letter urged the United Nations to reinforce government efforts by, among other things, "setting up as soon as possible an international tribunal to try the criminals." In addition to requesting and insisting that the UN create the ICTR, Rwanda attempted to shape this tribunal. During the 8 November 1994 Security Council meeting, which had on its agenda establishing the ICTR,[87] Rwanda, at that time a rotating, non-permanent member of the Security Council, explained the four reasons for which it had requested the establishment of the international tribunal as follows:[88]

First, in its search for accountability, the government of Rwanda wanted to involve the international community, which had also been harmed by the genocide and the grave and massive violations of international humanitarian law.

Second, the government framed its request as an appeal for an international presence in order to avoid any suspicion of its wanting to organize speedy and vengeful justice. It needed an exemplary justice that is completely neutral and fair.

Third, Rwanda wanted to make it easier to obtain custody of criminals who had found refuge in foreign countries.

Fourth, as it saw the genocide that had been committed in Rwanda as a crime against humankind, the government believed that this crime should be prosecuted and punished by the international community as a whole.

In spite of many meetings with the sponsors of the draft resolution on the statute of the ICTR, and some amendments to its initial text, the Rwandan government was not satisfied with the final resolution or the Statute of the ICTR as it was adopted. This is why it was the only country to vote against the resolution setting up the ICTR.[89] Seven reasons were provided by Rwanda to justify its vote:[90]

First, the resolution limited the *ratione temporis* competence of the tribunal to between 1 January 1994 and 31 December 1994. For the Rwandan delegation, such a limitation "refuses to consider the causes of the genocide in Rwanda and its planning, and refuses to consider the pilot projects that preceded the major genocide of April 1994" and therefore "cannot be of any use to Rwanda, because it will not contribute to eradicating the culture of impunity or creating a climate conducive to national reconciliation."

Second, the Rwandan delegation found "the composition and structure of the International Tribunal for Rwanda inappropriate and ineffective," especially because of the few trial chambers and judges, and its lack of an appeal chamber and its own prosecutor. The Rwandan delegation believed that "the establishment of so ineffective an international tribunal would only appease the conscience of the international community rather than respond to the expectations of the Rwandan people and the victims of genocide in particular."

Third, the Rwandan delegation found that the fact that nothing in the resolution and the statute indicated the order of priority for crimes to be punished by the tribunal could lead the latter to relegate genocide to a secondary level.

Fourth, Rwanda requested that the countries that may have taken part in its civil war be prevented from proposing candidates for the judges of the ICTR and participating in their election.

Fifth, the Rwandan delegation found that in proposing that those condemned by the ICTR be imprisoned outside Rwanda and that those countries be given the authority to make decisions regarding the detainees, the statute took away the right of the Rwandan people and that of the tribunal to decide on this issue.

Sixth, in ruling out the application of capital punishment, the statute enabled the planners, organizers, and devisers of the genocide to escape capital punishment, whereas those who simply carried out the plans were subjected to this sentence, as provided for in the Rwandan penal code. In the eyes of the Rwandan delegation, "that situation is not conducive to national reconciliation in Rwanda."

Last but not least, Rwanda felt that the tribunal itself should be based in Rwandan territory. To them, a tribunal without a seat in Rwanda was unlikely to bring about national reconciliation.

The statute of the ICTR gave this court the power to prosecute genocide, crimes against humanity, and violations of Article 3 Common to the Geneva Conventions and of Additional Protocol II committed in the territory of Rwanda as well as Rwandan citizens responsible for such violations committed in neighboring states between 1 January 1994 and 31 December 1994 (Art. 1, 2, 3, and 4). The ICTR had concurrent jurisdiction with national courts, including those of Rwanda, but it had primacy over them (Art. 8). This means that at any stage of the investigation or trial the ICTR could formally request that the national courts deferred to its competence

(Art. 8). No person could be tried by a national court if already tried by the ICTR on the same offense. However, a person who may have been tried before a national court for such acts could subsequently be tried by the ICTR (Art. 9). The ICTR statute provided also that states had the duty to cooperate with the ICTR in the investigation and prosecution of persons accused of committing serious violations of international humanitarian law (Art. 28).

Despite the reservations it expressed during the adoption of the resolution creating the ICTR, Rwanda tried as much as possible to fulfill its obligation to cooperate with the court, which had its seat in Arusha, Tanzania. The success of the ICTR's first trials, which today are hailed as having "extraordinary historic significance,"[91] were achieved thanks to Rwanda's cooperation. These trials include the *Akayesu* case, decided in 1998.[92] This is considered the first conviction for genocide since the adoption of the 1948 Genocide Convention. It introduced rape and sexual violence to international criminal law as acts that may constitute genocide. The groundwork by Rwanda's government and members of civil society, especially women's rights organizations, served as the foundation for the ICTR's trial of the *Akayesu* case. Other important cases were the *Kambanda* case[93] and the *Nahimana* case.[94] The former is considered the first case in history in which an accused acknowledged his guilt for the crime of genocide before an international criminal tribunal and in which a criminal tribunal convicted a head of government for the crime of genocide. The latter was hailed as the first judgment since the conviction of Julius Streicher at Nuremberg after World War II in which a court examined the role of the media in the context of international criminal justice.

Despite its early accomplishments, the cumulative achievements of the ICTR have remained modest. In its 21 years of existence, with an annual budget exceeding US$100 million – so, having spent, in total, more than US$ 2 billion[95] – the ICTR indicted only 93 people, among whom were 62 sentenced; 14 acquitted; 10 referred to national jurisdictions for trial; 2 deceased prior to judgment; 2 indictments withdrawn before trial; and 3 fugitives referred to the United Nations International Residual Mechanism for Criminal Tribunals,[96] a body created by the UN with the mandate to perform a number of essential functions previously carried out by the ICTR and the ICTY. Also, because of its distant location outside Rwanda, its poor outreach program, and its failure to involve Rwandans in its work and proceedings, the ICTR's work had very little direct impact on Rwanda, especially with regard to reconciliation and reparation for the victims.[97]

D. Domestic prosecution by both Rwanda and foreign courts

When Rwanda ratified the Geneva Conventions, as well as the Genocide Convention, nobody could have predicted that it would be the first country in the world to create a national criminal system to investigate, prosecute, and punish such crimes. As said earlier, Rwanda, like most countries, did very little to fulfill its obligation under the Geneva Conventions to "enact any legislation necessary to provide effective penal sanctions for persons committing, or ordering to be committed, any of the grave breaches" of the Geneva Conventions.[98] Rwanda's commitment was particularly lacking with regard to Article 1 of the Genocide convention related to the duty 'to prevent and punish' genocide, and its Article 5, which obliges parties to

> undertake to enact, in accordance with their respective Constitutions, the necessary legislation to give effect to the provisions of the present Convention and, in particular, to provide effective penalties for persons guilty of genocide or of any of the other acts [of genocide].

However, Rwanda managed to overcome the challenges of this unpreparedness and, obviously through trial and error, to come up with an approach that could be considered exemplary for any country confronting the challenge of investigating, prosecuting, and punishing such crimes. Rwanda's contribution to international criminal law can be summarized as two points: (1) Highlighting the limitations of a domestic criminal system to handle genocide, crimes against humanity, and war crimes, and (2) proving that the prosecution and punishment of such crimes in a domestic criminal system requires creative and innovative solutions.

1. *Domestic criminal systems were not designed to try crimes such as genocide, crimes against humanity, and war crimes*

International crimes, such as genocide, crimes against humanity, and war crimes, have special characteristics that make them challenging for a traditional domestic criminal system to handle. First, there is the time and place in which the prosecution and trial of such crimes take place. Second, there is the context in which such crimes were committed. Third is the number of perpetrators and the number of victims involved.

On the issue of time and place, it is a fact that prosecutions often take place in a post-conflict society when there is no human capacity and expertise, and where there is no infrastructure, either because it was destroyed during the conflict or because it did not exist in the first place. In the case of Rwanda, the Ministry of Justice and the courts began handling cases of genocide while seated in damaged buildings without windows, telephones, papers, or typewriters.[99] Before March 1994, there were 70 prosecutors and 758 judges in Rwanda; in November 1994, there were only 12 prosecutors and 244 judges.[100] Among them, only 16 were trained lawyers.[101] In April 1996, the country counted only 15 prosecutors supervising 225 untrained investigators.[102] Prisons and detention facilities that had existed before the genocide had been constructed to house around 12,000 persons[103] but were now hosting 124,000 detainees.[104] Furthermore, it was estimated that by July 1994, the country had only 30 practicing lawyers.[105] In addition to the lack of infrastructure, most Rwandans were not meeting their basic needs and were traumatized.

With regard to the context in which crimes were committed, although individuals were the ones who committed these crimes, they often acted with the State's active or passive support. This makes it difficult for the State to investigate and prosecute individuals while ignoring its own role. In the case of Rwanda, the role of the government and public officials in encouraging people to commit genocide has been well documented.[106] Some perpetrators even believed that they were operating under the governmental shelter of impunity.[107] During the Parliament discussion on the Organic Law No. 08/96 of 30 August 1996, on the Organization of Prosecution for Offenses Constituting the Crime of Genocide or Crimes against Humanity committed since 1 October 1990, some members of the Parliament wanted to include in the law the element of state responsibility. However, the adopted version focused on individual responsibility only.[108] In the early trials on genocide, victims attempted to bring the government to court for its role, but their efforts were fruitless.[109]

In terms of numbers, the figures of people involved in such crimes, as well as their victims, are often so high that it becomes impossible to fulfill, on the one hand, the constitutional guarantees of due process and fair justice to the suspects and accused, and on the other hand, provide justice and effective remedies for the victims. In the case of Rwanda, the number of victims of genocide was estimated to be 1 million. The ministry of justice estimated the number of perpetrators to be between 100,000 and 2,000,000.[110] By June 1996, the number of detainees was 75,000 and growing, and it appeared to be an impossible task for the couple dozen prosecutors, judges, and lawyers to handle this high number of cases and still guarantee the rights in the criminal procedure code.[111] Was it possible to apply procedure rules adopted for times of peace to a *sui generis* period of war and genocide? This code required, for example, that a suspect appear before the judge within five days of their arrest (Art. 39) and guaranteed them the right to be heard and represented by a lawyer during the preventive detention hearing (Art. 40).

In the immediate aftermath of the 1994 tragedy, the country struggled with basic, post-conflict needs, such as water, food, and rebuilding infrastructure destroyed during the conflict. Despite these challenges, the international community still pressured Rwanda for a flawless and timely justice for those involved in the genocide. With its limited number of investigators, prosecutors, and judges, and with its prisons built to host a limited number of prisoners, the country was expected not only to arrest, detain, and try thousands of suspects but also to follow international standards in this process. Often, the expectations of international human rights organizations could not be matched by the realities in the country. How do you expect a small number of investigators with no experience in criminal procedure to follow international standards when arresting more than one hundred thousand suspects in just a few months? How do you expect prisons built to host a few thousand people in times of peace to host hundreds of thousands of suspects and do so according to international prison standards? How do you create due process and fair trial in conditions described above? These serious questions should not be an excuse for violating human rights, but they are also real issues that should not be approached by hiding behind principles. They need to be addressed pragmatically by acknowledging that they are exceptional problems and therefore require exceptional solutions.

It is obvious that other countries learned from these challenges and solutions created through trial and errors by the Rwandan domestic criminal justice system. These lessons have informed and continue to inform national approaches in investigating, prosecuting and trying international crimes, especially by post-conflict societies.

2. *Prosecuting and trying crimes such as genocide, crimes against humanity, and war crimes requires creative solutions*

While in search of justice, the post-genocide Rwandan government was sure of two things: (1) That amnesty, a solution that Desmond Tutu and most South African scholars were advising for, was a nonstarter.[112] For Rwanda's government, "any consideration of blanket Amnesty would imply continued tolerance of impunity."[113] A retributive justice in which "perpetrators of genocide must be dealt with in accordance with the rule of law in appropriately formed courts of law"[114] was the only option possible. (2) That "classical judicial system was not adequate" to deal with challenges of mass atrocities such as genocide. As a consequence, the country had to find creative "alternative judiciary as well as prosecutorial institutions" to implement in dealing with genocide and other gross human rights violation cases committed in Rwanda in 1994.

The first creative solution was the adoption of the Organic Law No. 08/96 of 30 August 1996, on the Organization of Prosecution for Offenses Constituting the Crime of Genocide or Crimes against Humanity committed since 1 October 1990.[115] Considering its goal of forever eradicating the culture of impunity in Rwanda,[116] this organic law remained fundamentally retributive. However, it also introduced innovative common law concepts for speeding up trials in the Rwandan criminal system, which for so long had been based on civil law. These creative innovations included: (a) The categorization of suspects according to the gravity of their crimes (Article 2) with punishments that correspond to those levels (Art. 14). Category I was reserved for those suspects in political and administrative leadership, and the ringleaders who engaged in genocide, while Category II consisted of those accused of being perpetrators of and accomplices to murder. Category III applied to persons accused of serious assaults against other persons, and Category IV related to those suspected who had solely committed property offenses. (b) A procedure that allows those who confess or plead guilty to receive less severe punishment (Art. 4). And (c) The establishment of specialized chambers in Rwanda's ordinary and military courts with exclusive jurisdiction over genocide and crimes against humanity committed in Rwanda.

The trials under this organic law that started in December 1996 were historic. Although the ICTR takes credit for being the first international court to enforce the 1948 Genocide Convention when it found Jean-Paul Akayesu guilty of genocide on 2 September 1998,[117] the very first time in the history of the world in which a person was found guilty of genocide under this convention was in 1997 by the Rwandan court. By 1998, when ICTR rendered its first historic decision, Rwanda had already tried more than 300 people for genocide, with more than 130 sentenced to the death penalty.[118] Among the early cases was that of Frodouald Karamira, one of the key politicians in the regime behind the 1994 genocide. Karamira was found guilty by the Rwandan court for genocide on 14 February 1997 and was executed with others by firing squad on 24 April 1998.

However, the creativity introduced in the Organic Law No. 08/96 of 30 August 1996 proved to be insufficient in speeding up trials and trying suspects in "accordance with the rule of law in appropriately-formed courts of law." In mid-1999, the government estimated that of the 135,000 people in prison, only 1,000 had been tried. Also, the number of those who had confessed or pled guilty did not exceed 7,000.[119] According to the Rwandan League for Promotion and Defense of Human Rights (LIPRODHOR), one of the local human rights organizations that monitored genocide trials, the number of people tried in 1997 was 346; this number increased to 928 in 1998, and then to 1318 by the end of 1999.[120] At this time, it was estimated that the national courts had heard only 1% of the total number of detainees then held in custody.[121] The hope for guilty pleas dropped in 2000, when it was realized that only 20% of the accused had pled guilty.[122] In 1999, the government estimated that, given the high number of people in prison and the slow speed at which the trials were moving, it was going to take about 200 years to try them all.[123] In the meantime, the maintenance of this number of prisoners was estimated to cost $20 million a year.[124]

Confronted with these realities, the government of Rwanda needed to be even more creative in moving beyond the innovations it had introduced in the Organic Law No. 08/96 of 30 August 1996. It was time to find a solution that softened the principled commitment on retribution, a system that, without giving in to impunity, could maintain the need for accountability while promoting truth, justice, forgiveness, and reconciliation. This solution was found in the homegrown system of *Gacaca* courts. These courts are discussed in chapter two on homegrown solutions.

Notes

1 We use Rwandan International Law (RIL) not to mean that there is a specific branch of international law for Rwanda but to mean international law that is binding in Rwanda.

2 Statute of the International Court of Justice, 26 June 1945, 59 Stat. 1055, 33 U.N.T.S. 933 (hereinafter: ICJ Statute).

3 UN, *Treaty Series: Treaties and international agreements register or filed and recorded with the secretariat of the UN*, vol. 1155 (New York: United Nations, 1987), 331.

4 https://treaties.un.org/Pages/ViewDetailsIII.aspx?src=TREATY&mtdsg_no=XXIII-1&chapter=23&Temp=mtdsg3&clang=_en (accessed August 5, 2019).

5 Mary Ellen O'Connell, Richard F. Scott, and Naomi Roht-Arriaza, *The International Legal System, Cases and Materials*, 6th edn (St. Paul: Foundation Press, 2010), 62.

6 Ibid., 109.

7 The Paquete Habana, 175 U.S. 677 (1900) "reproduced in," in *International Human Rights in Context: Law, Politics, Morals*, ed. Henry J. Steiner, Philip Alston, and Ryan Goodman, (3rd edn, Oxford University Press, 2008), 67.

8 Nicaragua v. United States, 1986 I.C.J. Rep. 14 (ICJ 1986) para. 207.

9 The Paquete Habana, 67.

10 For example, the Cabinet meeting approving the draft law ratifying the Protocol to the Treaty establishing the African Economic Community relating to free movement of persons, right of residence, and right of establishment signed in Kigali, Rwanda, on 21 March 2018. Republic of Rwanda, "Statement on Cabinet Decisions of 11/04/2018," Republic of Rwanda, http://gov.rw/newsdetails2/?tx_ttnews%5Btt_news%5D=1921&cHash=0c6caa52bc848fdddd808710c1e8b012.

11 Myres McDougal, "The Impact of International Law upon National Law: A Policy-Oriented Perspective," *South Dakota Law Review* 4 (1959): 27–31.

12 Constitution, "France 1958 (rev. 2008)," Constitute, www.constituteproject.org/constitution/France_2008?lang=en.

13 Constitution, "Germany 1949 (rev. 2014)," Constitute, www.constituteproject.org/constitution/German_Federal_Republic_2014?lang=en

14 Constitution, "Netherlands 1815 (rev. 2008)," Constitute, www.constituteproject.org/constitution/Netherlands_2008?lang=en.

15 Constitution, "Poland 1997 (rev. 2009)," Constitute, www.constituteproject.org/constitution/Poland_2009?lang=en.

16 Accession on 16 April 1975. L.D. no. 8 / 75 of 12/02/1975 O.G. no. 5 of 12/02/1975, 231.

17 Accession on 16 April 1975. D-L. no. 8 / 75 of 12/02/1975 O.G. no. 5 of 01/03/1975, 230.

18 Accession on 16 April 1975 D-L. no. 8/75 of 12/02/1975 O.G. no. 5 of 01/03/1975, 230.

19 Ratified on 2 March 1981. P.O. no 431/16 of 10/11/1980 O.G. no. 4 of 15/02/1981, 132.

20 Accession on 15 December 2008. P.O. no. 51/01 of 05/09/2008 O.G. no. 19 of 01/10/2008, 75.

21 Ratified on 24 January 1991. P.O. no. 773/16 of 19/09/1990 O.G no. 21 of 01/11/1990, 1160.

22 Accession on 15 December 2008. P.O no. 33/01 of 17/05/2010 O.G. no. 24/06/2010, 37.

23 Accession on 15 December 2008. P.O. no. 131/01 of 27/12/2012 O.G no. Special of 31/12/2012.

24 Rwanda had made reservation on Article 13 of this instrument specifically on issues related to education: "However, on the subject of education, Rwanda considers itself only bound by its Constitution." The reservation was withdrawn by P.O. no. 50/01 of 05/09/2008, O.G. no. 19 of 01/10/2008, 68.

25 Rwanda had made the following reservation: On Article 22 of the Convention "Rwanda does not consider itself bound by Article 22 of this Convention." The reservation was withdrawn by P.O. no. 49/01 of 05/09/2008, O.G. no. 19 of 01/10/2008, 64.

26 Rwanda had made the following reservation: On Article 9 of the Convention "Rwanda does not consider itself bound by Article 9 of this Convention." The reservation was withdrawn by P.O. no. 48/01 of 05/09/2008, O.G. no. 19 of 01 October 2008, 71.

27 Reservation of Rwanda on Article 26 of the 1951 Convention: "For reasons of Public policy, the Republic of Rwanda reserves the right to establish a residence and limit movement of refugees." The reservation was withdrawn by P. O. no. 31/01 of 17 May 2010, O.G. no. 24 of 14 June 2010, 29.

28 Rwanda made reservation on Article 4 of Additional Protocol Convention relating to the status of refugees of 1967: "For all disputes between the parties, recourse to the International Court of Justice can be introduced only with the prior agreement of the Rwandese Republic." The reservation was withdrawn by P. O. no. 32/01 of 17/05/2010, O.G. no. 24 of 14 June 2010, 33.

29 Accession on 31 December 2012, P.O no. 131/01 of 27 December 2012 O.G no. Special of 31 December 2012.

30 Accession on 31 August 2009; P.O. no. 34/01 of 14 July 2009 O.G. no. 35 of 31 August 2009, 5.

31 Article 20 on the Protocol on Torture; Art. 6 and 7 of the Protocol on Disabilities.

32 Ratified on July 22nd, 1983. L. no. 10/1983 of 01 July 1983 O.G. no. 13 of 01 July 83, 343.

33 Ratified on 28 April 2003; Presidential Order no. 12 January, 27 March 2003 O.G. Spec. no. of 28 April 2003, 17.

34 Ratified on 15 November 2001 Ratified on P.O. no. 11/01 of 30 May 2001 O.G. no. 22 of 15 November 2001, 58.

35 Ratified on 24 June 2004 P.O. no. 11/01 of 24 June 2004 O.G. Spec. no. of 24 June 2004, 19.

36 UN General Assembly, Sixtieth Session, Resolution Adopted, *60/251. Human Rights Council*, A/Res/60/251, 2006.

37 UN Human Rights Council, "First cycle," under "Universal Periodic Review- Rwanda," United Nations, www.ohchr.org/EN/HRBodies/UPR/Pages/RWindex.aspx.

38 UN Human Rights Council, "Second cycle," under "Universal Periodic Review- Rwanda," United Nations, www.ohchr.org/EN/HRBodies/UPR/Pages/RWindex.aspx.

39 Institution-building of the United Nations Human Rights Council, A/HRC/RES/5/1 para. 4.

40 Ibid., para. 15.

41 See infra.

42 African Commission on Human and Peoples' Rights State Reporting, available at www.achpr.org/states/. (accessed August 18, 2019).

43 Id. at www.achpr.org/states/detail?id=38 (accessed August 18, 2019).

44 African Commission, 33rd Ordinary Session, *227/99 Democratic Republic of Congo/Brundi, Rwanda, Uganda*, held in Niamey: Niger, 2003. www.achpr.org/files/sessions/33rd/comunications/227.99/227_99_democratic_republic_of_congo___burundi_rwanda_uganda.pdf.

45 African Commission, 33rd Ordinary Session, *157/96: Association pour la sauvegarde de la paix au Burundi / Kenya, Uganda, Rwanda, Tanzania, Zaire (DRC), Zambia*, held in Niamey: Niger, 2003. www.achpr.org/files/sessions/33rd/comunications/157.96/achpr33_157_96_eng.pdf.

46 African Commission, 20th Ordinary Session, *27/89–46/91–49/91–99/93: Organisation mondiale contre la torture, Association Internationale des juristes démocrates, Commission internationale des juristes, Union interafricaine des droits de l'Homme/Rwanda*, held in Grand Bay: Mauritius, 1996. www.achpr.org/files/sessions/20th/comunications/27.89-46.91-49.91-99.93/achpr20_27.89_46.91_49.91_99.93_eng.pdf.

47 "Protocol to the African Charter on Human and Peoples' Rights on the Establishment of an African Court on Human and Peoples' Rights," www.african-court.org/en/images/Basic%20Documents/africancourt-humanrights.pdf.

48 See www.african-court.org/en/; and List of countries that have signed, ratified/acceded to the Protocol to the African Charter on Human and Peoples' Rights on the Establishment of an African Court on Human and Peoples' Rights, as of 15/06/2017 https://au.int/sites/default/files/treaties/36393-sl-protocol_to_the_african_charter_on_human_and_peoplesrights_on_the_estab.pdf.

49 African Court on Human and Peoples' Rights, The Gambia becomes the Ninth Country to allow NGOs and individuals to access the African Court Directly, Press release, 23 November 2018. www.african-court.org/en/index.php/news/press-releases/item/257-the-gambia-becomes-the-ninth-country-to-allow-ngos-and-individuals-to-access-the-african-court-directly.

50 Republic of Rwanda, *Declaration under Article 34(6) of the Protocol to the African Charter on Human and Peoples' Rights on the Establishment of an African Court on Human and Peoples' Rights*, May 2003. http://en.african-court.org/images/Declarations/Declaration%20Rwanda.PDF.

51 Republic of Rwanda Ministry of Justice, *Clarification* (2016). www.minijust.gov.rw/fileadmin/Documents/Photo_News_2016/Clarification2.pdf.

52 In its ruling in the Application 003/2014 (Ingabire Victoire Umuhoza v. Republic of Rwanda) the African Court on Human and Peoples' Rights held that the withdrawal of Rwanda's declaration under Article 34(6) of the Protocol shall take effect one year after its submission, that is, from 1 March 2017. Para. 67. http://en.african-court.org/images/Cases/Ruling%20on%20Jurisdiction/Appl.%20003-2014%20Ingabire%20Victoire%20Umuhoza%20v.%20Rwanda%20Ruling%20on%20Jurisdiction%20ENG.pdf.

53 African Court on Human and Peoples' Rights, "Current Judges," African Court on Human and Peoples' Rights, www.african-court.org/en/index.php/judges/current-judges.

54 www.african-court.org/en/index.php/cases/2016-10-17-16-18-21#finalised-cases.

55 *Mulindahabi Fidele v. Republic of Rwanda*, App. No 008/2017 (2017). www.african-court.org/en/index.php/55-finalised-cases-details/1014-app-no-008-2017-mulindahabi-fidele-v-republic-of-rwanda-details.

56 *Rutabingwa Chrysanthe v. Republic of Rwanda*, App. No. 003/2013 (2013). www.african-court.org/en/index.php/55-finalised-cases-details/943-app-no-003-2013-rutabingwa-chrysanthe-v-republic-of-rwanda-details.

57 *Ingabire Victoire Umuhoza v. Republic of Rwanda*, App. No. 003/2014 (2018). www.african-court.org/en/index.php/56-pending-cases-details/867-app-no-003-2014-ingabire-victoire-umuhoza-v-republic-of-rwanda-details.

58 *General Kayumba Nyamwasa and others v. Republic of Rwanda*, App. No. 016/2015 (2017). www.african-court.org/en/index.php/55-finalised-cases-details/881-app-no-016-2015-general-kayumba-nyamwasa-and-others-v-republic-of-rwanda.

59 www.african-court.org/en/index.php/55-finalised-cases-details/866-app-no-002-2014-faustin-uwintije-v-republic-of-rwanda-details.

60 African Union Executive Council, *Report on Activities of the African Court on Human and Peoples' Rights*, Thirtieth Ordinary Session, 2017. www.african-court.org/en/images/Activity%20Reports/AfCHPR_Activity_Report_2016_E.pdf.
61 See Frederic Sebihuranda, LE Droit Internatinal Conventionnel a Travers la Constitution Rwandaise, Revue Juridique du Rwanda, Vol. IX, No. 2, 1 April 1985, 127.
62 Id. 128.
63 *Black's Law*, s.v. "judiciary."
64 In 2009, the constitution that was in force was that of 2003, which placed only the constitution above international treaties.
65 See, Human Rights Committee, Replies of the Government of Rwanda to the list of issues (CCPR/C/RWA/Q/3/REV.1) to be taken up in connection with the Consideration of the Third Periodic Report of Rwanda (CCPR/C/RWA/3), CCPR/C/RWA/Q/3/Rev.1/Add.1 of 29 March 2009, 2.
66 *BRD v. Mwubahamana, RSOCA 0194/13/HC/KIG – RSOCA 0202/13/HC/KIG* Rwanda Law Report vol. 2 (2015), 89.
67 The Government of Rwanda (Minecofin) v. Vuzimpundu, Rwanda Law Reports vol. 1 (2017), 33–52.
68 Ibid., 38.
69 See Article 18, para.3 of the CCPR.
70 Ibid., 43.
71 Armed Activities on the Territory of the Congo (Democratic Republic of the Congo v. Rwanda) 2002 Application.
72 36(1) of the ICJ Statute gives the Court jurisdiction over "matters specifically provided for … in treaties and conventions in force." In this sense, a compromissory clause is a clause in a specific treaty providing for the submission of a dispute resulting from that treaty to the ICJ.
73 These conditions are required by Article 20, paragraph 2 of the Convention.
74 This article provides that

> 1. Any dispute between two or more States Parties concerning the interpretation or application of the present Convention, which is not settled by negotiation, shall, at the request of one of them, be submitted to arbitration. If within six months from the date of the request for arbitration the parties are unable to agree on the organization of the arbitration, any one of those parties may refer the dispute to the International Court of Justice by request in conformity with the Statute of the Court.

75 Article 75 provides that

> Any question or dispute concerning the interpretation or application of this Constitution which is not settled by negotiation or by the Health Assembly shall be referred to the International Court of Justice in conformity with the Statute of the Court, unless the parties concerned agree on another mode of settlement.

76 Article XIV provides that "Any question or dispute concerning the interpretation of this Constitution shall be referred for determination to the International Court of Justice or to an arbitral tribunal, as the General Conference may determine under its Rules of Procedure."
77 UN Treaty Collection, "Human Rights," United Nations, https://treaties.un.org/Pages/ViewDetails.aspx?src=IND&mtdsg_no=IV-1&chapter=4&clang=_en#EndDec (accessed April 2, 2019).
78 UN Treaty Collection, "Declarations and Reservation," under "Human Rights," United Nations, https://treaties.un.org/pages/ViewDetails.aspx?src=TREATY&mtdsg_no=IV-2&chapter=4&clang=_en#EndDec (accessed April 2, 2019).

79 International Court of Justice, "Declarations recognizing the jurisdiction of the Court as compulsory," International Court of Justice, www.icj-cij.org/en/declarations (accessed April 3, 2019).
80 See Article 8 Rome Statute of International Criminal Court.
81 See Antonio Cassese, *International Criminal Law* (Oxford: Oxford University Press, 2003), 69–74.
82 See supra.
83 Ibid.
84 See M. Cherif Bassiouni, *International Crimes: Digest/Index of International Instruments, 1815–1985* (New York, London, Rome: Oceana Publications, Inc., 1986).
85 For the dates on Rwanda's ratification of these treaties, see International Committee of the Red Cross, "Rwanda," under "Treaties, States Parties and Commentaries," International Committee of the Red Cross, https://ihl-databases.icrc.org/applic/ihl/ihl.nsf/vwTreatiesByCountrySelected.xsp?xp_countrySelected=RW.
86 Permanent Representative of Rwanda to UN President of the Security Council, letter, September 28, 1994, S/1994/1115.
87 The Situation concerning Rwanda, Establishment of an international Tribunal for the Prosecution of persons responsible for serious violations of international humanitarian law committed in the territory of Rwanda and Rwandan citizens responsible for such violations committed in the territory of neighboring States. UN Security Council, 49th year, 3453rd meeting, *S/PV.3453*, November 1994.
88 Ibid., 14.
89 By a vote taken by show of hands, Argentina, Brazil, Czech Republic, Djibouti, France, New Zealand, Nigeria, Oman, Pakistan, Russian Federation, Spain, UK, and the US voted in favor, while Rwanda voted against, and China abstained. UN Security Council, *S/PV.3453*, 3.
90 Ibid., 14–16.
91 Leila Nadya Sadat, "The Legacy of the International Criminal Tribunal for Rwanda" (paper presented at the ICTR, July 3, 2012), 6.
92 Akayesu, ICTR, Trial Chamber I, Judgment of 2 September 1998, case no. ICTR-96-4-T.
93 Kambanda (Judgment and sentence) ICTR, Trial Chamber, judgment and sentence of 4 September 1998 (Case no.ICTR 97-23-S).
94 The Prosecutor v. Ferdinand Nahimana, Jean-Bosco Barayagwiza, Hassan Ngeze (Judgment and Sentence), ICTR-99-52-T.
95 United Nations Meetings Coverage and Press Releases, "Press Briefing-Headquarters Briefing on the International Criminal Tribunal for Rwanda, July 24, 2002," United Nations, www.un.org/press/en/2002/rwandabrf.doc.htm. Most years the ICTR budget was around $200 million. United Nations Meetings Coverage and Press Releases, "Fifth Committee takes up 2004–2005 budget for Rwanda, Former Yugoslavia Tribunals," United Nations, www.un.org/press/en/2003/gaab3594.doc.htm.
96 United Nations International Residual Mechanism for Criminal Tribunal, "The ICTR in Brief," United Nations, http://unictr.unmict.org/en/tribunal (accessed June 25, 2018).
97 J.M. Kamatali, "The Challenge of Linking International Criminal Justice and National Reconciliation: The Case of the ICTR," *Leiden Journal of International Law* 16 (2003): 116–133; J.M. Kamatali, "From the ICTR to ICC: Learning from the ICTR Experience in Bringing Justice to Rwandans," *New England Journal of International and Comparative Law* 12, no. 1 (2005): 89–103.
98 Article 49: Geneva Convention I; Art. 50: Geneva Convention II; Article 129: Geneva Convention III; and Article 146: Geneva Convention IV.

99 Bornkamm, *Rwanda's Gacaca Court*, 22.
100 Gacaca Report Summary, "Summary."
101 Marc Cousineau, "L'Établissement de L'État de Droit au Rwanda: Un but Irrealisable," *Ottawa Law Review* 28, no.1 (1997): 175.
102 Ibid., 177.
103 Ibid., 176.
104 Paul Christoph Bornkamm, *Rwanda's Gacaca Court: Between Retribution and Reparation* (Oxford; New York: Oxford University Press, 2012), 22.
105 Cousineau, "L'Établissement de L'État de Droit au Rwanda," 179.
106 See Alison Des Forges, *Leave None to Tell the Story: Genocide in Rwanda* (New York: Human Rights Watch, 1999).
107 Cousineau, "L'Établissement de L'État de Droit au Rwanda," 175.
108 Francoise Digneffe and Jacques Fierens, ed., *Justice et Gacaca. L'expérience Rwandaise et le Génocide* (Namur: Presse Universitaire de Namur, 2003), 54.
109 Digneffe and Fierens, *Justice et Gacaca*, 69–70.
110 Cousineau, "L'Établissement de L'État de Droit au Rwanda," 175.
111 Law No 31/198 of 8 November 1985 modifying the law of 23 February 1963 instituting the Criminal Procedure Code, J.O.R.R. 25th Year, No.4, 155.
112 Desmond Tutu, *No Future without Forgiveness* 1st edn (New York: Doubleday, 1999), 257; Jeremy Sarkin, "The Tension Between Justice and Reconciliation in Rwanda: Politics, Human Rights, Due Process and the Role of Gacaca Courts in Dealing with the Genocide," *Journal of African Law* 45, no. 2 (2001): 167.
113 Republic of Rwanda: Office of the President, "Recommendations of the Conference," 16.
114 Ibid.
115 Official Gazette No. 17 of 1 September 1996.
116 The preamble of this organic law stressed that "to achieve reconciliation and justice in Rwanda, the culture of impunity must be eradicated forever."
117 Historic Judgment finds Akayesu guilty of Genocide, ICTR press release 2 September 1998. http://unictr.irmct.org/en/news/historic-judgement-finds-akayesu-guilty-genocide.
118 Amnesty International, *Imminent Executions: Rwanda 33 people sentenced to death, including Silas Munyagishari and Frodualdo Karamira* (Amnesty International, 1998), 2.
119 Republic of Rwanda, *Report on the reflection meetings*, 51.
120 Digneffe and Fierens, *Justice et Gacaca*, 65.
121 Nicola Palmer, *Courts in Conflict: Interpreting the layers of justice in post-genocide Rwanda* (Oxford: Oxford University Press, 2015), 101.
122 Ibid.
123 Republic of Rwanda, *Report on the reflection meetings*, 51.
124 President Paul Kagame, quoted in Stef Vandeginste, "A Truth and Reconciliation Approach to the Genocide and Crimes against humanity in Rwanda" Working Paper 1998/1, Center for the study of the Great Lakes Region of Africa, University of Antwerp, May 1998, 45.

5 Organization, jurisdiction, and functioning of Rwanda's judiciary

Introduction

The constitution of the Republic of Rwanda provides that the judiciary is independent and exercises financial and administrative autonomy (Art. 150). It organizes the judiciary into ordinary courts and specialized courts. The former comprise the Supreme Court, the High Court, Intermediate Court, and Primary Courts. The latter include commercial courts and military courts (Art.149 and 152). This list is not exhaustive, however, because the constitution allows the establishment or removal of any court by organic law. It is in this spirit that Organic Law No. 002/2018 of 04 April 2018 established the Court of Appeals.

This chapter will discuss Law No. 012/2018 of 04 April 2018, which regulates the organization and functioning of the judiciary in Rwanda (LOFJ), as well as Law No. 30/2018 of 02 June 2018, which determines the jurisdiction of courts (LJC). More specifically, it will cover the court system and other key organs of the judiciary as well as their jurisdiction and responsibilities.

The following chart illustrates the judiciary of the Republic of Rwanda.

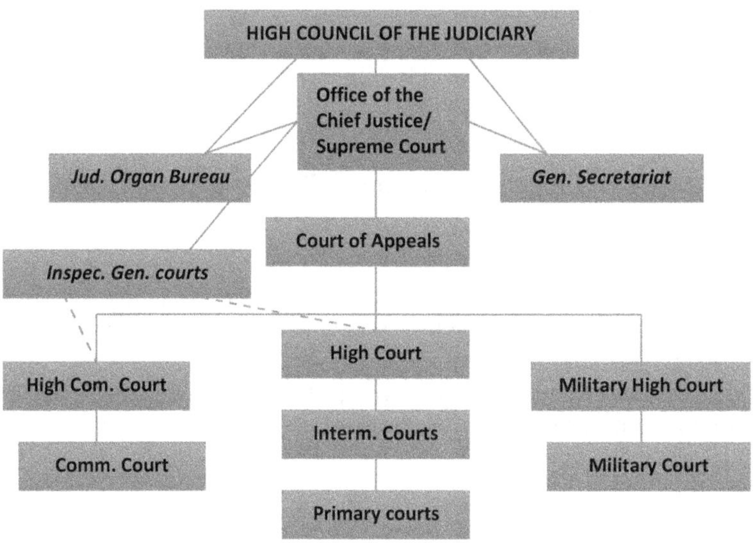

Section 1. The High Council of the judiciary

The High Council of the Judiciary (HCJ) is the supreme organ of the judiciary. It sets general guidelines governing its administration. It is composed of 30 members. Its organs include the General Assembly, the Bureau, the Executive Secretariat, and three permanent committees.

A. Members of the HCJ (Art. 6–10 LOFJ)

The HCJ comprises the following members: The president of the Supreme Court, who is also its chairperson; the vice president of the Supreme Court; the president of the Court of Appeals; one judge from the Court of Appeals, elected by their peers; the president of the High Court; the president of the Commercial High Court; the chief registrar of the Supreme Court; the executive secretary of the HCJ; one judge from the high court, elected by their peers; one judge from the Commercial High Court, elected by their peers; one judge representing judges of commercial courts, elected by their peers; five judges representing judges of Intermediate Courts, elected by their peers; five judges representing judges of Primary Courts, elected by their peers; one judge from military courts, elected by their peers; two deans of the faculties of law of recognized universities and institutions of higher learning, elected by their peers; the president of the Rwanda Bar Association; one representative of the Ministry of Justice appointed by the minister in charge of justice; the president of the National Commission for Human Rights; the ombudsman; one registrar representing registrars of ordinary courts, elected by their peers; and one court registrar representing commercial court registrars, elected by their peers.

Members of the HCJ, through election by their peers, must have at least five years' experience in the legal profession. To be elected, they must submit their application at least 30 days before elections to the executive secretariat of the HCJ. Elections are presided over by the president of the HCJ, except those of two law faculty deans, which are chaired by the minister in charge of institutions of higher education. The term for elected members is four years, renewable only once, if consecutive.

B. Organs of the HCJ and their responsibilities

1. The General Assembly (Art.12, 16, 20–23 LOFJ)

The general assembly is the supreme organ of the HCJ. It comprises all members of the HCJ. It is specifically responsible for: (1) Examining and, either on its own motion or upon request, advising on matters relating to the functioning of the justice system; (2) making decisions relating to the appointment, promotion, or removal from office of judges and the practicing of the profession of judges, other than judges of the military courts, and making decisions as a body in charge of their discipline, except those appointed by other organs; (3) making decisions on the appointment, promotion, and removal from office of registrars; (4) providing advice on any bill relating to the establishment of a new court or removal of an existing court, or to the statutes of the judges and judicial personnel for whom it is responsible; (5) assessing the delivery of services and making decisions to improve their quality; (6) advising the president of the Republic on the nomination of judges appointed by a Presidential Order; (7) adopting the rules of procedure of the HCJ; and (8) approving members of committees of the HCJ.

Ordinary sessions of the general assembly of the HCJ are held quarterly. It can, however, hold an extraordinary session, whenever necessary, with an initiative from its chairperson or upon request by at least seven members. Other individuals may be invited to attend the general assembly but without voting rights. The general assembly of the HCJ is held if at least two-thirds of its members are present. Members are not allowed to attend the meetings of the general assembly by proxy.

The general assembly of the HCJ makes decisions by consensus; failing that, decisions are made by an absolute majority of votes of members present. A decision to remove a judge from office is made by a majority of two-thirds of the votes of members present. Such voting is secret.

2. *The Bureau (Art. 13 and 17 LOFJ)*

The Bureau of the HCJ comprises the following persons: (1) The president of the Supreme Court, who is also its chairperson; (2) the vice president of the Supreme Court; (3) the deputy chairperson of the HCJ; (4) the president of the Court of Appeal; (5) the president of the High Court; (6) the president of the Commercial High Court; and (7) the executive secretary, who is also its rapporteur.

The Bureau has the following responsibilities: (1) Determine members of committees to be approved by the General Assembly of the HCJ; (2) follow up on the implementation of decisions of the HCJ; (3) take urgent decisions that are of the HCJ powers, in the interim when the latter has not yet met; (4) carry out the performance appraisal of judges and registrars at the last instance in accordance with the law governing the statutes of judges and judicial personnel; and (5) propose to the HCJ the extension of the term of the office of presidents of ordinary and commercial courts, except those appointed by other organs.

Decisions made by the Bureau of the HCJ that fall under the powers of the General Assembly of the HCJ are definitively approved by it in its first meeting following the period in which the decisions were made. If such decisions are not approved, they become null and void.

3. *The Executive Secretariat (Art. 15 and 19 LOFJ)*

The Executive Secretariat of the HCJ is headed by the Executive Secretary, recruited on a competitive basis and approved by the General Assembly of the Council.

The responsibilities of the Executive Secretary of the HCJ are as follows: (1) Carry out the secretariat duties for the HCJ and its Bureau; (2) prepare files for consideration by the HCJ and its committees; (3) prepare and send invitation letters to members of the HCJ; (4) prepare files from the Inspectorate General of Courts for submission to the HCJ; (5) manage, file, and track records of judges and court registrars; (6) receive and review applications of judges and registrars aspiring to be members of the HCJ and organize their election; (7) prepare draft orders of the president of the Supreme Court implementing the decisions of the HCJ and notify the concerned parties; (8) prepare draft rules of procedures of the HCJ; and (9) perform any other duties as may be assigned to them by the HCJ.

4. *Permanent committees of the HCJ (Art. 14 and 18 LOFJ)*

The HCJ has three permanent committees: (1) The disciplinary committee, (2) the committee responsible for the profession of judges and registrars, and (3) the committee responsible for the functioning of the judicial system.

The HCJ may, if necessary, establish ad hoc committees with a specific mission and time limit.

Section 2: The Judicial Organ Bureau (Art. 26–28 LOFJ)

The general administrative and financial responsibilities of the judiciary are managed by the Judicial Organ Bureau, which is composed of eight people: The president of the Supreme Court, who is also its chair; the vice president of the Supreme Court; the president of the Court of Appeals; the president of the High Court; the president of the Commercial High Court; the Inspector General of Courts (IGC); the secretary general of the Supreme Court; and the chief registrar of the Supreme Court, who also serves as its rapporteur.

The Bureau has two key responsibilities: (1) To adopt strategies and make decisions aimed at improving the functioning of courts and other organs of the Judicial Organ, and follow up on the implementation of such strategies and decisions, and (2) to approve the action plan and the draft budget for ordinary and commercial courts.

The Bureau meets once a month and whenever necessary. Its decisions are generally made by consensus or, failing that, by a two-thirds majority of members present in the meeting.

Section 3: General Secretariat (Art. 35–37 LOFJ)

This organ serves as the General Secretariat of the Supreme Court as a court but also as the general secretariat of the judiciary with regard to budgetary and general managerial issues of judicial organs. It is composed of the secretary general, senior officials, officials, and other necessary personnel.

The secretary general in the Supreme Court is the chief budget manager of the judicial organ. He or she also has the following responsibilities: (1) Coordinate all activities of the organs in charge of the management of the support staff of courts; (2) ensure the management of finances, property, and equipment of ordinary and commercial courts; (3) implement the policy of the judicial organ as well as its strategies and plans; (4) ensure technical cooperation with other public institutions; (5) manage organs responsible for support services for courts; (6) take necessary measures falling within their duties and relating to the organization of courts; and (7) prepare the draft budget for ordinary and commercial courts.

The secretary general performs their duties under the supervision of the president of the Supreme Court and reports to the latter as the head of both the judiciary and the Supreme Court. Although appointed by the president of the Republic upon proposal by the president of the Supreme Court, the secretary general is not a member of the judiciary. Like other members of the General Secretariat, they remain under the general statute of the public service.

Section 4: Inspectorate General of Courts (Art. 31–34 LOFJ)

The IGC comprises the inspector general and at least four other inspectors, researchers, and other necessary staff members assisting inspectors in the performance of their duties. The IGC, inspectors, and researchers are usually temporarily detached from the judiciary and therefore continue to be governed by the statutes of judges and judicial personnel.

The IGC is specifically in charge of: (1) Carrying out the inspection of the functioning of ordinary and commercial courts, with the exception of the Supreme Court and the Court of Appeals; (2) monitoring and following up on the discipline of judges and registrars, with the exception of those of the Supreme Court and the Court of Appeals; (3) following up on the implementation of laws and regulations governing courts; (4) ensuring the fairness of judgments and examining injustice alleged in the judgments submitted for review; (5) advising on required measures to improve upon the performance of the judicial organ; and (6) organizing training for judges and registrars.

The law places the following responsibilities specifically in the hands of the IGC: (1) Ensure the effective organization and functioning of the inspectorate; (2) file to the HCJ, through the president of Supreme Court, cases of suspected misconduct by judges or registrars, after making a report;

(3) assign additional responsibilities to the units of the inspectorate, whenever necessary. The IGC decides, based upon their own motion or request by the president of the Supreme Court, the conduct of inspection and submits his or her report to the president.

In addition to the IGC, who is also the head and coordinator of the activities of the inspectorate, the four additional members are in charge of the following: (1) The unit in charge of the inspection of the fairness of decisions of courts and the examination of injustice alleged in the judgments submitted for review; (2) the unit in charge of the preparation and publication of court decisions to provide guidance for the harmonization of court rulings; (3) the unit in charge of fighting corruption and ensuring the administration and functioning of courts, monitoring the conduct of judges and registrars, providing advice on possible sanctions for misconduct by judges and registrars when necessary, and acting as the link between the judicial organ and the citizens; and (4) the unit in charge of training judges and registrars, following up on law reform, and drafting regulations relating to courts as well as their implementation modalities. Every inspector also has courts in the jurisdiction of a chamber of the high court that they have has to inspect personally.

Section 5: Organizational and functioning features common to all courts

Whether they are ordinary or specialized, or higher or lower, there are organizational and functioning features that are applicable to all courts. These are related, for example, to their composition, the responsibilities of their president and those of the court registrars, and other administrative requirements general to all courts.

A. Hearing and composition of the court (Art. 40–42 LOFJ)

Except for the Primary Courts, which have no vice presidents, every court is governed by a president and a vice president, who head the court, other judges, registrars, and staff members in charge of various duties. The staff of the courts are governed by the law governing the statutes of judges and judicial personnel, except those governed by the general statutes for public service.

Courts may be structured into specialized chambers. Except for the Supreme Court, these chambers are established or removed by the HCJ

Hearings are conducted at the courts' seats. With the exception of the Supreme Court and the Court of Appeals, courts may conduct hearings in any other place within their jurisdictions if the presidents of such courts deem it necessary in order to achieve fair justice. The conduct of hearings in a place other than the seat of a court shall cause no disruption of operations at the court's habitual seat.

B. The president of the court (Art.43–45 LOFJ)

At the head of every court is a president, whose responsibilities include case adjudication, administration, organization and smooth running of activities, and the conduct of the staff. With the exception of the military courts, if the president of a court is absent or unavailable, these responsibilities fall to the vice president. If he or she is absent or if the court has no vice president, the president is replaced by the senior judge. In case there are judges with the same seniority, the president is replaced by the senior judge with the highest law degree. In cases where such judges have the same qualifications, precedence is given to the one with age seniority.

The president of the court has the following key responsibilities: (1) Presiding over the hearings in which they are taking part; (2) setting dates for hearings; (3) determining the judges on a bench and distributing cases to the judges who adjudicate them; (4) adopting appropriate strategies to improve court functioning and expedite the trying of cases; (5) supervising each staff member of the court, in accordance with the disciplinary procedure provided by law; (6) convening and chairing the meetings of all court judges and other staff on a monthly basis; and (7) monitoring and supervising the functioning of lower courts.

Every president of a court submits to the president of the Supreme Court monthly and annual activity reports and any other required reports, with copies sent to the IGC, the president of the immediate higher court, and the director of planning services.

C. Court registry (Art. 46–49 LOFJ)

Every court has a registry, comprising the chief registrar and other registrars.

The chief registrar is the coordinator of the registry's activities. In this regard, he or she is responsible for (1) developing and implementing plans related to the registry, keeping court documents, following up on the registry's activities, and preparing court reports, and (2) the discipline of registrars. In particular, the chief registrar of the Supreme Court is responsible for coordinating activities and developing appropriate strategies relating to the organization and functioning of the registry of courts in the country. The president of the Supreme Court may also delegate to the chief registrar the powers to sign some documents and decisions related to the smooth management of the registry of courts.

The chief registrar of the Supreme Court or the Court of Appeals has the power to help parties if they opt for settling their case if they opt to and to make decisions on the costs of proceedings associated therewith.

In case of the absence or unavailability of the chief registrar, the senior registrar replaces him or her. Where there are registrars with the same seniority, the chief registrar is replaced by the one with the highest academic degree. If registrars have the same academic degrees, they are replaced by the eldest registrar.

Registrars have the following responsibilities: (1) Receive complaints and verify whether they fulfill the required conditions for entry into the register; (2) receive and respond to the complaints of the population; (3) summon parties and notify them of court decisions; (4) provide other services that the population requires in the court; (5) examine whether case files fulfill the necessary conditions for being heard; (6) prepare the draft of the pre-trial conference schedule, conduct the pre-trial conference, and help parties settle cases if they opt to (7) prepare the pre-trial conference report; (8) assist judges in preparing cases whose dates for hearing are set; (9) carry out the legal research necessary for the case draft report, to be used for hearing purposes; and (10) record proceedings and prepare the case draft report to be submitted to the bench that tried the case.

Section 4: The Supreme Court

A. *Organization and functioning of the Supreme Court (Art. 3, 50–54 LOFJ)*

The Supreme Court is the highest court in the country. Its seat is located in the city of Kigali, and its jurisdiction covers the whole country.

The Supreme Court comprises a president; a vice president; and at least five other judges, court registrars, and staff members in charge of the various duties of the Supreme Court. The president and the vice president of the Supreme Court are appointed for a five-year term, renewable only once.

The president of the Supreme Court is both the head of the judiciary organ and the top judge of the Supreme Court. As the head of the judiciary, the president of the Supreme Court:

1 Signs decisions relating to the appointment, promotion, and dismissal of judges, inspectors, and registrars of ordinary and commercial courts as well as other members of the staff governed by the law governing the statutes of judges and judicial personnel, except those appointed by other organs;
2 May, in the interest of justice, for the sake of adjudicating national cases, and in conformity with international jurisprudence in relation to similar cases – upon their own motion or upon request by the accused, their counsel, or by the national, or foreign prosecution authority – seek the judicial cooperation of the United Nations or of any other international organization or a foreign country to send judges to Rwanda to sit with Rwandan judges in cases of international and transnational crimes committed on Rwandan territory or abroad, referred to in the law determining the jurisdiction of courts and in the criminal laws of Rwanda. The chief justice may also send a judge from Rwanda to hear cases in another country that requested it, upon approval by the HCJ;

3 Publishes the annual activity report on the general functioning of the judicial organ;
4 Issues instructions and makes decisions relating to the administration and functioning of the judicial organ;
5 Issues, upon approval by the General Assembly of the Supreme Court, instructions governing court procedure in cases not provided by laws governing it, to be published in the official gazette;
6 Convenes and chairs the Bureau of the Judicial Organ;
7 Presides over elections of judges and court registrars running for membership in the HCJ, except those from military courts;
8 Determines, upon approval by the HCJ, the dress worn by judges of all ordinary and commercial courts during hearings and official ceremonies;
9 Designates the spokesperson for the Judicial Organ;
10 Issues an order determining the ceremonies to be followed in the funerals of a judge or a court registrar;
11 Issues an order determining the responsibilities of the personnel of the office of the president of the Supreme Court;
12 Convenes and presides over the meeting of the presidents of courts at least once a quarter and any time when this is deemed necessary;
13 Convenes and presides over the annual retreat of judges and court registrars; and
14 Presides over the ceremonies marking the official opening of the judicial year.

As the top judge of the Supreme Court, its president is responsible for: (1) Convening and chairing the meeting of all judges of the Supreme Court at least once every quarter, and whenever this is deemed necessary, to discuss legal issues raised during the adjudication in different courts and to set up guidelines to solve any issues; (2) incorporate the decisions taken in recent meetings of Supreme Court judges, in the manual containing instructions for all courts; (3) ensuring the implementation of the decisions made during meetings referred to under item (2) above; (4) issuing instructions governing the organization and functioning of the Supreme Court upon approval by all judges of the Supreme Court; (5) delegating, in the interest of work, to the judges and registrars from lower courts the powers to work in the higher courts for not more than six months, except in the Supreme Court; (6) delegating, in the interest of work, to the judges and court registrars from specialized courts the powers to work in ordinary courts or to those from ordinary courts the powers to work in specialized courts for not more than six months, with the exception of military courts; and (7) administering the oath of office to the president of the Republic.

The Supreme Court bench consists of three judges assisted by its registrar. However, the bench may consist of an odd number of more than three judges, depending on the importance that the president of the Supreme Court attaches to the case at hand. Supreme Court decisions are binding on all other courts of the country. They are neither appealable nor revocable, except in cases of review or presidential pardon.

The Supreme Court also has a vice president, whose main responsibilities are assisting its president and deputizing for them in case of their absence. Other responsibilities of the vice president of the Supreme Court include: (1) Monitoring the functioning of the registry, (2) monitoring the functioning of the general secretariat, (3) coordinating the implementation of strategies meant to enhance the fairness of judgments, and (4) performing other duties as may be assigned by the president of the Supreme Court.

In addition to its president and vice president, the office of the president of the Supreme Court is composed of the following staff: (1) The adviser to the president of the Supreme Court, who is the head of the office; (2) the adviser to the vice president of the Supreme Court; (3) the executive secretary of the HCJ; (4) staff members in charge of research assisting the judges of the Supreme Court; (5) staff members of the translation department; (6) the secretaries of the president and vice president of the Supreme Court; and (7) other necessary staff members.

B. Jurisdiction of the Supreme Court

The jurisdiction of the Supreme Court is primarily in reviewing the judgments of the lower courts either because (1) they are vitiated by injustice, or (2) the interest of the law requires a new precedent to be developed. The Supreme Court's jurisdiction includes hearing at the first and last instance important cases related to (3) offenses committed by the highest officials of the country, (4) cases related to some constitutional issues and powers, and (5) cases related to procedures in the appointment and removal of officials.

1. Review of lower courts judgments vitiated by injustice (Art.53–64 LJC)

Upon approval by the president of Supreme Court, the Supreme Court hears applications for review of judgments rendered at last instance on the grounds of their being vitiated by injustice.

The law considers a judgment vitiated by injustice in the following cases: (1) If there is unequivocal evidence of corruption, favoritism, or nepotism that had effects on the judgment and were unknown to the losing party over the course of the proceedings; (2) if, during the trial, the judge showed blatant disregard for legal provisions and evidence; or (3) if the judgment cannot be executed as it was decided. Unless in exceptional cases identified by the IGC, the application for review of judgments vitiated by injustice must follow appeals and other legal deadlines.

The persons empowered to apply to the president of the Supreme Court for review of judgments on the grounds of their being vitiated by injustice are: (1) The office of the ombudsman, upon request by one of the parties; (2) the president of the court, having examined the case and identified the injustice therein; (3) the party that is not satisfied with the judgment rendered by the Court of Appeals; and (4) the IGC for other possible cases that no one else can raise.

Any person wishing to have their case reviewed on the grounds of its being vitiated by injustice files, to that effect, a reasoned written application to the competent organ. Which organ receives applications for review depends on the level of jurisdiction that rendered the vitiated judgment. For judgments of lower courts, the application is submitted to the president of the court immediately above the one that tried the case at the last instance. For cases rendered by the Court of Appeals, the application is submitted to the president of the Supreme Court. This application must be submitted within 30 days of notification of judgment. However, in case of application for review because the judgment cannot be executed as it was decided, the time limits begin from the time this impossibility is confirmed in a statement made by a bailiff.

When the president of the court with which an application is filed for consideration of alleged injustice finds that there is such injustice, they promptly inform the president of the Supreme Court thereof in writing, applying for review of the judgment on the grounds of its being vitiated by injustice. After receiving this application, the president of the Supreme Court examines it; if there is no *prima facie* case of injustice, the president informs the applicant of this. In case there is a *prima facie* case of injustice, the president can decide that (a) the case must be heard by the Supreme Court, mainly if it can serve as precedent for other courts, or (b) the case must be sent to another court higher than the one that heard it in the last instance. The decision on the determination of whether a case is vitiated by injustice must be made within three months of the filing of the application. It should, however, be understood that the deadline provided here concerns the determination on whether or not the vice exists. It does not concern the substantive review of the case.

If the applicant is not satisfied by the decision of the president of the Supreme Court, they may address a written request to the office of the ombudsman for consideration of the alleged injustice. If the office finds that there has been no injustice, it informs the applicant of this. However, if the office of the ombudsman finds that there has been such injustice, it informs the president of the Supreme Court in writing and applies for review of the judgment. The office prepares and submits a report on the specific nature of the issue, along with evidence of injustice. The president of the Supreme Court then makes a decision based on the report of the inspectorate-general of courts.

The office of the ombudsman cannot be involved in the examination of instances of injustice with respect to a case to which it is a party. Such alleged injustice is examined by the president of the court above the one that heard the case upon application by the office of the ombudsman or a party to the case. If either party is not satisfied with the decision of the court president, they inform the IGC and request that he or she examine the alleged instance of injustice. Where the IGC finds that there has been injustice in a judgment rendered, the latter applies to the president of the Supreme Court for review of such a judgment.

Where the IGC considers the judgment and finds that there has been injustice, and that there is no other remedy to resolve this, they prepare a report and submit it to the president of the Supreme Court. The report on injustice must contain facts evidencing such injustice and the reasons for the impossibility of other remedies.

Where, upon considering a report on the judgment vitiated by injustice that is submitted to them, the president of the Supreme Court decides that the case must be re-adjudicated, he or she forwards the file to the chief registrar of the Supreme Court, who sets a date for the necessary hearing or refers it to another court, as provided and decided by the president.

When the Supreme Court, or any other court designated by its president, receives an application for review of a judgment on the grounds of its being vitiated by injustice, it examines the merits of the case anew and in the presence of all parties. The applicant seeking remedy against injustice is exempted from the payment of court fees.

An application for review of a final judgment on the grounds of its being vitiated by injustice does not entail the stay of the execution of the judgment. However, if the president of the Supreme Court orders the review of a judgment on the grounds of injustice when the judgment has not yet been executed, the execution is immediately suspended, even if the proceedings to execute the judgment have already been initiated.

The Supreme Court president's decision made after consideration of the alleged injustice is final and not open to any further appeal.

2. *Review of lower courts' judgments to develop a new precedent (Art. 65 LJC)*

The Supreme Court has jurisdiction to review cases decided by lower courts with goal of developing, confirming or changing a precedent. In this case, the Supreme Court acts upon request by the Rwanda Bar Association or the National Public Prosecution Authority. In their application, both entities must indicate errors or problems in the challenged cases as well as the reasons for the need to change the rules. Such cases are not intended to change the *res judicata* in the challenged cases. Parties cannot use any review, including the injustice review, as a reason. Such cases are not subject to the payment of court fees.

3. *Offenses committed by highest officials of the country (Art. 66–68 LJC)*

The Supreme Court has the exclusive jurisdiction to try, in the first and last degree, criminal cases involving the president of the Republic, the president of the Senate, the speaker of the chamber of deputies, the president of the Supreme Court, and the prime minister. It also has jurisdiction to try their co-offenders or accomplices. The Supreme Court has the jurisdiction to try, in the first and last degree, the president of the Republic on charges of treason or gross and deliberate violation of the constitution. When trying these officials, its bench should be composed of at least five judges.

The prosecution and trial of high-ranking officials requires some other formalities from the legislative power: In the case of the president of the Republic, the latter cannot be subject to prosecution and trial for criminal acts unless charged by both Chambers of Parliament in a joint sitting by a two-thirds majority vote of the members of each chamber. The same majority is required for the prosecution of the president of the Supreme Court and the prime minister. In the case of the president of the Senate and the speaker of the chamber of deputies, the latter cannot be prosecuted or tried unless authorized by a two-thirds majority vote of members of their respective chambers present in the sitting. The vote is not required, however, if these leaders of the legislative power are caught red-handed committing a felony or misdemeanor.

4. *Constitutional issues and disputes on conflict of powers (Art. 69 LJC)*

The Supreme Court also has first and last jurisdiction over the following disputes: (1) Make decisions on petitions on the unconstitutionality of organic laws, international instruments, laws, and decree laws; (2) resolve disputes relating to interpretation of the constitution; (3) resolve disputes relating to the preservation of public interest; (4) provide authentic interpretation of laws; (5) give authentic interpretation on traditional unwritten customs if the written law is silent; (6) resolve disputes relating to referendum, presidential elections, and Parliamentary elections; and (7) decide that there is a force majeure that prevents the chambers of Parliament from sitting in the national capital city.

5. *Administering oaths of some high officials and other special powers (Art. 70–71 LJC)*

The Supreme Court is also vested with the jurisdiction to administer the following oaths of offices: (1) Chief gender monitor and deputy-chief gender monitors (2) commissioners of national commissions; (3) registrars of land titles; and (4) other officials as determined by the law.

The Supreme Court is vested with the following special jurisdiction: (1) Approve the list of senatorial candidates, except those appointed by the president of the Republic; (2) declare vacant the office of the president of the Republic if the president in office dies, resigns, or is sentenced by a court for treason or gross and deliberate violation of the Constitution; and (3) hear petitions relating to a decision to expel a senator or a deputy from the Parliament or from a political organization.

Here, a distinction must be made between the powers of the Supreme Court as a court and the powers vested in the hands the chief justice by the Constitution as the head of the judiciary. These powers include, for example, administering the oath of the president of the Republic.

Section 6: The Court of Appeals

A. Organization and functioning of the Court of Appeals (Art. 55–58 LOFJ and Art. 90 LJC)

In May 2018, the Court of Appeals was added to the existing court system of Rwanda as a new ordinary court to adjudicate, at the appeal level, cases handled by the High Court, the Commercial High Court, and the military High Court. This court was created with its jurisdiction covering the national territory to maintain the appeal benefits that parties received during their appeals at the Supreme Court, as was the case under the pre-2018 law on the organization and functioning of courts, and free the Supreme Court from continuing to serve as the appeals level for every case. As was the case at the Supreme Court level, cases tried by the Court of Appeals are not subject to appeal unless otherwise stated by the law.

The Court of Appeals comprises a president, vice president, at least 11 other judges, the chief registrar, registrars, and other necessary support staff members performing the various duties of the court provided by the law. The president, vice president, and other judges of the Court of Appeals are appointed by the president of the Republic after consultation with the Cabinet and the HCJ, and after the approval of the Senate. The president and vice president of the Court of Appeals are appointed for a five-year term renewable only once. Other judges of the Court of Appeals have no fixed term.

In addition to being the top judge of the Court of Appeals and managing the court, the president has the responsibility of harmonizing the courts' rulings. In this regard, the president presides at least every six months over a meeting of the judges of the Court of Appeals, the High Court, the Commercial High Court, and the Military High Court to discuss legal matters raised during the adjudication of cases and to set up guidelines at each level.

B. Jurisdiction of the Court of Appeals (Art.52 LJC)

The Court of Appeals has jurisdiction to hear at the first level of appeals cases tried at first instance by the High Court, the Commercial High Court, and the military High Court.

It also has jurisdiction to hear at the second level of appeal cases tried by the High Court, the Commercial High Court, and the Military High Court, if such cases: (1) Have an impact on national security; (2) have ordered penalties that are not provided by law; (3) are decided based on a non-existing law, refer to repealed legal provisions, or are tried by a court lacking jurisdiction; (4) are decided based on evidence, a document, or submissions that were presented after the conclusion of the hearing without any reopening of the hearing; (5) are decided by a bench with no required minimum number of judges provided by law; (6) were pronounced by a judge other than the one that heard them; (7) are tried in-camera hearing though not so ordered; or (8) have ordered the award of damages of at least 75 million Rwandan francs (Frw 75,000,000) or, in the case of disagreement between the parties, had the same amount ordered by the judge. When the monetary value of the dispute was not determined in earlier cases, it must have a value of at least 75 million Rwandan francs (Frw 75,000,000), determined by an expert, if necessary. Last but not least are cases that (9) involve a term of imprisonment of at least fifteen (15) years. The determination of such a term is made only with reference to the imprisonment sentenced and not the one proposed by the law.

An appeal at the second level can be admitted only: (1) If approved by the chief registrar of the Court of Appeals and if the appellant has not admitted to the charges brought against them, or (2) if they have not lost their case in both courts for the same reason. In cases where the appellant is dissatisfied with the decision of the chief registrar, they have the right to appeal in writing against the decision to the president of the Court of Appeals within five days of notification of the decision.

Cases tried by the Court of Appeals are not appealable.

Section 7: The High Court

A. Organization and functioning of the High Court (Art. 59–61 LOFJ and Art. 88–89 LJC)

The High Court has its seat in the city of Kigali, and its jurisdiction covers the entire national territory. In addition to its seat in the capital, it also has five (5) chambers: (1) The special chamber, hearing international and transnational crimes, with its seat in *Nyanza*; (2) the High Court chamber of *Nyanza*; (3) the High Court chamber of *Musanze*; (4) the High Court chamber of *Rwamagana*; and (5) the High Court chamber of *Rusizi*. Every chamber has its own administration.

The territorial jurisdiction of the following High Court seats is as follows: (1) The High Court: The Intermediate Courts of *Nyarugenge*, *Gasabo*, and *Gicumbi*; (2) the High Court chamber of *Musanze:* The Intermediate Courts of *Musanze* and *Rubavu*; (3) the High Court chamber of *Nyanza*: The Intermediate Courts of *Muhanga*, *Huye*, and *Nyamagabe*; (4) the High

Court chamber of *Rwamagana*: The Intermediate Courts of *Ngoma* and *Nyagatare*; (5) the High Court chamber of *Rusizi:* The Intermediate Courts of *Rusizi* and *Karongi*; and (6) the international and transnational crimes High Court chamber that covers the entire national territory.

The president of the Supreme Court may designate other chambers in the High Court, if this is deemed necessary, upon approval by the HCJ.

The High Court comprises a president, vice president, at least 30 other judges, the chief registrar, registrars, and other support staff members in various duties of the court provided by the law. The president and vice president of the High Court are appointed for a five-year term, renewable only once.

The president of the High Court has the following specific responsibilities: (1) Monitoring the functioning of the High Court, Intermediate Court, and Primary Courts; (2) presiding over the bench of judges in each chamber of the High Court, if considered necessary; (3) convening and presiding over the meeting of all judges of the High Court at least once every six months; (4) convening and presiding over the meeting of all staff of the High Court chambers at least once every six months; and (5) making decisions, when necessary and in the interest of work, that enable judges and court registrars in the High Court and lower courts to work in other courts of the same level as those to which they are assigned for a period of not more than six months.

B. Jurisdiction of the High Court

The High Court is primarily the Court of Appeals for most cases from the Intermediate Court. It is also a first degree court for some specific serious offenses, transnational and international cases or offenses, and administrative cases. The law also gives the High Court some special jurisdiction related to providing administrative instruction and administering oaths.

1. The High Court as the appellate court for cases from Intermediate Courts (Art. 41, 43, 45, 46, 51 LJC)

The High Court has jurisdiction to hear at the first level of appeal criminal, civil, and administrative cases decided at first instance by the Intermediate Court. It also hears appeals of cases on the genocide against the Tutsi, genocide ideology, and other related crimes rendered by the Intermediate Court.

As a second level of appeal in criminal matters, the High Court hears cases rendered at the first level of appeal by Intermediate Courts if such cases: (1) Have been decided based on a non-existing law or rendered by an incompetent court; (2) involve a penalty that is not provided by law; (3) have been decided based on evidence, documents, or submissions presented after the trial without any reopening of proceedings; (4) have been rendered by a bench with no required minimum number of judges; (5) have been pronounced by a judge other than the one that heard them; or (6) haven been tried in-camera hearing though it was not so ordered. In civil matters, this second level of appeals applies if such cases (1) have been decided based on a non-existing law or pronounced by an incompetent court; (2) have been decided based on evidence, documents, or submissions presented after the trial without any reopening of proceedings; (3) have been decided by a bench with no required minimum number of judges; (4) have been pronounced by a judge other than the one that heard them; (5) have been tried in-camera hearing though it was not so ordered; or (6) have awarded or have the value of at least 50 million Rwandan francs (Frw 50,000,000).

The appeal at the second level is not, however, automatic, even when the above conditions are met. To be admissible, (1) a second level of appeals must be approved by the chief registrar of the High Court; (2) parties must not have admitted to the charges brought against them; (3) the party must not have lost their case in both lower courts for the same reason; and (4) the value, in civil cases, must be at least 50 million Rwandan francs (Frw 50,000,000). The decision of the chief registrar is appealable in writing to the president of the High Court within five (5) days of notification of the decision. The decision of the president of High Court on this appeal is not appealable.

2. *The High Court as the first level court of special cases (Art. 39, 40, 42, 44, 47, 49 LJC)*

At the first degree, the High Court has two categories of jurisdiction: Cases in which the High Court is the first-level jurisdiction, but there is an option for appeal, and cases in which the court hears the case as the first and last instance.

The general rule is that the High Court has jurisdiction to try at first instance the following offenses committed by civilians, other than minors: (1) Offenses of high treason, (2) offenses against state security, and (3) terrorism offenses. The law also gives the High Court jurisdiction to try at first instance cases transferred to Rwanda from the International Criminal Tribunal for Rwanda/Mechanism for International Criminal Tribunals or transferred by the courts of other countries.

Furthermore, the High Court has jurisdiction over all persons, including foreign nationals, and non-governmental organizations or associations, whether national or foreign, alleged to have committed, within or outside the territory of Rwanda, any of the following international or transnational crimes: (1) Terrorism and hostage taking; (2) human trafficking; (3) slavery and other related crimes; (4) torture or inhumane or degrading treatment; (5) crimes of genocide, except crimes of genocide against the Tutsi and crimes against humanity perpetrated between 1 October 1990 and 31 December 1994; (6) crimes against humanity; (7) war crimes; (8) genocide denial or revisionism; or (9) inciting, mobilizing, aiding, and facilitating or otherwise participating, whether directly or indirectly, in the commission of any of the aforementioned crimes listed under points (1)–(8).

The jurisdiction to hear exequatur cases also belongs to the High Court. In considering exequatur cases, it must ascertain whether: (1) The foreign judgment comprises an element incompatible with public order and Rwandan law principles; (2) the judgment has acquired the force of *res judicata* in accordance with the laws of the country of origin; (3) the copy of the judgment fulfills all the necessary conditions for its authenticity in accordance with such laws; and (4) the rights of defense have been respected. The High Court hears applications relating to the extradition of foreign nationals suspected of having committed offenses. It also adjudicates cases relating to applications for asylum.

In administrative issues, the High Court hears at first instance: (1) Applications seeking the annulment of administrative decisions made in the last instance by the president of the Republic, president of the Senate, speaker of the chamber of deputies, prime minister, ministers, and ministers of state and other cabinet members that are illegally made, made by incompetent authorities, or made by authorities who act *ultra vires*; (2) applications seeking damages based on the decisions made under (1); (3) applications seeking the annulment of administrative decisions or seeking damages arising from non-compliance with laws governing public service decisions made by the authorities referred to in (1); and (4) applications relating to the incompatibilities between elective and non-elective public functions.

The cases that the High Court hears at the first and last instance include reviews of decisions of the meetings of the Bar Association as well as petitions arising from the elections of members of the organs of that association and matters related to the rehabilitation of persons convicted by ordinary courts.

Although the law did not specify if the High Court hears, in the first and last degree of jurisdiction, the following administrative cases the basic rule of statute interpretation makes one assume that because the law did not say that they are not appealable, they are open to appeal. These cases are related to: (1) Election petitions of administrative leaders at the provincial and Kigali city levels; (2) disputes relating to political organizations, whether among themselves or between a political organization and its members, or between a political organization and the administration; and (3) adjudicate cases relating to political organizations' having undermined the national unity, territorial integrity, and national security; having been involved in discrimination on the grounds of political affiliation; or having identified themselves with any element such as race, ethnic group, region, sex, or anything else that may serve as a basis for discrimination.

3. Special jurisdiction related to administrative instruction and oaths (Art. 50 LJC)

With regard to the jurisdiction of the High Court related to administrative instructions and oaths, this court has the power to (1) instruct through a written order any administrative organ to perform or to not perform a given act; (2) indicate in its written decision that it has authorized an administrative organ to choose between paying compensation in kind and paying compensation in cash; (3) issue certain written instructions related to the kind of conduct expected from a given administrative authority in order to comply with an order provided under point (2); under penalty for this administrative authority to be personally liable for damages; and (4) administer oath of office to members of the council and the executive committee of the city of Kigali, members of the Bar Association, and other persons authorized by law.

Section 8: The Commercial High Court

A. Organization and functioning of the Commercial High Court (Art.69–70 LOFJ)

The jurisdiction of the Commercial High Court covers the entire national territory. It has its seat in the city of Kigali. The Commercial High Court comprises a president and a vice president, at least five other judges, a chief registrar, registrars, and other necessary staff members. The president and vice president of the High Court are appointed for a 5-year term, renewable only once.

The president of the Commercial High Court has the responsibility of convening and presiding over the meeting of all personnel of commercial courts every three months and whenever it is deemed necessary for the purpose of exchanging views on modalities to deliver effective and prompt justice, on challenges encountered, and on appropriate strategies.

B. Jurisdiction of the Commercial High Court (Art. 81–82 LJC)

The primary responsibility of the Commercial High Court is to hear the appeals of judgments rendered at first instance by commercial courts.

The Commercial High Court also has the jurisdiction to hear at first instance the following cases:

- Cases seeking execution in Rwanda of decisions and judgments rendered by foreign courts on commercial, financial, and fiscal cases. The examination of such applications is conducted in consideration of whether (1) the foreign judgment contradicts the public order and legal principles of Rwandan laws; (2) the case was finally heard and determined in accordance with the laws of the country in which the judgment was rendered; (3) the copy of the judgment is by all means authentic in accordance with the laws of the country in which the judgment was rendered; and (4) the right of defense was respected;

- Cases seeking execution in Rwanda of authentic deeds that have proof that they were written by foreign authorities, if they have the following evidence: the reasons for seeking the execution of the authentic deeds are not contrary to public order and legal principles of Rwandan laws; and/or according to laws of the country in which they were written, they have all the necessary evidence to prove their authenticity; and
- Cases examining the legality of awards rendered by the arbitrators. Cases in this category are not, however, subject to appeal.

Section 9: The Military High Court

A. Organization and functioning of the Military High Court (Art. 72–79 LOFJ)

The judges of military courts, in exercising their judicial duties, are fully independent. They have full discretion to hear cases and decide on them.

The military high court comprises a president, a vice president, at least seven judges, a chief registrar, and other necessary registrars. It has its seat in the city of Kigali. Its jurisdiction covers the entire national territory.

The president, the vice president, and the judges of the military courts are selected from the army and appointed by a Prime Minister's Order upon request by the minister in charge of the army. They are appointed for an unspecified period. However, they may be dismissed at any time in accordance with similar procedures of their appointment, in the interests of court or due to incompetence, misconduct, or other reasons as provided by law.

The Military High Court, as well as the Military Tribunal, consists of a registry composed of registrars with at least a rank of sergeant and other necessary support staff appointed by an order of the minister in charge of the army.

For the military courts to legally hear cases, the bench must be constituted by an odd number of no fewer than three judges, assisted by a court registrar. The judge presiding over the bench shall be at least of the same military rank as the accused. In military courts, if the president of the court is absent or unavailable, they are replaced by the vice president and, in the absence or unavailability of the latter, by the judge with the highest military rank. If there are judges with equal ranks, the president is replaced by the most senior judge. The president of the Military High Court prepares the draft annual budget of military courts and submits it to the minister in charge of the army.

The judges of the military courts must, over the course of performing their judicial duties, put on the appropriate uniform and their rank insignia.

B. Jurisdiction of the Military High Court (ART 84 LJC)

The primary jurisdiction of the Military High Court is to hear appeals in all cases tried by the military court.

The Military High Court tries at first instance all offenses that constitute a threat to national security committed within the territory of the Republic of Rwanda and beyond by soldiers, irrespective of their ranks, and their co-perpetrators and accomplices.

The Military High Court also hears cases regarding damages arising from criminal offenses under its jurisdiction, unless the party decides to bring this before a civil court. It also hears cases regarding the rehabilitation of persons tried by military courts.

Section 10: Intermediate Courts

A. Organization and functioning of Intermediate Courts (Art. 62–65 LOFJ)

Rwanda has 12 Intermediate Courts (Art. 87 LJC). In addition to its main chamber, every intermediate court counts at least three specialized chambers: (1) The chamber hearing children and family cases, (2) the chamber hearing cases on corruption and economic crimes, and (3) the chamber hearing labor and administrative cases. Judges that sit in chambers may, however, adjudicate other cases not assigned to their chambers, as may be decided by the president of the court.

Each Intermediate Court is composed of its president, vice president, at least seven other judges, the chief registrar, other registrars, and other support staff in various duties of the court provided by the law.

The president of the Intermediate Court closely monitors the functioning of the Primary Courts located under the jurisdiction of the court that they head as well as the conduct of judges, registrars, and staff of such courts. Every quarter, the president convenes and presides over a meeting of judges and registrars operating under their jurisdiction, and exchanges views on modalities to deliver prompt and effective justice, and on the challenges they encounter and appropriate strategies.

B. Jurisdiction of the Intermediate Court

The jurisdiction of the Intermediate Court is divided into two levels. The first one hears appeals in both criminal and civil cases rendered by the Primary Courts located within their territorial jurisdiction, and the second hears, at the first instance, cases specifically attributed to the law. The categories of cases specifically attributed to the Intermediate Court's jurisdiction are (1) General criminal cases, (2) general civil cases, (3) cases about minors and families under the specialized chamber for minors, (4) labor and administrative cases under the specialized chamber for labor and administrative matters, and (5) economic crime cases under the specialized chamber for economic crimes.

1. *General criminal matters (Art. 29–30 LJC)*

Intermediate Courts try at the first instance the following offenses: (1) Offenses punishable by a term of imprisonment exceeding five years, except those that are exclusively preserved for other courts by this law, and (2) crimes of genocide perpetrated against the Tutsi as well as crimes against humanity committed in Rwanda between 1 October 1990 and 31 December 1994 by the following persons: a) Any person having committed offenses or acts of complicity that place them in the category of the masterminds, planners, instigators, supervisors, or leaders of genocide or other crimes against humanity, with their accomplices, or b) any person who was at that time in the administrative organs at the national or prefectural level, and their accomplices.

2. *General civil matters (Art. 31–32 LJC)*

Intermediate Courts hear at the first instance all cases that are outside the jurisdiction of other courts. They also hear civil actions relating to road traffic accident insurance disputes.

3. *Minors and family matters (Art. 33–34 LJC)*

The specialized chamber for minors and family hears at the first instance the following offenses: (1) Any offense committed by a minor at the time of the commission of such an offense, and their co-perpetrators and accomplices, except those tried in the first and last instances by the Supreme Court; (2) domestic violence; (3) abortion; (4) infanticide; (5) patricide; and (6) spousal homicide. The specialized chamber for minors and family also hears, at first instance, applications seeking an order for abortion provided under the law.

At the appeals level, the specialized chamber for minors and family has appellate jurisdiction over all cases related to the minor child's interests tried at first instance by the Primary Court, if they are appealable. It also hears appeals related to (1) the status of persons and family, (2) the petition to establish paternity for an adult child according to the procedure provided for by law, (3) the distribution of marital property and change of matrimonial property regime, (4) distribution or management of marital property, and (5) succession to property with a value that exceeds 3 million Rwandan francs (Frw 3,000,000).

4. *Labor and administrative matters (Art. 35–37 LJC)*

With regard to labor and social security, the chamber for labor and administrative cases hears, at first instance, all labor and social security cases as well as cases pertaining to the following: (1) Individual or collective disputes arising out of employment between private employers and their employees; (2) employment contracts, apprenticeship contracts, collective agreements, or alternative administrative decisions; (3) disputes between social security organizations, between social security organizations and their insurees, and between employers and employees with regard to the application of social security laws; and (4) claims for damages arising out of the breach of labor laws, without prejudice to the laws that confer such jurisdiction on criminal courts if a criminal action is filed against them.

With regard to administrative matters, the specialized chambers of the intermediate courts for labor and administrative cases have jurisdiction to try at first instance the following cases related to administrative decisions taken at last instance by the administration: (1) All claims relating to disputes arising from elections of administrative leaders, except those who are tried in other courts; (2) all claims for damages arising from extra-contractual liability as a result of the actions of government employees and government institutions; (3) applications for revocation of decisions made at last instance by administrative authorities on the grounds of the breach of substantive and procedural rules, those made by incompetent authorities, or those made by those acting as *ultra vires*; (4) applications for revocation of administrative decisions or for damages arising from non-compliance with laws governing public service; (5) all claims relating to civil liability, if the damage arises from an act or omission of the administration or is caused by public works; (6) all claims relating to contracts between government authorities, whether governed by administrative or civil laws, except for contracts relating to public tenders; (7) all claims relating to labor disputes between individuals and the government or its corporations; (8) all claims relating to seizure, in the public interest, of private persons' movable or immovable property; (9) all claims arising from expropriation in the public interest; (10) cases relating to immovable property and succession thereto in cases where the subject matter is based on other contradictory decisions made by a government institution on such property; and (11) claims against the State, except where the law provides otherwise.

In addition to adjudicating cases, this chamber can take some administrative orders and administer some oaths of office. These include: (1) Indicating in the operative provisions of its written order that it grants to the administration the right to choose between paying compensation in kind and paying compensation in cash; (2) order any administrative organ to perform or not perform a given act; and (3) administer the oath of office to members of the Council and Executive Committee of Districts, and other officials determined by law.

5. *Economic crimes (Art. 38 LJC)*

The chamber for economic crimes hears at first instance the following offenses: (1) Corruption and related offenses; (2) misuse of public property;

(3) money laundering; (4) embezzlement or destruction of public property; (5) tax evasion; (6) fraudulent bankruptcy and related offenses; (7) illegal award of public tenders; (8) award of unjustified advantages during the execution of public tenders; (9) counterfeiting, using, or putting into circulation objects that can be mistaken for money or negotiable instruments; (10) putting counterfeit money into circulation; (11) counterfeiting, falsification, or alteration of money; and (12) other offenses related to the embezzlement of public property provided for by law.

Section 11: Commercial Court

A. *Organization and functioning of the Commercial Court (Art. 71 LOFJ)*

The territorial jurisdiction of the Commercial Court covers the entire national territory with its seat in the city of Kigali. The Commercial Court comprises a president, a vice president, at least 13 other judges, a chief registrar, some registrars, and other necessary staff members.

B. *Jurisdiction of the Commercial Court (Art. 81 LJC)*

Excluding commercial matters involving amounts not exceeding 5 million Rwandan francs (Frw 5,000,0000) that are within the Primary Court's jurisdiction, the Commercial Court hears in the first instance all other commercial, financial, and fiscal cases, and other related matters in connection with: (1) Disputes arising from commercial contracts or commercial activities between individuals or business entities; (2) disputes arising from the use of negotiable instruments; (3) disputes arising from contracts between individuals and financial institutions; (4) disputes related to liquidation, dissolution, and recovery of business firms facing bankruptcy; (5) disputes related to insurance, with the exception of those related to accident compensation claimed from insurance companies by those who have no contract with such companies; (6) disputes related to taxes and duties; (7) disputes related to the transportation of persons and goods; (8) any dispute that may arise between persons who own or manage registered entities and other business companies, namely: (a) members of the board of directors, (b) directors, (c) auditors, (d) liquidators of a dissolved company, and (e) administrators of the property of a bankrupt firm; (9) cases related to bankruptcy; (10) disputes related to intellectual property, including trademarks and names; (11) disputes related to registration and deregistration of business people from commercial registers; (12) disputes related to the appointment or dismissal of auditors of firms; (13) disputes related to business competition and consumer protection; (14) business-related issues arising in cooperative organizations; (15) any dispute arising in the preparation and execution of administrative contracts between public organs and the private sector on business and financial affairs; and (16) cases related to public tenders.

The Commercial Court also hears at the first instance tax cases referred to under the East African Community Customs Management Act.

Section 12: The Military Tribunal

A. Organization and functioning of the Military Tribunal (Art. 73–78 LOFJ)

The military tribunal comprises a president, a vice president, at least eight (8) judges, a chief registrar, and other necessary registrars. The territorial jurisdiction, the appointment, and the dress code of judges at the military tribunal are similar to those of judges at the military high court.

B. Jurisdiction of the military tribunal (Art. 83, 85 LJC)

The military tribunal has jurisdiction at the first instance over all offenses committed in the territory of the Republic of Rwanda and abroad by soldiers, irrespective of their ranks, and their co-perpetrators and accomplices, unless such offenses were committed with children and persons tried in the Supreme Court at first and last instance.

The military court also tries former soldiers and former gendarmes who are prosecuted for having committed the crimes of genocide against the Tutsi and other crimes against humanity that were committed in Rwanda between 1 October 1990 and 31 December 1994.

Furthermore, the Military Court hears cases on damages arising from criminal offenses under its jurisdiction, unless the party decides to bring it before a civil court.

Section 11: Primary courts

A. Organization and function of Primary Courts (Art. 66–67 LOFJ)

Rwanda counts 60 Primary Courts. Each Primary Court comprises at least two (2) judges, one of whom is the president of the court. The court also has a chief registrar, a registrar or registrars, and other necessary staff members. The Primary Court hears cases by a bench of one (1) judge assisted by a court registrar, unless otherwise provided for by the law.

B. Jurisdiction of Primary Courts (Art. 26–28; 86 LJC)

The Primary Court is the lowest formal court in the Rwandan judiciary. It is therefore the lowest jurisdictional level for most small civil cases and criminal offenses.

In civil matters, Primary Courts try at first instance: (1) Disputes between physical and non-governmental entities or corporations whose monetary value does not exceed 20 million Rwandan francs (Frw 20,000,000); (2) cases relating to movable property that is worth more than 3 million Rwandan francs (Frw 3,000,000) but does not exceed 20 million Rwandan francs (Frw 20,000,000), and those relating to succession in respect thereof; (3) cases relating to immovable property, other than land, used for agriculture and livestock worth a value of more than 3 million Rwandan francs (Frw 3,000,000) but not exceeding 20 million Rwandan francs (Frw 20,000,000), and succession in respect thereof, as well as disputes between the emphyteutic lessee and the landowner with no certificate; (4) all commercial matters involving amounts of not more than 5 million Rwandan francs (Frw 5,000,000); and (5) cases relating to the status of persons and families.

In criminal matters, Primary Courts have jurisdiction over the following offenses: (1) Offenses punishable by a term of imprisonment not exceeding five years, except those that are exclusively preserved for other courts; (2) crimes of genocide against the Tutsi and crimes against humanity committed in Rwanda between 1 October 1990 and 31 December 1994, as listed below: (a) acts of torture; (b) homicide; (c) acts of rape or genital mutilation; (d) degrading acts on a dead body; (e) serious harm to persons, resulting in death; (f) acts that cause injuries or serious harm to persons, with an intent to inflict death, even if the purpose is not accomplished; (g) any other criminal acts against persons without any intent to inflict death; and (h) other crimes committed by any person who was in the administrative organs at the sub-prefecture or commune level, in political organizations, in the communal police, or in any militia and who committed or incited other people to commit such crimes with their accomplices; and (3) review of cases tried by *Gacaca* courts that fulfill the conditions required by law.

Primary Courts also hear applications for provisional detention and release at first instance.

6 Persons, family, matrimonial regimes, and succession

Section 1. Historical development of Rwandan written law on persons, family, matrimonial regimes, and succession

Until 1988, the laws concerning persons, family, matrimonial regimes, and succession in Rwanda were defined according to the Belgian colonial decree of 4 May 1895[1] and the Ordinance of 14 May 1886 of the colonial general administrator of Congo.[2] While the former provided a detailed Civil Code that will be discussed here, the latter had only two provisions. The first provision provided that issues not regulated by a promulgated decree, ordinance, or order shall be settled using indigenous customs, and general principles of law and equity. The second provision provided that in cases where an indigenous custom must be applied, the colonial judge could consult competent indigenous notables for their opinions on the issue. This is what often happened in most issues related to persons and family, and in almost all matters related to matrimonial regimes and succession. It resulted, therefore that for many years, customary law continued to regulate some aspects of family, matrimonial regimes, and succession in Rwanda, even after the introduction of the written law.[3]

The above-mentioned 1895 Decree, which for more than 40 years governed the issues of persons and family in Rwanda, was passed on the basis of colonial foundations, and it treated foreigners differently from indigenous people. It even categorized the indigenous people into those emancipated, meaning civilized, and those who were non-emancipated.[4] It was also based on gender discrimination, and it treated women as legally inferior to men.

Following are some provisions of the 1895 Code that clearly discriminated against women. Article 29 provided that only the father could register his child, and only in the absence of the father could the mother make such a registration. Article 58 required the wife to have the same domicile as her husband. Article 96 set the marriage age for men at 18and that for women at 15. Article provided that the husband was the head of the family; he owed protection to his wife, and the wife owed him obedience. Article 120 provided that the wife was obliged to live with her husband and to follow him wherever he wanted to reside. Article 122 provided that the wife must receive authorization from her husband for every legal act that imposed a duty on her and expected her to personally perform any obligation. Article 124 provided that, except for exceptional cases, a woman has no right to legal proceedings in court, to acquire or sell property, or to take up a legal obligation without the authorization of her husband. Article 134 provided that the husband could request a divorce for cause of adultery by his wife. However, the wife could not request a divorce for her husband's adulterous acts unless she can prove that those acts were accompanied by circumstances that caused her grave insults. Article 150 provided that, during a divorce proceeding, a wife could leave her home and reside somewhere else only if she had the authorization of the judge. Articles 238–248 considered parental authority as exclusively paternal. Article 240 provided that the parental authority was exercised by the father, and in the absence of the father, by the mother.

The majority of the above provisions were modified in 1988, 26 years after independence, by the Law No. 42/88 of 27 October 1988 instituting Civil Code I.[5] However, not all discriminatory provisions were repealed.[6] For example, Article 206 of the 1988 law maintained that the husband was the head of the household. Article 83 maintained that the wife must have the same domicile as her husband. Although Article 345 recognized the parental authority to both the father and the mother of the child, it further provided that, in case of disagreement on this authority between the father and the mother, the former must prevail. Article 352 provided that the father, and in the absence of the latter, the mother administer the property of their minor children. Article 427 provided that non-married minors who attained the age of 18 can be led to emancipation by their father, and in the absence of the father, by their mother.

With the Law No. 32/2016 of 28 August 2016 governing persons and family, the above discriminatory provisions were corrected.

With regard to matrimonial regimes and succession, this field remained governed by customary law until 1999 when the Law No. 22/99 of 12 November 1999[7] was adopted. Article 3 of the Law No. 42/88 of 27 October 1988 instituting Civil Code I had maintained the colonial provision that provided that in the absence of written legal provisions, judges must apply customary law, or, in the absence of the latter, the rules that they would create as if they are the legislator. As discussed in Sections 12 and 16 of this chapter, this 1999 law was updated and improved in 2016.[8]

The following sections summarize the Law No. 32/2016 of 28 August 2016 Governing Persons and Family (LPF), and the Law No. 27/2016 of 08 July 2016 governing Matrimonial Regimes, Donations, and Successions (LMDS).

Section 2. Legal personality (Art. 9–34 LPF)

The legal personality is the foundation of civil rights. Every person, Rwandan or foreigner, is free to exercise civil rights recognized by law and perform their obligations in good faith. Abuses and excessive or unreasonable exercise of civil rights with the intent to inflict harm upon others are not protected. The legal personality commences from the time of birth. However, a conceived child is entitled to civil rights recognized for every person, provided they are born alive. This means that a child, simply by virtue of being conceived, is deemed to have been born whenever its interests so dictate.

Legal personality terminates at death or, in the event of absence or disappearance, by a declaratory judgment of death. The law defines disappearance as a "situation where a person is absent from their domicile or residence to such an extent that the person's death is taken as certain, or virtually certain, even if their body is yet to be found." This means that the declaration of disappearance requires absence and its declaration is a prerequisite.

An absent person is first presumed alive before being presumed dead. The presumption of life for a person who has appointed an authorized representative is for four years, but that for the person who has been absent without having appointed an authorized representative is for two years. When the presumption of life ceases, any interested person may apply to the competent court of the last domicile or residence of the person presumed to be alive for the declaration of absence. When five years has elapsed since the delivery of the declaratory judgment of absence, and it is uncertain whether the absentee is alive, any interested person who presumes that the absentee is dead can apply to the court of the last domicile or residence of the absentee for declaration of the absentee's death.

When a person has disappeared such that their death is established beyond a reasonable doubt, even if their body is yet to be found or has not been identified, any interested person may, by unilateral petition, apply to the court for a declaratory judgment of their death. This judgment orders the civil registrar to issue the disappeared person's death record. If, however, the person whose death has been judicially declared reappears, any interested person may request the court that delivered the judgment to annul it.

The declaration of absence does not entail the dissolution of marriage of the absentee, nor changes the administration of their property, unless otherwise declared by the court. The declaration of death of the disappeared or absentee entails the surviving spouse's right to enter into a new marriage. This declaration entails also the opening of succession. The existing heirs on the day fixed as the date of death of the disappeared person or absentee have the right to share the disappeared person's or absentee's estate in accordance with relevant laws.

Section 3. Elements of a person's identification (Art. 35–60 LPF)

A person is identified by their name, origin, sex, residence, and domicile.

A person's name is the one mentioned on their birth record. It must be composed of a surname and a post-name. The post-name may consist of a first name, a family name, or both. This order must be strictly followed in the drafting of administrative documents; if not so followed, the document is invalid.

Every child is entitled to have a name. Every parent or any other person having parental authority over the child has a duty to freely choose a name for the child. It is prohibited, however, for a child to bear all names, including those of the father, mother, or sibling. It is also forbidden to give to a child a name that is offensive to good morals or to people's moral integrity.

Marriage or religious vows in no way change a person's name. However, by consent of both spouses, a spouse can add the other spouse's surname to their other names, but this has to be done before the civil registrar. This consent can be withdrawn anytime during the marriage or after divorce. Legal marriage or religious vows can also be annulled in case of divorce or the death of one of the spouses.

Any person has, however, the right to change their name: (1) if the name infringes upon the honor of the person bearing it; (2) if the name is offensive to good morals or people's moral integrity; (3) when the name is used by another person such that it may infringe upon their honor or cause injury to their property; and (4) if there are other reasons deemed valid by the minister in charge of the civil status. The application for name change must be submitted to the minister in charge of the civil status. Once the minister approves the change, the name becomes effective only from the date the new name is recorded in the registry of birth records

A person's origins refer to filiation as the relationship between a child and their father or mother. Paternal or maternal filiation of a person is proved by their birth record. However, in the absence of a birth record, uninterrupted possession of status is sufficient to prove filiation. Possession of status is established by an adequate combination of facts indicating the filiation relationship. The main facts establishing possession of status are the following: (1) The presumed father or mother of the child has always treated the child as theirs, and has in that quality catered for their education, maintenance, and possession of personal assets; (2) the child has been treated as such by the family; and (3) the child has permanently been treated as such by the community. Nobody can claim a filiation different from the one registered in the birth record and matching uninterrupted possession of status.

Maternal filiation of a child born out of wedlock is proved in the same way as that of a child born in wedlock. However, the paternal filiation of a child born out of wedlock is proven by (1) oral or written acknowledgment of the child done before the civil registrar, or (2) judgment declaring paternal filiation or copy of civil register in which the judgment was recorded. With regard to an adoptive child, its proof is an adoption record issued by the civil registrar and approved by the court. In the absence of such a record, however, it is proved by a declaratory judgment in lieu of civil status records.

A person's sex refers to the human physiological state of being male or female. The sex of a person is the one recorded in their birth record.

A person's domicile is the place where a person is registered in civil registers. The domicile of a minor is the same as the domicile of those exercising parental authority over them unless otherwise authorized by them in the minor's interest. Similarly, the domicile of a person deprived of the capacity to exercise their rights is the same as the domicile of their guardian. Although no person is allowed to have more than one domicile in Rwanda, parties to a judicial act may, in writing, elect a domicile with a view to execution of an act or the exercise of the rights arising therefrom.

A person's residence is the place where a person lives for occupational or any other purposes, but which is different from their place of domicile. Unlike their domicile, a person can have more than one residence. Spouses have the same residence unless otherwise dictated by the family's interests. Also, minors are deemed to have the same residence as that of the persons who exercise parental authority over them unless otherwise authorized by the parental authority in the best interest of the minors.

Section 4. Civil status (Art. 61–112 LPF)

Civil status for persons is established and proved by civil status records. The civil status record is an authentic document intended to serve as proof of certain main identifying particulars of a person within the family and country, especially with regard to the enjoyment and exercise of civil rights. The civil status records are contained in civil status registers. Under Rwandan law, civil status registers are the following: (1) register of birth records, (2) register of death records, (3) register of marriage records, (4) register of guardianship records, (5) register of acknowledgment of children born out of wedlock, (6) register of adoption records, and (7) register of other records.

The civil registrar is responsible for the civil status record. The duties of a civil registrar are as follows: (1) issuing civil status records with regard to statements that they, correcting errors, and submitting copies thereof; (2) keeping and preserving civil status registers; (3) recording all judgments related to civil status; (4) approving the application for emancipation of a minor; (5) heading the Guardianship Council and approving the guardian; (6) producing statistics with regard to civil status; (7) officiating over civil marriages after ensuring that the intending spouses fulfill the conditions required by law; (8) performing any other acts relating to the civil status provided for by the law. The civil registrar only records facts in their jurisdiction, as well as declarations made to them in conformity with the law. The registrants as well as witnesses guarantee the accuracy of facts they certify or corroborate in civil status records. The civil registrar may neither refuse to issue a record required by law, nor record declarations other than those made by the involved parties. The civil registrar issues civil status records only by request and never on their own initiative. Civil registrars cannot draw a civil status record and also get involved in their execution or in any other capacity. It is, for example, prohibited for a civil registrar to officiate their own marriage, that of their spouse, ascendants, descendants, collaterals, and in-laws up to the second degree inclusively. Civil registrars are individually liable for any malpractices and offenses committed intentionally or through negligence in the performance of their duties. Without prejudice to civil or criminal liability for acts or omissions, the civil registrar may be liable to administrative sanctions provided for by laws.

Particular civil status records are worth highlighting here: the civil status record for foreigners and those drawn abroad, birth records, and death records.

A. Civil status records for foreigners and those drawn abroad (Art. 96–99 LPF)

Any foreign national having their domicile or residence in Rwanda can have their civil status record drawn up by a Rwandan civil registrar. In the specific case of a marriage record, when a marriage is celebrated in Rwanda and one or both spouses are foreign nationals, the civil registrar must, in thirty days following the celebration of the marriage, transmit the copy of the marriage record to the minister in charge of foreign affairs, who in turn transmits it to the diplomatic or consular representation of the country of origin of the spouse of foreign nationality in Rwanda.

With regard to records drawn abroad, any civil status record of a Rwandan or a foreign national drawn up in a foreign country and drafted in the forms followed in that country is authoritative in Rwanda, except in cases where other documents or data held from abroad or elements drawn from the record itself establish that the record is irregular and falsified, or that the facts declared in it do not correspond to reality. In case of doubt, the Rwandan court, by way of exequatur procedures, must examine the contested record. Upon request by the concerned person, a civil status record drawn up abroad concerning a Rwandan national is entered into the civil status register of the place of their domicile, or if the latter is unknown, of the place of their residence.

B. Birth records (Art. 100–105 LPF)

Every child must be declared within 30 days after birth. The declaration of birth is made by the child's father or mother or, in the case of impossibility, by a person to whom they have granted authorization, or any person exercising parental authority over the child. In the absence of the persons referred to above, the declaration is made by any other person present at the child's birth or a close relative.

The declaration of birth is made upon presentation of a medical birth certificate issued by the health facility where the child was born. In case the child was not born in a health facility, the declaration is made upon presentation of a birth certificate issued by a competent authority of the place of birth of the child, indicating the names of the child's parents and date of birth, and in the presence of two witnesses of at least 18 years of age. For births occurring in health facilities, a special register was designed to record births at those facilities. For children born in prisons, the director of the prison, with the permission of the child's parent, has the responsibility to register them with the civil registrar of the place of location of the prison. For children born to unknown parents, they are registered by the person who found them within 30 days after they are found, at the civil registrar of the place where the child was found.

The civil registrar issues a provisional birth record indicating the child's name and gender, as well as the presumed place and date of birth. The registrant must explain or attach to the declaration a note on the facts and circumstances in which the child was found. If the above information is unknown, the civil registrar determines the place and date of birth depending on a medical report or the child's condition. The provisional record remains until the child's birth is found or declared by the court.

With regard to a child born out of wedlock, the registrar indicates the names of the child's father and mother if both agree. When the presumed mother or father of the child is not present at the time of registering the birth of the child, the registrar informs the presumed absent parent about this presumption, and if the latter agrees to be registered as parent, then the registrar proceeds with the registration. In cases where the informed presumed parent refuses to be registered as the parent of the child, the matter is referred to the competent court. In any case, unless it is declared by the father himself or the mother herself, when the child's parents are not legally married, the declaration of birth of the child with the civil registrar's office by indicating the names of the child's father or mother should not in any way be construed as the recognition of the child. With regard to stillborn babies, or when a child dies immediately after birth, they are not required to be declared before the civil registrar.

C. Death records (Art. 106–112 LPF)

Death is recorded based on the declaration of one of the relatives or the spouse of the deceased, or any other person who has sufficient information on the civil status of the deceased. In cases where the civil status of the deceased is unknown, the death record is drawn up according to the declaration made by the authorities of the cell of the place of death. The death record must be signed by the following persons: the registrant, two witnesses who are at least 18 years of age, and the civil registrar. Death is declared within a period of 30 days following the occurrence thereof upon presentation of a medical certificate of death or a death record issued by the competent authority. In cases where the identity of the dead person is unknown, the declarant should provide the probable place, date, and hour of death, and any other information known to them, such as name, age, profession, place of birth, and domicile, based on the report of a judicial police officer or a medical report. If the place of death is unknown, the presumed place of death is where the body is found. In cases where the death occurred in a health facility, it is recorded in a register kept for that purpose. For deaths that occur in a prison, the prison director must, within 72 hours, transmit the death certificate issued by an authorized medical doctor to the civil registrar of the place of death.

Section 5. Capacity of persons

The capacity of persons depends on whether they have attained the age of majority; are under guardianship, or advisory for a prodigal adult person.

A. Majority age (Art. 113–118 LPF)

The age of majority in Rwanda is 18 years, unless provided otherwise by law. A person having attained that age is fully qualified for all acts of civil life. In case of justifiable grounds, a minor having attained the age of 16 years may be emancipated upon application by the following persons: (1) both their parents and the surviving parent; (2) their adoptive parents; (3) their guardian, upon approval by the Guardianship Council; or (4) children's rights organizations. A minor who has attained the age of 16 years can also individually apply for their emancipation if they have neither parents nor a guardian.

A child who has not achieved the age of majority, or who is not emancipated, is considered a minor. Except in cases the law allows them to act alone, minors are represented by the person who exercises parental authority over them. Any act performed by minors while they are not legally empowered to act alone is absolutely null. However, a minor having attained the age of 16 years may enter alone into an agreement relating to their employment, and exercise their artistic or any occupational activity, or any other activity useful to them.

B. Guardianship (Art. 119–153 LPF)

Guardianship is a procedure used to help a minor or an adult with a mental disability to enjoy rights generally recognized for every person, and ensure administration of their property, if any. Guardianship is exercised in the interest of the person under guardianship. There are two categories of guardianship: the guardianship of a minor and the guardianship of an adult with mental disabilities.

1. Guardianship of a minor (Art. 120–146 LPF)

The guardianship of a minor is established due to the following grounds: (1) in cases of loss, absence, or disappearance of both parents or when they are unknown; (2) in cases where paternity and maternity are denied; (3) when both parents are still alive, but deprived of parental authority; or (4) when the surviving parent has a disability preventing them from fulfilling their parental responsibilities. Two key organs intervene in the guardianship of a minor: (1) the Guardianship Council and (2) the guardians.

The Guardianship Council is composed of three representatives from the paternal family of the minor and three representatives from the maternal family of the child, as well as the civil registrar of the place of the minor's domicile or residence. Members of the Guardianship Council are chosen by the Family Council from those having attained the age of majority who are close relatives of the minor, who will apparently be helpful to the minor, and whose morality ensures the minor's good upbringing and education. If the minor has siblings having attained the age of majority, they are automatically members of the Guardianship Council regardless of their number. When the number of the minor's relatives by blood or marriage on their mother's or father's family is insufficient, the civil registrar invites citizens known to have had usual relationships of friendship with the minor's father or mother. If there are no such persons, the civil registrar invites the person who usually takes care of the minor or persons of integrity of the place of the minor's domicile or residence. The Guardianship Council has the following duties: (1) to monitor and oversee the exercise and administration of guardianship; (2) to consider and authorize the sale of or creation of a mortgage on the minor's property in order to care for the minor's needs; (3) to terminate the responsibilities of a guardian and replace them in case of failure to fulfill their duties; and (4) to present to the minor a final statement on the property when the minor attains the age of majority or is emancipated. The meeting of the Guardianship Council is held at least once a year and whenever necessary.

Guardians discharge their duties voluntarily and free of charge. To be a guardian, a person must be at least 21 years of age and helpful to the minor and have moral integrity guaranteeing the minor's good upbringing. A guardian is appointed as follows: (1) The surviving spouse has the right to appoint a guardian in a will. The guardians appointed must, before taking up their duties, notify the will to the civil registrar for them to draw up a guardianship certificate; (2) the surviving spouse may, in case of a disability preventing them from fulfilling their parental responsibility, appoint while before the Guardianship Council, a guardian from their relatives or persons outside their family by recording in a guardianship certificate made by a civil registrar. Such a certificate has an immediate effect; (3) in case of the death of both parents before appointing a guardian in their will, their absence, disappearance, or disqualification from exercising parental authority, guardianship is awarded by the Guardianship Council. The chosen guardian is free to accept or refuse the responsibility conferred by the Guardianship Council. The following persons are not allowed to be guardians: (1) a person under 21 years of age, (2) a person declared by courts to be legally incapacitated, (3) a person involved in or person whose parents are involved in court proceedings with that minor, (4) persons deprived of their civic rights as a result of a conviction, (5) a person deprived of parental authority, (6) a person sentenced to imprisonment for crimes against children, (7) a person sentenced to imprisonment for the crime of genocide, or (8) a person sentenced to imprisonment for the crime of genocide ideology and related crimes.

The guardian has a number of powers and duties. The guardian has the following powers: (1) to represent the minor in acts involving civil life unless otherwise provided by law and (2) to administer the minor's property and be liable for any damage to the property as a result of poor administration. However, the guardian is not allowed to administer the minor's occupational earnings from an activity unrelated to the guardian's duties, as well as the property acquired through such earnings. Among the duties of the guardian include being responsible for the minor's custody. When a guardian takes up their duties, they make an inventory of the minor's immovable and movable property in the presence of members of the Guardianship Council meeting. This inventory must be submitted to the civil registrar of the place where the property is located within a period of 30 days in order to be certified and attached to the guardianship deed.

The guardian alone undertakes all acts of protection and administration of the property in the minor's best interests. The guardian uses this property in such a way as to generate income for the minor. The guardian is not allowed, however, to perform acts of transfer, sale, mortgage, or any other acts likely to adversely affect the minor's property without prior authorization from the Guardianship Council. Income from the minor's property is allocated as a matter of priority to the minor's maintenance and education. When the income moves into surplus, the guardian is required to notify the Guardianship Council thereof for it to decide on how to allocate the surplus. If such income is insufficient, the additional amount needed to compensate for the shortfall may be obtained using income from the minor's personal work, subject to the authorization from the Guardianship Council. When the guardian has interests that conflict with those of the minor, the case is subject to review by the Guardianship Council, which may, if necessary, appoint an ad hoc guardian to represent the minor or represent the minor itself in such a situation. When one of the Guardianship Council members has interests that conflict with those of the minor, the case is referred to the Guardianship Council for decision. When considering this case, the person whose interests conflict with those of the minor is excluded.

A guardian may be dismissed for the following reasons: (1) notorious misconduct, (2) inability or poor management of the minor's property,

(3) no longer satisfying the conditions which served as the basis for their appointment as guardians, (4) falling into one of the categories of those the law forbids from becoming guardians, or (5) any other serious reason left to the discretion of the Guardianship Council. The removal of a guardian is within the competence of the Guardianship Council, which at the same time appoints a new guardian. Such removal is mentioned in the margin of the corresponding guardianship certificate. The appointment of another guardian is subject to a new guardianship record.

Guardianship can come to an end when (1) the minor attains the age of majority or is granted emancipation, (2) the minor dies, (3) the minor's parent who had disappeared or were absent reappear, (4) one of the parents acknowledges the child, (5) there is a release of the withdrawal of the parental authority, or (6) the minor is adopted.

2. *Guardianship of an adult with mental disability (Art. 147–153 LPF)*

A competent court may declare legally incapacitated an adult with mental disability and appoint a guardian for that adult when the latter lives in a habitual state of mental deficiency, even if such deficiency shows lucid intervals. The application for declaring an adult person to be legally incapacitated for their placement under guardianship is admissible for the following persons: (1) one of the parents, if filed with respect to an unmarried adult; (2) one of the spouses, if filed with respect to the other spouse; (3) adult children, if filed with respect to their parents; or (4) any interested person.

The court seized of the application for declaring a person to be legally incapacitated appoints their guardian after having heard and conducted observation of the person in respect of whom the guardianship is applied for, as well as having heard witnesses and Family Council, and examined medical records indicating their mental condition. A judgment declaring a person to be legally incapacitated is entered in the margin of the birth certificate of the person declared to be legally incapacitated. Guardianship for an adult declared to be legally incapacitated takes effect vis-à-vis third parties from the date the judgment declaring a person to be legally incapacitated has become final.

The guardianship over a married adult or a person declared to be legally incapacitated is exercised by one of the spouses with respect to the other spouse, and by parents with respect to their unmarried adult child still living at their home, unless otherwise determined by the court. In this case, the Guardianship Council shall not be necessary.

Guardianship for an adult ends with the discontinuation of the causes that gave rise thereto or their death. The guardian or any other interested person applies for the reinstatement of capacity to the court having pronounced the judgment.

C. Advisor for prodigal adult person (Art. 154–157 LPF)

Prodigality refers to the misuse of property that is visible to everyone by wasting it or misusing it in any other manner whatsoever. An advisor for a prodigal adult person is therefore a person responsible for advising a prodigal adult person in order for them to perform legal acts related to their property. An advisor for an adult person is appointed by the court of the place of the prodigal person's residence upon request by any interested person after having consulted their spouse, witnesses, and the Family Council. The advisor for an adult person may be chosen from among the parents of the person in respect of whom the advising is instituted, their children, or from the Family Council in the absence of the former. If the adult who needs an advisor is one of the spouses, the other spouse serves as the advisor.

An advisor for an adult person intervenes in all acts in respect of which they are required to provide advice to the person they assist. Such acts include pleading before the court, transaction acts, loan application, acquisition, disposition, and mortgage. However, the advisor has no responsibility to administer the property of the person they advise. When the court appoints an advisor, the adult person in respect of whom the advisor is appointed shall in no way act alone without the advisor's assistance. However, any act performed by an adult person alone, while the advisor's assistance is required, may only be annulled if it adversely affects the person being assisted.

Section 6. Family Council (Art. 162–165 LPF)

The Family Council is an organ within the family especially responsible for ensuring the safeguarding of the interests of the family members, and settling the disputes arising in the family. The Family Council is composed of the following: (1) father and mother of the concerned person; (2) siblings who have attained the age of majority; (3) at least two of the relatives from his father's or mother's family, depending on which family is closely related; and (4) two wise people chosen by the concerned person. Where people mentioned under points (1), (2), and (3) are not available, two people are chosen among the friends of the family recognized for their honesty.

The Family Council has the following responsibilities: (1) to protect the interests of the family; (2) to listen to and settle disputes relating to succession and any other dispute arising in the family; (3) to appoint the members of the Guardianship Council; (4) to give advice at the time of appointing the guardian of an adult person; (5) to appoint the administrator of the property of the absent or disappeared person, if the concerned person or the court did not appoint any; (6) to approve the adoption of the child who does not have both parents, or when the parents are unable to express their consent; (7) to mediate when the parents of the child have disputes over parental authority; (8) to consider petitions in connection with maintenance obligation; (9) to perform any other responsibility as may be determined by other laws or the family.

The Family Council meets any time when deemed necessary, and its decisions are made by consensus and recorded in minutes signed by members present. In cases where there is no consensus, decisions are made by a majority vote of participants to the meeting. Any person who is not satisfied by the decision of the Family Council refers the matter to the competent organ.

Section 7. Relation between parents and children (Art. 253–286 LPF)

The meaning of the term "children," as far as their relationship with their parents is concerned, includes any person born, either naturally or through medically assisted techniques, to a parent, irrespective of their age. Although a distinction can be made between children born during marriage and those born out of wedlock, the general rule is that all children whose filiation is established have equal rights and duties vis-à-vis their parents, irrespective of the circumstances of their birth. Children, born either in a marriage or out of wedlock, have the duty to honor their parents, respect them, and care for them when in need.

As far as children born during a marriage, the relation with their parents is governed by the presumption of paternity, providing that a child born during marriage is presumed to be the child of their mother's husband, and the presumption of maternity, providing that the mother of a child is presumed to be the one who gave birth to the child and who is registered in the birth record. A child is presumed to have been conceived during marriage if born after the 180th day following the celebration of marriage or within 300 days following the dissolution of marriage. A presumed father can, however, deny paternity if (1) he can prove that during the period between the 300th day and 180th day before the child's birth, it was physically impossible for him to cohabit with his wife because of his living away from home or due to an accident; (2) the child was born after 300 days following the judgment granting separation of residence of spouses involved in divorce proceedings or legal separation; (3) the child was born before 180 days since the final judgment rejecting the application for divorce or since the conciliation of spouses who lived separately; (4) he proves that his wife has committed adultery; or (5) he never consented to medically assisted reproduction, or he proves that the child was not born as a result of such reproduction. A husband cannot, however, deny a child born 180 days before marriage in each of the following cases: (1) if the husband had knowledge of the mother's pregnancy before marriage; (2) if he registered the child's birth; (3) if, before and after birth, he conceded that he is the child's father, either verbally or in writing; (4) if spouses have cohabited again for a period of between 300 and 180 days before the child's birth.

As far as children born out of wedlock are concerned, they have a biological mother whose name is entered on the birth record, while their father is the one who readily acknowledges them, or is so declared by the court. Recognition of a child is a voluntary and personal act and is not subject to any condition or time limits. It can happen for (1) a living child; (2) a conceived child, provided that he or she is born alive; or (3) a deceased child if he or she left descendants. The act of recognition is done before a civil registrar, who then establishes a related record. Recognition of a child by one spouse does not require the other spouse's consent. It has effect only in respect of the spouse having recognized the child. However, the other spouse must be notified of such recognition by the civil registrar.

A parent having deliberately abandoned a child can recognize the child if they make themselves known. However, such recognition in no way entails restoration of their parental authority if the child has been adopted.

Recognition of a child born out of wedlock can also happen through the marriage of their parents. A child born out of wedlock is deemed to be legitimized through their father's and mother's subsequent marriage, if both parents recognize the child at the time of the marriage celebration. Legitimization of a child must be registered in a civil register at the place of celebration of the marriage, or at the place of the child's birth. Such legitimization is registered in the margin of the legitimized child's birth record. Legitimization becomes effective from registration. Legitimization may also occur in favor of deceased parents having left behind descendants. In such a case, the legitimization benefits such descendants.

A petition for paternity or maternity can be instituted by the presumed parent denying it, or by the child claiming it.

A petition to deny paternity or maternity of a child is solely instituted by a husband or a wife. Nobody else can file such a petition on the husband's, or wife's, behalf. However, when a husband or a wife dies after having filed a petition to deny paternity or maternity, their heirs may continue the petition within a period of six months. A petition to deny paternity or maternity is brought against the child. The child is represented by either the mother or the father, or, in case of their absence or incapacity, by the guardian, the adoptive parent, or a child's rights organization if the child is a minor. The court competent to hear the action to deny paternity or maternity is that of the place of the child's domicile.

The petition to deny paternity or maternity is filed within a period of six months from the date the husband or wife finds out that the child is not theirs. A child whose non-paternity or non-maternity is established loses rights and duties with regard to their presumed parents.

A paternity and maternity petition can be filed by a child, if the child attained the age of majority, or by one of the child's parents or the child's representation if the child is a minor requesting the court to establish paternity. The grounds for admissibility of the paternity petition are notably (1) if the child was born between 180 and 300 days from the kidnapping, unlawful detention, or rape of the child's mother; (2) if the child's mother was enticed into sex using fraudulent tactics, abuse of authority, or promise of marriage; (3) if clear written or verbal declaration of paternity recognition exists; (4) if the child's mother engaged in cohabitation with the child's presumed father; (5) if the child has possession of status of a legitimate child; or (6) if there is confirmation by DNA test or other scientific evidence. The grounds for admissibility of the maternity petition are notably (1) if there is possession of status of a legitimate child, (2) if the child's birth and the delivery of the defendant are connected based on any form of evidence, or (3) if there is confirmation by DNA test or other scientific evidence.

The prescription for a paternity or maternity petition is five years starting from the day the minor, having attained the age of majority, becomes aware of their presumed father or mother. For a petition against a deceased presumed father or mother however, this period of five years starts running from the day the presumed father or mother died.

Section 8. Parental authority (Art. 319–329 LPF)

Parental authority over a child born in wedlock is vested in the father and the mother of the child. In cases of non-consent over the exercise of parental authority, one of the spouses refers the matter to the Family Council, which in turn attempts to conciliate them. The unsatisfied party is allowed to refer the matter to the competent court which decides with particular regard to the interest of the child. If either spouse dies, is missing, or is deprived of parental authority, parental authority is exercised by the other parent. However, in case both parents die, disappear, are absent, are legally incapacitated, or are deprived of parental authority, parental authority is exercised by the guardian or any other person who has the legal custody in respect of the child.

Parental authority over a child born out of wedlock is placed in the hands of the parent who has custody over the child.

Parental authority comprises the duties to cater for, educate, manage, and use the child's property, in accordance with the law. The parents have the duties to cater for and educate the child under 21 years of age. The same duties apply to the custodian. The place of education for any minors is the family of their parents or that of other persons with parental authority over them. No minor may leave family home to reside or settle somewhere else without parental consent.

The father and mother, or any other person exercising parental authority over a child, ensures the administration of the property of their child and represents the child in all civil acts. All these civil acts must be conducted in the interest and for the normal economic use of the child's own property. A transfer, sale, or mortgage on the child's property requires the consent of both parents or others exercising parental authority over the child. In case of disagreement, either spouse may refer the matter to the Family Council. A person who is not satisfied with the decision of the Family Council is allowed to refer the matter to the competent court that decides with particular regard to the interest of the child. The parents of the child or other persons vested with parental authority have the right to the legal enjoyment of the revenues accrued from their child's personal property in the interest of the child. However, the legal enjoyment is neither extended to professional revenues that a child got from a particular activity different from that of the child's parents or other persons vested with parental authority, nor extended to the property the child generates from these revenues.

The duties of parents or persons with parental authority to ensure the administration of the child's property are terminated: (1) when guardianship is vested in another person, (2) when the child attains the age of majority, (3) when the child is emancipated, (4) when the parents or other persons vested with parental authority are deprived of parental authority by the court or die, or (5) when the child dies.

In cases of divorce, the legal enjoyment of the revenues accrued from the child's property is conveyed to the parent in charge of the child's custody. The legal enjoyment of the child's property is terminated at the same time as its administration.

Parental authority can be temporarily or permanently removed in the following cases: (1) where persons with parental authority abuse their parental authority or ill-treat the child or (2) where the persons with parental authority are no longer worthy of exercising parental authority due to their notorious misconduct.

Section 9. Adoption (Art. 287–318 LPF)

The Rwandan law recognizes two forms of adoption: (1) simple adoption and (2) full adoption.

Simple adoption is a form of adoption that consists in maintaining filiation ties with the adoptee's family of origin. It requires the consent of both parents of the adoptee if they are still alive, even in cases where they are divorced. If one of the parents is dead or in a state of incapacity to express consent, or has been absent or has disappeared, the consent of one spouse is sufficient. If a child has neither father nor mother, or both of them are in a state of incapacity to express their will, or if they have been absent or have disappeared, the consent is given by a Family Council or by a person vested with the child's custody. In case such a child lives in a foster family or orphanage, the consent of the foster family or orphanage is enough. However, while the only requirement for a foster family to be valid is that it must be expressed before the civil registrar, the consent of the orphanage must be authorized by the civil registrar.

In cases of simple adoption, the adopted children keep their names, continue to belong to their family of origin, and retain all rights and duties toward their family. The parental authority is, however, exercised by the adopting parent only.

Full adoption is a form of adoption that completely severs filiation ties with the adoptee's family of origin. This severance does not affect, however, the rights of the adoptee in their country of origin. Full adoption is only granted in the best interests of the child under the following circumstances: (1) The child's parents are unknown or have abandoned the child as declared by the court, (2) the child is an orphan and has no siblings, or (3) the child is a ward of the State. A consent by an adoptee is required if they are 12 years of age. A full adoption entitles adopted children and their descendants to the same rights and duties as if the adoptive parents were their biological parents. However, full adoption does not create any retroactive effects.

Whether simple or full, adoption must meet a number of requirements and follow specific procedures.

A person intending to adopt a child must meet the following conditions: (1) to be a person of integrity; (2) to have enough resources for them to meet the duties that arise from adoption; (3) to be at least 21 years of age; (4) to be at least seven years older than the child to be adopted, except when the adopting person and the adoptee are related up to the seventh degree, in which case this age is reduced to three years; (5) to have a fixed address; (6) not to have been sentenced to imprisonment for offenses against the family; (7) not to have been sentenced to imprisonment for the crime of genocide; (8) not to have been sentenced to imprisonment for the crime of genocide ideology and related crimes; and (9) not to have been deprived of parental authority. Also, consent by the adopting parent's spouse is required when the adoption is by one of the spouses. This consent does not, however, necessarily imply a joint adoption. Also, to be adopted, a child must be younger than 18 years.

With regard to the adoption procedure, an application for adoption is made before the civil registrar of the domicile of the child to be adopted, in the presence of the person or persons applying for adoption, the parents of the child if they are alive, or the head of the Family Council and at least two witnesses. The application for approval of the adoption record is settled by the relevant court by summary proceedings, after examining whether it was done in the child's interest and whether other prerequisites regarding age and consent were fulfilled. The death of an intended adoptive parent after filing the application but before the ruling of the court halts the proceedings. The adoption judgment is filed in the register of adoption records and mentioned in the margins of the birth record of the adopted child. The adoptive parent having been granted the adoption by the court must register that order in the civil register within two months from the date on which the judgment became final.

Adoption, whether simple or full, can be revoked on the following grounds: (1) if cogent evidence exists to the effect that the adoption was granted following or with the aim of kidnap, making her/him a wife or husband, human trafficking, or slavery; (2) if it is evident that it was done in contradiction with the child's interests, or when the adoptive parent no longer fulfills the necessary requirements to adopt a child; (3) if the relationship between the child and the mother or father is established, even when the final judgment granting adoption was rendered, unless the adoption resulted from the fact that the natural mother or father had deliberately abandoned the adoptee. The right to revoke an adoption belongs to the parents, the representative of the Family Council of the adoptee, or any interested person.

Inter-country adoption requires more specific conditions and procedure. Inter-country adoption is a form of simple or full adoption that creates a relationship between a child and an adoptive parent with whom they have no kinship or relationship, but both are not domiciled in the same country. Inter-country adoption occurs when the child to be adopted: (1) usually resides in Rwanda and has to be transferred to a foreign country, (2) has to be moved from the country of origin to Rwanda, or (3) resides in Rwanda without being authorized to settle there. For an inter-country adoption to occur, it must be ensured that (1) the adoption is aimed at the interests of the child; (2) there is no other person in the country of origin of the child to be adopted who wishes to adopt the child; (3) the consent of those required to consent to the adoption was freely given and that all of them got the necessary advice and were duly informed of the consequences of their consent; (4) the receiving State where the adopted child is to be transferred has proven that the intending inter-country adoptive parent has enough capacity to care for the child and is of good moral integrity required for adoption; (5) the country of the intending adoptive parent has approved that the child will be allowed to enter and reside in such a country on a permanent basis.

Section 10. Marriage: conditions, effects, and nullity (Art. 166–177; 181–188; 192–213 LPF)

Civil monogamous marriage contracted upon mutual consent before the public administration is the only marriage recognized by law. Such a marriage is publicly officiated by the civil registrar of the domicile or residence of one of the intending spouses.

Civil marriage may be preceded by traditional ceremonies consistent with the values of Rwandan society, which include the following: (1) the preliminary engagement ceremony that brings together families of the partners consenting that there is no impediment to the marriage of their children; (2) the ceremony of engagement and payment of the bride price, which demonstrates the agreement between the two families, which agree that their son and daughter will get married, and that both families will continue to support their marriage and be witnesses thereof. However, the validity of the marriage is not conditional on the payment of the bride price.

To be valid, a marriage must meet both of the following basic and formal conditions. The minimum legal age for marriage is 21 years. Marriage between persons in direct lineal kinship is prohibited. In addition, marriage between persons in collateral kinship up to the seventh degree is prohibited. Marriage between a person and their parent-in-law is prohibited. In case of adoption, marriage is prohibited between (1) the adoptive parent and the adopted child, (2) the adoptive parent and the descendants of the adopted child, (3) the adopted child and the spouse of the adoptive parent, (4) the adoptive parent and the spouse of the adopted person, (5) the adopted persons from the same adoptive parent, or (6) the adopted person and the children of the adoptive parent. Prohibitions provided under points (5) and (6) may be lifted for valid reasons upon authorization by the civil registrar.

Prior to officiating at a marriage, the civil registrar ensures that spouses have chosen their matrimonial regime. The registrar must also require the following: (1) birth certificate of each of the intending spouses; (2) certificate of celibacy, or extract of death certificate of the former spouse, or extract of judicial decision of divorce or annulment of the former marriage; or (3) an authorization of marriage without publication for justified reasons. The marriage certificate must mention all of the above documents. Also, prior to officiating at a marriage, the civil registrar must (1) verify if all formalities required for marriage are fulfilled and (2) inform the intending spouses of the matrimonial regime at least seven days prior to officiating at the marriage per se. After the intending spouses have agreed with the civil registrar on the date and time of the marriage, the civil registrar publishes the marriage by posting a notice at the civil registrar's office of the residence or domicile of the intending spouses and that of the intended location for the celebration of marriage at least 20 days prior to the marriage. The civil registrar may, in case of critical and exceptional circumstances, authorize the shortening of the period for marriage notification, or authorize the celebration of marriage without notice. Such circumstances must be indicated in the notice and registered in the margin of the marriage certificate. If, within four months after the expiry of the period provided in the notice, the marriage does not take place, it may not be celebrated without publication.

The marriage notice must indicate the following: (1) names of the intending spouses, (2) their occupations, (3) their domicile and residence, (4) their age, and (5) their father's and mother's names, as well as their domicile and residence. The notice must also indicate the date, place, and time, as well as the intended civil registrar's office for the celebration of the marriage.

If, prior to officiating at marriage, the civil registrar finds a legal evidence to bar the ceremony, they must refuse to officiate the marriage. In this case, they must issue a note thereof and immediately inform the intending spouses. If the civil registrar indicates the reasons for refusing to officiate the marriage, any of the intending spouses is entitled to lodge a complaint before a senior hierarchical authority. If the intending spouses are not satisfied with the decision taken, the matter is referred to the competent court, which settles it by summary proceedings. The civil registrar may not refuse to celebrate the marriage if their reasons are found unjustified by the court.

Marriage celebration follows a specific procedure. The intending spouses accompanied by a representative from each family and by two adult witnesses, enjoying all civil rights, appear all together before the civil registrar. The civil registrar reads to them all documents related to their civil status and their rights and duties as married spouses. The intending spouses declare to be each other's husband and wife as per the following oath: "I........................., having heard what the law requires the spouses, agree without any coercion that you.......... be my wife/husband and we live together as per our agreement and in accordance with the law of the Republic of Rwanda." After the spouses take the oath, the civil registrar declares that they are legally married in the following terms:

> I.......... the civil registrar of......... having heard the vows made between......... and..........as agreed in my presence and in public, pursuant to powers conferred to me by the law, hereby declare that from today .... and ..... are married in accordance with the law.

The oath of the spouses and the oath of the civil registrar are taken by raising the right hand holding the national flag with the left hand. In case of impossibility to hold the flag due to disability, the concerned party is required to wear it.

A marriage certificate records the marriage unless the law provides for any other type of evidence. The civil registrar, the spouses, the representatives of each family, and two witnesses must sign the marriage certificate. If the marriage certificate is not obtained for any reason, it may be replaced by a rendered judgment upon request by any interested person in a competent court where the claimant resides. The court may conduct an investigation if deemed necessary.

From the day the marriage is celebrated before the civil registrar, the spouses acquire the same rights, including the patrimonial rights and obligations. They owe each other mutual fidelity and assistance. Spouses jointly provide management of the household, including moral and material support, as well as its maintenance. Spouses contribute to the household expenses in accordance with their capacity and means. Each spouse also has the obligation to pay alimony to the other. It must be paid in kind or in cash and in proportion to the needs of the claimant and resources of the provider. Marriage also creates a marital community with a duty of cohabitation. A marriage not followed by cohabitation within one year, without reasonable grounds, gives one of the spouses the right to lodge a divorce case. By marriage, spouses are also bound by the obligation of catering for and educating their children based on Rwandan cultural values.

Anyone can oppose the celebration of a marriage as long as they can justify it. Opposition to the celebration of a marriage is made either orally or in writing before the civil registrar, as long as the marriage has not yet been celebrated. Opposition to the celebration of marriage may be motivated by at least one of the following grounds: (1) lack of one of the conditions of form or substance or (2) existence of any of the prohibitions to marriage. Once any of these two reasons are available, the marriage celebration must be suspended unless (1) a court decides otherwise or (2) the identified defects are fixed or no longer exist. In case the court confirms the opposition, the marriage celebration continues to be suspended until the necessary requirements for marriage celebration are met or if the obstacles are eliminated. However, in case the court finds the opposition non-justifiable, it may also condemn the bad faith opposition claimant to pay damages.

A celebrated marriage can be nullified by a court decision, or by the request of one of the spouses, if conditions for nullity are present. The effect of nullification depends on whether the guilty party acted in good or bad faith. The nullity of a marriage can be absolute or relative. The court must declare absolute nullity when (1) either spouse in the marriage is under the age of 21, (2) the entered marriage is between relatives by kinship or allies to the prohibited degree, (3) the celebrated marriage is bigamous, or (4) the marriage was entered into without the consent of one or both spouses. Nullity based on point (4) is, however, not possible if the married couple has been in a continuous cohabitation for at least 12 consecutive months. The court will declare a relative nullity, however, if (1) there has been consent, but it was vitiated; (2) the marriage was celebrated clandestinely; (3) the marriage was officiated by a usurper or an incompetent civil registrar; or (4) there is any other reason that may be related to the lack of fulfillment of celebration formalities. The law provides that there is vitiated consent when the consent of one of the spouses has been given by mistake, or if it has been ensnared by fraud, or extracted under duress. Although the court has the discretion in the determination of relative nullity, it cannot pronounce a relative nullity of marriage when the concerned couple has been in continuous cohabitation for at least six consecutive months from the date the cause for relative nullity was known.

Section 11. Marriage: foreigners in Rwanda or Rwandans outside Rwanda (Art. 179–1180; 189–191 LPF)

The law provides for specific provisions governing marriages celebrated in Rwanda between foreigners or between a foreigner and a Rwandan, and marriages celebrated outside Rwanda between Rwandans or between a foreigner and a Rwandan.

On the one hand, the marriage between foreigners celebrated in Rwanda is governed by (1) Rwandan law, with regard to the marriage celebration; (2) the national law of each of the spouses if it does not contravene public order and good morals of Rwandans, with regard to substantive requirements;

(3) the law of the country where they reside, with regard to the matrimonial right of each person and the right of children, when there is no common agreement; or (4) the law of the country where the property is located, with regard to effects on marital property, when there is no marital property agreement. On the other hand, the marriage between a foreigner and a Rwandan celebrated in Rwanda is governed by (1) Rwandan law with regard to the marriage celebration and (2) Rwandan law for a Rwandan and by the law of the country of which the foreigner is a national, if it does not contravene public order and good morals of Rwandans, with regard to substantive requirements.

The marriage between a Rwandan and a foreigner celebrated in a foreign country is governed by (1) the law of the country where the marriage is celebrated with regard to the form and (2) Rwandan law, with regard to the substantive requirements for a Rwandan. However, marriage between Rwandans celebrated in a foreign country at a Rwandan embassy or consulate is governed by Rwandan law, with regard to the form and substantive requirements. When the marriage is celebrated in a foreign country where there is no Rwandan representative, it is governed by the law of the country where marriage is celebrated with regard to the form, and by Rwandan law with regard to substantive requirements.

A monogamous marriage legally celebrated abroad is recognized in Rwanda. To be recognized, this marriage must be registered by the Rwandan civil registrar in the register of marriage records. If the marriage of Rwandans celebrated abroad contravenes public order and good morals, it is nullified in accordance with the provisions of this law.

Section 12. Matrimonial regimes

The Rwandan law recognizes the following matrimonial regimes: community of property regime, limited community of property regime, and separation of property regime.

A. Community of property (Art. 5–8 LMDS)

The community of property regime is a contract by which the spouses opt for joint ownership of all of their property. Spouses under the community of property regime manage the property together and have the same right to recover property together. Spouses are jointly liable for debts contracted before and after their marriage.

Once there is a divorce or a change in the type of matrimonial regime, if under the community of property regime, the couple shares equally or shares according to any other agreed-upon method. If one of the spouses dies, the property is owned by the surviving spouse until succession execution. Items that are of personal and professional use are preferably included in the share of the spouse that utilizes them.

A creditor has the right to claim payment for debts contracted by the spouses before the dissolution of marriage. If the dissolution of the property regime occurs while there are some creditors who are not aware, the creditors may opt to claim the total payment from either or both of spouses.

B. Limited community of property (Art. 9–13 LMDS)

Limited property regime is a contract by which spouses agree to pool their respective properties owned from the day of the marriage celebration, as well as the property acquired during marriage.

At the moment of the marriage contract, the spouses created an inventory of property of each spouse, and property, if any, each spouse has set apart for the basis of their household. The inventory is signed by both prospective spouses and the civil status registrar. Anything that is not listed is considered personal property.

Spouses under the limited community of property regime manage property based on their common agreement; they both have the same right to use legal representative of this common property. Each spouse has their own power of administration, enjoyment, and free disposal of their personal property. Any fruits of that personal property that produce revenue are part of that spouse's property.

For loans and debts contracted by one of the spouses under the limited community of property regime, the benefits of the household are borne by the community property. If the debt cannot be paid from the jointly owned property, the outstanding balance is paid in equal parts from the property of each spouse. Loans and debts contracted for one spouse are paid with that spouse's personal property. However, if the spouses are jointly liable while contracting the debt, it is paid by the community property.

Fines and debts from criminal responsibility linked with the spouse's personal property are personal, and the payment of such fines and debts is carried out from the personal property of the concerned spouse.

Dissolution of limited community of property regime occurs due to divorce or change in the type of matrimonial regime, and spouses share equally the property acquired during marriage. Each spouse keeps their personal property. If the dissolution occurs due to the death of one spouse, the personal property is managed by the surviving spouse until succession execution. If dissolution occurs, the provisions of sharing property apply to common property.

C. Separation of property (Art. 14–17 LMDS)

Separation of property regime is a contract in which spouses agree to contribute to the expenses of the household in proportion to their respective abilities while retaining their own personal rights over their personal property.

Where one of the spouses married under the separation of property regime transfers the power of administration of their property to the other spouse, the governing power of attorney applies. Each spouse is liable for personal debts contracted before or after marriage, unless they have contracted such debts for the benefits of the household. Joint debts are repaid by each spouse from their own property according to the modalities they agreed upon while contracting those debts.

If the dissolution of separation of property regime occurs due to divorce, each spouse enjoys ownership of their personal property. If dissolution occurs due to the death of one spouse, succession of property is to be carried out in accordance with the provisions of this law.

D. Common provisions on matrimonial regimes (Art. 18–26 LMDS)

Spouses must fulfill their rights and the expected duties that result from the marriage. The civil status registrar prepares and provides the prospective spouses with detailed instructions and explains the nature of each type of matrimonial regime, at least seven days before the ceremony itself.

On the day of the marriage, the type of matrimonial regime chosen by the spouses is recorded in the registry and on the marriage certificate. The type of matrimonial regime chosen must be recorded in the contract of marriage celebrated before the civil status registrar in the presence of the concerned spouses and upon their common consent. The type of matrimonial regime takes effect immediately after marriage.

The type of matrimonial regime may be modified upon the request by one of the spouses or by both. They are required to establish that the modification is requested in the interests of the household or due to important changes in the living conditions of both or only one of them. The request is submitted under summary procedure before a competent court of the place where the spouses reside. In the case of the final rejection of the request, any other request cannot be re-submitted before the expiry of a one-year period, and upon the addition of new elements.

Within one month from the date on which the final decision modifying the type of matrimonial regime cannot be appealed, upon request by the plaintiff, the court order regarding that change is sent to the civil status registrar of the place where the marriage was celebrated for being recorded on the marriage certificate. Creditors may file before the court a claim requesting not to be bound by such medications when they realize that the changes in the marriage contract are prejudiced against them. Such a claim is prescribed after one year from the date they are notified of such changes.

Irrespective of the type of matrimonial regime, if one of the spouses compromises the interests of the household by depreciating the family property of their own property or misusing it, they may be deprived of the rights of administration, enjoyment, disposal, and sale of the property upon request by the other spouse or any interested third party. A request is submitted through appropriate procedures before a competent court where the spouses reside. Unless it is necessary to appoint a judicial administrator, the judge grants the plaintiff spouse with the right to administer the personal property and use the profits for the benefit of the household; any excess profits are saved. The spouse deprived of such rights may subsequently petition the court for restoration of their rights once the underlying cause of the divestment no longer exists. In case of the death of one of the spouses to whom the right to administer the property as per the provisions of Paragraph One of this Article was awarded, an interested party must make a request before the court assigns another person the right to administer the personal property of the spouse divested of such right.

Types of matrimonial regimes are dissolved for the following reasons: divorce, modification of the type of matrimonial regime, and the death of one of the spouses. Types of matrimonial regimes for foreigners, whether they are nationals of the same country or those of different countries who celebrate their marriage in Rwanda, are governed either by the law of the country of one of the spouses, depending on their choice, or by Rwandan law. For the case of a Rwandan marrying a foreigner, whether in Rwanda or in a foreign country, the type of matrimonial regime is governed by the laws of the foreign country or by the law of the country in which the marriage was celebrated. When the marriage is not concluded before the Rwandan representative abroad, the prospective spouses choose the type of matrimonial regime to be governed either by Rwandan law or by the law of the country in which the marriage was celebrated.

Matrimonial regimes apply to monogamous legally celebrated marriages. The division of assets in a *de facto* union is governed by Article 39 of the Law No. 59/2008 on prevention and punishment of gender-based violence, providing that:

> Those people entertaining unlawful marriages shall be married in accordance with the monogamous principle. If a person concerned with the provision of previous paragraph of this Article was living with many husbands/wives, he shall first of all share the commonly owned belongings with those husbands/wives equally.

To clarify this provision, the Supreme Court has ruled that "the division of assets in de facto union is not only based on the fact that the couple has been living together; parties must also prove that they co-own the asset or have acquired it together."[9]

Section 13. Marriage: legal separation and dissolution (Art. 214–217; 248–252 LPF)

Legal separation can be by (1) mutual consent or for (2) any of the grounds provided by law. Grounds for legal separation are similar to those for divorce. Legal separation relieves spouses of the duty of cohabitation, but does not entail the severance of a marriage bond or the dissolution of matrimonial regime. Legal separation does not affect the matrimonial regime, as well as spouses' duty of support, fidelity, and parenting. The legal separation judgment determines alimony for the spouse in need, irrespective of the spouse with whom the fault rests. After two years of legal separation from the final judgment, the court, upon joint application by the spouses or either of them, converts the legal separation judgment into a divorce judgment. The application for the conversion of a legal separation into a divorce is filed in accordance with the ordinary rules relating to the application for divorce.

Unlike legal separation, marriage dissolution puts an end to all effects of marriage, including the dissolution of the matrimonial regime. A marriage can be dissolved on the following grounds: (1) divorce or (2) death of one of the spouses.

The death of one of the spouses dissolves the marriage. Although acknowledging the right to a widowed spouse to enter into a new marriage after dissolution by death, Rwandan law seems to make a discrimination based on whether the surviving spouse was the wife or the husband. In this regard, Article 215 of the 2016 Law on Persons and Family provides that

> A widowed spouse has the right to enter into a new marriage. However, the wife may enter a new marriage after a period of three hundred completed days from the death of her first husband. This period is interrupted by childbirth or a pregnancy certificate issued by a recognized medical doctor.

Section 14. Divorce (Art. 218–247 LPF)

Divorce can be by mutual consent or for cause.

Divorce by mutual consent is the one jointly applied for by both spouses, after they agree on ending their marriage and its effects, while submitting to the judge a written agreement settling the effects of the divorce on the spouses and their property, as well as their children. However, divorce applied for by one of the spouses can be converted into a divorce by mutual consent when the respondent recognizes the relevance of the application and consents to such a divorce. The spouses who choose to apply for divorce by mutual consent must first make a written inventory of their movable and immovable property, indicate its value, and determine each spouse's share of the property depending on their matrimonial regime. Through a notarized agreement, the spouses must agree about (1) the custody of the children born or adopted as a result of their marriage, during the divorce proceedings, and after the pronouncement of divorce; (2) the contribution of each spouse to the maintenance and education of the children; (3) the residence of each of the spouse during divorce proceedings; and (4) the alimony that the spouse with inadequate income to meet their needs has to get from the other spouse during divorce proceedings regardless of their matrimonial regime.

For action in divorce by mutual consent to be admissible, concerned spouses must have been married for at least two years. Spouses who agree to a divorce by mutual consent must appear in person in court and declare their intention to divorce. If the court is fully convinced that the spouses are genuinely willing to divorce and that their consent is free and the best interests of children are sufficiently safeguarded, the court pronounces the divorce. However, if the court is not convinced, it does not grant the divorce. The refusal of the court to grant a divorce by mutual consent is appealable, but the appeal is admissible only if lodged by both spouses.

Divorce for cause is admissible only in case of (1) adultery; (2) desertion for a period of at least 12 consecutive months; (3) conviction for an offense severely tainting the honor; (4) refusal to provide for household needs; (5) excess, abuse, or serious insults by one toward another; (6) gender-based violence; (7) *de facto* separation for a period of at least two years; and (8) non-cohabitation for more than 12 consecutive months from the day of the celebration of the marriage on unjustifiable grounds. Rwandan law does not consider it to be desertion when a spouse leaves their home following mistreatment by the other spouse as long as the nearest local administration was informed and a record thereto has been drawn. To this list has been added Article 6 of the GBV Law as a cause of divorce. Gender-based violence is defined by this law as

> any act that results in a bodily, psychological, sexual and economic harm to somebody just because they are female or male. Such act results in the deprivation of freedom and negative consequences. This violence may be exercised within or outside households them.

In principle, a divorce for cause should be based on at least one of the above reasons; Rwandan courts have, however, often taken a liberal interpretation of these causes.[10]

Only spouses have the right to lodge an action for divorce. The competent court for such an action is the one where the spouses had their last conjugal residence or where the defendant is domiciled. This action expires after five years from the time the cause of divorce is discovered. At any stage of the hearing, the judge may take provisional measures related to the parties, their children, and their property.

A criminal case may not suspend the action for divorce. However, if the offense prosecuted is the cause for the application for divorce, the action for divorce is suspended until the criminal judgment becomes final.

With regard to children, the judge may assign one of the spouses or third party the provisional custody of their children and determine the contribution of each spouse to the support of their children. Any of the spouses may request the judge to give the order to another spouse to vacate the conjugal residence and decide on the means enabling them to find a separate residence. However, the spouse in charge of the provisional custody of children must remain in the conjugal residence pending the final judgment authorizing divorce. With regard to property, where the court orders separate residence, except in cases where spouses are married under the regime of separation of property, movable and immovable assets are provisionally shared, after the inventory signed by both parties, taking into consideration the best interests of the children and the professions of the spouses. The assigned property must be kept diligently with no right to sell, dispose of, or mortgage it.

Whether it is by mutual consent or for causes, every action in divorce must be preceded by a conciliation procedure. During the first hearing, which must be held in camera, the judge tries to conciliate the concerned spouses, and gives them pieces of advice and observations considered necessary with respect to the effects of their intended divorce. The conciliation of spouses entails the termination of divorce proceedings. It results from the spouses' declaration before the judge, indicating their intention to restore their living together or resume cohabitation for a period of more than three months. However, any of the spouses may file a new petition based on a new reason that arises after conciliation, and then base it on the grounds previously given to substantiate their new petition. If, after three months since the conciliation attempt or the advising session by the judge, parties still maintain their willingness to proceed with the divorce, the court register makes a report of the failure of conciliation. Then, the judge authorizes the divorce hearing to proceed.

Divorce creates a number of effects on the divorced couple, their children, and their property.

A divorce entails the dissolution of the marriage and matrimonial regime of the spouses. The property is shared according to the law governing matrimonial regimes. The custody of children is awarded to the spouse that obtained the divorce, while the other spouse gets visitation rights. While rendering the judgment, the judge determines appropriate terms to ensure respect for such rights. However, the court may, on its own motion or upon request by either spouse or any other interested person, order that the child be entrusted to the spouse who lost the case, or to a third party, if the interests of the children dictate such a decision. Still, children under the age of six years must live with their mother unless the interests of the children are in danger. The court may also order that the custody of children be shared between both spouses if it is in the best interests of the children. Regardless of which person the children are placed with, parents retain the right to supervise the maintenance and education of their children. They must also contribute to the alimony in proportion to their means. In case of divorce by mutual consent, children retain the usufruct right over half of each spouse's property which, if they are minors, is administered by the parent to whom the court grants custody of them until they attain the age of majority.

Section 15. Family donations

Family donation refers to a voluntary act by which a spouse or spouses transfer to, or receive from, another person a gratuitous valuable property or patrimonial right.

The family donation may be made between spouses themselves or between spouses and another person, or may be made between parents and their children, whereby they donate a portion of their property. When parents donate to their children, they do it without any discrimination between girls and boys. Family donation is made by an authentic deed, written agreement, or simple transfer.

The types of family donations are the following: *inter vivos* donations and legacy.

A. Inter vivos *donations (Art. 30–38 LMDS)*

The *inter vivos* donation is a charitable contract by which the donor irrevocably transfers a patrimonial right to another person who accepts it. The *inter vivos* donation takes effect on the date of its acceptance. The receiver of the donation may accept it in writing or verbally. The transfer of ownership of movable or immovable property is done in accordance with relevant laws.

Any donation is void if the donation is made, but is conditional to the single will of the donor; it does not conform to rules of public order and good morals; it is made by a person other than its owner; the receiver is required to pay extraneous debts or charges to the donor unless those preceded the donation and that are mentioned in the act of donation; or the donor makes a gift but retains the right to dispose of any of the rights or items donated.

An action to nullify an *inter vivos* donation is filed by the donor, the receiver, or any other interested person within a period not exceeding one year from the day the grounds for the nullity of the donation has arisen. A nullified donation is deemed to have never existed. All components of the donation and its fruits still in the possession of the receiver are returned. The nullification of the donation does not affect holders of security stemming from a property formally given as a donation, or any other parties enjoying entitlements to the same property.

Any *inter vivos* donation is revocable for the following reasons: The receiver fails to fulfill any of the obligations required under the terms of the donation, or because of the ingratitude of the receiver. An action to revoke the donation is lodged within a period not exceeding one year from the day grounds for revocation arise, or the day the said grounds were brought to the knowledge of the plaintiff. This action is personal to the donor and they may not sue their heirs for revocation. However, if the donor dies after they files the action, their heirs may continue the claim in the name of the *de cujus*.

If revocation occurs, the receiver is required to return anything they received by virtue of the donation. However, the receiver is not required to compensate the donor, neither for the value of any items that were disposed of or sold before the action of revocation is instituted, nor for fruits and other benefits of any kind from the items. If a donation is revoked, the receiver is reimbursed for expenses made to improve the property. Such revocation does not affect any creditor to whom a donated property has been formally given as security or any other parties enjoying entitlements to the same property.

B. Legacy (Art. 39–45 LMDS)

A legacy is a donation made in the form of a will, the full ownership of which is acquired by the legatee only after the death of the testator. A legacy can be under a universal title, general title, or particular title. A legacy under a universal title is that by which the legatee is entitled to the whole property the *de cujus* is authorized to donate. A legacy under a general title is that by which the legatee is entitled to a portion of the property the *de cujus* is authorized to donate. The legacy under a particular title is that by which the legatee is entitled to one or more specified components making up the property the *de cujus* is authorized to donate.

The legatee of the property of the *de cujus* is not liable for the obligations of paying debts of the testator.

When the person bequeaths their property to a linked group living in a particular place, the legacy is, at the time of liquidation, collected by the district administration where the place is located, who in turn hands it over to the legatees. Where the testator has not mentioned the address of the people making up the group, the district administration where the testator was domiciled or resided collects the legacy and hands it over to the legatees making up the linked group. Where the legatees are located in different districts, the legacy is collected by the ministry in charge of social affairs, which hands it over to the legatees.

The bequeathed property and all its appurtenances and insurance compensations are enjoyed by the legatee from the opening of succession, unless otherwise required by the testator. A legacy to a creditor is not deemed in satisfaction of the testator's debt.

A legacy is void if the legatee predeceases the testator, unless they can be represented during the lifetime of the testator, the bequeathed property is completely destroyed, or the legatee renounces the legacy or is declared unworthy.

A legacy may be revoked in whole or in part where the conditions for its validity are not met.

C. Common provisions on family donations (Art. 46–50 LMDS)

Legal provisions relating to the capacity to contract and the validity of deeds are applicable to family donations in conformity with the regulations of matrimonial regimes.

In case of community of property regime or limited community of property regime, any donation from a family property by one of the spouses requires consent of the other. Consent is also required for the acceptance of such a donation.

Spouses have the right to make donations, provided that they do not exceed the disposable portion. The disposable portion is a portion of the property that a person is not allowed to exceed when making donations. Notwithstanding the chosen matrimonial regime, the disposable portion cannot exceed one-fifth of the property if the donor has children, and the remaining four-fifths of property comprises the reserved portion of succession designated for the children and spouse. However, where the donor has no children but the spouse is alive, the disposable portion cannot exceed one-third of that spouse's property, and the remaining two-thirds are the spouse's reserved portion of the estate. The reserved portion of a succession comprises the personal property of the donor that remains after paying any debts the donor owes on the date of donation.

An authentic donation between foreigners of the same or different nationalities made in Rwanda is governed by the laws of Rwanda, either regarding its form, meaning, characteristics, and effects. However, in the case of a written form, the donation may be governed by the laws of the countries as may be chosen by parties to the donation act, provided that they conform to the rules of public order and good morals of Rwanda. In case of a donation made from a Rwandan national to a foreign national, its form is governed by the law of the place where it is made. In regard of its substance, characteristics, and effects, it is governed by Rwandan law, the law of the country in which it is made, or the law of the country of origin of that foreigner.

Section 16. Succession

Succession is the transfer of rights and obligations on the assets and liabilities of the *de cujus*. Succession opens upon the death of a person at their domicile or residence or with a declaratory judgment of death, in the event of absence or disappearance. However, succession for spouses opens when they are both deceased, or in case one of them remarries, unless otherwise provided by law. After the opening of succession, the liquidator must be appointed.

The succession has no legal personality. The liquidator is responsible for all succession matters.

A. Person eligible for succession (Art. 53–59 LMDS)

A person alive or represented at the moment succession opens is eligible to succeed, including any unborn children, provided that they are born alive. The disappeared persons may be entitled to succeed where they are assumed to be alive. Government and public or private entities with legal personality may be entitled to succeed under a will where the estate comprises property to which they are eligible. Legitimate children of the *de cujus* succeed in equal portions without any discrimination between male and female children.

Starting from the day of the opening of succession, a person entitled to succeed by way of a will or under law is called an heir as long as they accept it. Heirs are automatically deprived of succession rights if they are convicted of intentionally killing the *de cujus* or of attempting to kill them; are convicted of a false accusation or perjury that could have resulted in the *de cujus* being sentenced to at least six months of imprisonment; have deliberately abandoned the child whose succession is open; and committed an indecent assault, sexual abuse, exposed the child to sexual exploitation, or sexually abused the child. A court judgment convicting the legitimate heir of one of the offenses referred to in this paragraph is sufficient to deprive a person of the right to be among heirs.

Any legitimate heir or legatee may be debarred from succession if during the lifetime of the *de cujus*, they broke off parental relationships with the *de cujus*; they deliberately failed to take care of the *de cujus* in need; they took advantage of the physical or mental inability of the *de cujus* to take over the whole or a part of the inheritance; intentionally disposed of, destroyed, or altered the last will of the *de cujus* without consent, or took advantage of a revoked or voided will. Any person entitled to succession, within a period not exceeding one year from the day of the opening of succession or the day they became aware of one of those reasons, may petition the competent court to debar the heir or legatee responsible for one of the acts mentioned above. The claim is filed in the form of summary procedure. An heir cannot be debarred from succession if, before death, the *de cujus* knew the reason for debarment from succession and did not raise such debarment.

A person debarred from succession is excluded from succession to the estate of the *de cujus*. The supposed portion of the debarred person is added to the respective portions of other heirs. Debarment from succession only affects the right to succeed to the estate of the person offended and may not affect the right to succeed to other property of the family. However, any person debarred from succession for criminal acts mentioned in the previous paragraph loses the right to succeed the whole estate of the family, disregarding the management of the property regime. The heir or the legatee excluded from succession as a result of debarment from succession during their lifetime is bound to return all inherited or bequeathed property or the value thereof.

B. Testamentary succession (Art. 60–71 LMDS)

Succession of the de cujus may be wholly or partially testamentary or intestate. Any property of the *de cujus* not given by way of a will is devolved according to intestate succession.

A will is a revocable unilateral deed intended to have a legal effect that is drawn up in accordance with one of the procedures prescribed by law, by which a person determines the disposition of their property after their death. The testator gratuitously transfers their property, the full ownership of which is acquired by the legatee after the testator's death.

A will is made by any person prior to their death. The testator disposes of their property at no cost, and the heir enjoys sole and full ownership thereof, upon the testator's death.

Any person with the required legal capacity may dispose of all or part of their property by a will in accordance with the provisions of the law. However, a will made by one spouse married under community of property regime or limited community of property regime related to common property must be allowed by the other spouse through written consent. The testator, as well as their spouse, must have the legal capacity at the time of making a will.

The legatee must possess legal capacity on the day of acceptance of the will. The acceptance by a minor or an incapacitated person of a will is done in compliance with the rules relating to the representation of incapacitated persons.

A will is either authentic or private. An authentic will is the one made by the testator before the notary or the civil registrar of the testator's place of residence or domicile. The civil registrar or the notary keeps the original document and records the date on which the will is made, along with the testator's name and domicile or residence in the appropriate register. The original document and the register are kept confidential and only made accessible to those involved in the will after the testator's death. A private will is the one entirely handwritten by the testator in the presence of at least two witnesses, dated and signed by the testator and the witnesses. If the testator cannot write or is unable to draw up and sign the will, they can designate a person of their choice to draw up the will on their behalf.

A will may be amended and recorded under testamentary provisions found in several wills that are, to the extent practicable, executed jointly. Where the provisions of two or more wills are inconsistent with one another, those contained in the most recently drawn up will prevail.

The head of the family must set the date for the disclosure of the will to the heirs of the *de cujus* within a period not exceeding 30 days from the testator's death. Any interested person may attend the disclosing session. On that date, they establish a succession council. The testator may, however, appoint in the will one or several testamentary executors responsible for liquidating the estate.

Wills made by a Rwandan residing outside Rwanda when the estate is in Rwanda are governed by the law of the country in which they are made, as to the form. However, a Rwandan may also choose to comply with the forms laid down by Rwandan law, as to the substance and effects.

Wills made by a foreign national residing in Rwanda are governed by the law of the country in which they are made, as to the form. However, a foreign national who makes their will in Rwanda may choose to comply with the forms laid down by the law of their country of origin, as to the substance and effects.

A will may be revoked in whole or in part by the court upon request by the interested party when it is the result of force, fraud, or does not conform to the provisions of the law. Revocation of a will automatically entails its annulment. If no other will was made, the succession of the *de cujus* is conducted in accordance with the provisions of the law.

C. *Interstate succession (Art. 72–75 LMDS)*

Interstate succession is a succession opened in accordance with the law, in the absence of a will. Under interstate succession, heirs are entitled to inherit in the following order: (1) children of the *de cujus*, (2) father and mother of the *de cujus*, (3) full-blood brothers and sisters of the *de cujus*, (4) half-brothers and half-sisters of the *de cujus*, (5) grandparents of the *de cujus*, (6) paternal and maternal uncles and aunts of the *de cujus*. Full-blood children of the *de cujus* inherit from both parents, while consanguineous and uterine children inherit only from the parent to whom they are related.

Apart from the father and mother, grandfather and grandmother of the *de cujus*, the heirs who predeceased the *de cujus* are represented in succession by their descendants. Representation is unlimited among direct descendants, and the partition is done following the generation.

The surviving spouse is entitled to take part in the succession of the deceased spouse's estate and inherits in equal portions with the heirs of the first category. If there are no heirs of the first category, the spouse has the same right of succession as heirs in the second category, and in the absence of heirs of the second category, the spouse co-inherits with those of the third category, and so forth.

D. *Succession and its impact on property in matrimonial regimes (Art. 77–79 LMDS)*

Succession of spouses married under the community of property regime is as follows: (1) If one of the spouses dies, the surviving spouse is entitled to the entire property and fulfills the duty of taking care of their children and that of the legitimate children of the *de cujus*; (2) if both spouses die leaving children, the children inherit the entire property of their deceased parents. When there are children who were not born to both spouses, the property is divided into two equal parts, and each child succeeds their parent; (3) if both spouses die leaving no children, the property is divided into two equal parts, one half being allocated to the heirs of the husband and the other being allocated to the heirs of the wife; (4) if the surviving spouse has no children with the *de cujus* and gets remarried, this spouse has the right to receive half of the property by virtue of the community of property regime and co-inherits the other half with the heirs of the *de cujus*. In this case, the spouse receives three quarters of the property of the *de cujus*. If the surviving spouse does not get remarried, they are entitled to the whole property, which enables them to raise children voluntarily or judicially acknowledged by the *de cujus*, if any; (5) if the surviving spouse gets remarried when there are children they have had with the *de cujus* or children voluntarily or judicially acknowledged by the *de cujus*, succession to the deceased spouse's succession is open in such way that the surviving spouse receives one half of the property by virtue of the matrimonial regime and inherits the remaining half on an equal basis with all children left behind by the *de cujus*. In this case, the spouse continues to administer the portion inherited by minor children, unless otherwise decided by the court; (6) if the surviving spouse fails to fulfill the duties of raising some or all of the children left behind by the *de cujus*, the competent court strips the spouse of such duties and of half of the whole property, and determines the guardian of the children who will be in charge of ensuring the management of the property until they attain the age of majority.

For the spouses married under the limited community of property regime, the succession modalities for community of property regime apply to their common property and modalities for separation of property regime apply to their separate property.

Subject to some conditions provided by the law, when one of the spouses married under the separation of property regime dies, the surviving spouse retains ownership on their own property, while the property of the *de cujus* is inherited by the legitimate children of the *de cujus*. If the *de cujus* leaves minor children, the surviving spouse continues to ensure the administration of their property. If the *de cujus* leaves no child, the surviving spouse co-succeeds with other heirs by receiving half of the *de cujus*' property. The other half is inherited by the other heirs of the de *cujus*. In case of partition, the surviving spouse may ask to be granted the pre-emptive right to receive the family house and equipment therein as part of their inheritance. Where the values of the house and equipment therein exceed their portion, the surviving spouse retains ownership of the house provided that they pay the compensation. The family house means a dwelling in which spouses lived as husband and wife, and which is listed among the property of one of the spouses.

If the *de cujus* leaves minor children, the surviving spouse continues to ensure the administration of the inherited property on behalf of the minor children until they all attain the age of majority and succeed their deceased parent and inherit their property. In case the surviving spouse does not comply with this obligation, the competent court debars them from administering the whole property of the *de cujus* and designates a guardian who administers the property on behalf of the minors until they attain the age of majority. The surviving spouse continues to live in the family house and uses all the equipment therein as long as they still have the custody of the legitimate children of the *de cujus*. The surviving spouse continues to enjoy these rights until they get remarried or the children attain the age of majority and succeed their deceased parent and inherit their property.

E. Fate of unclaimed succession (Art. 80–82 LMDS)

The succession is said to be unclaimed when there is no heir or when the heirs renounce their right of succession. In case of unclaimed succession, the estate is vested in the State. The State must execute the obligation of the *de cujus* up to the value of the property received.

The procedure for succession in the case of unclaimed succession is as follows: (1) The competent court or the *Abunzi* Committee declares that the property is escheated following the petition of the executive secretary of the sector where succession is expected to take place or where the estate is located; (2) within a period of one month of receiving the petition, the court or the *Abunzi* Committee must provisionally declare the succession unclaimed. In this case, the property is administered in accordance with the provisions of the law relating to the management of abandoned property; (3) the decision is posted at the office of the sector of the place of the opening of succession or of the location of the estate; (4) after three years for movable property and five years for immovable property from the date of the order to temporarily administer the property, the court or the *Abunzi* Committee, upon petition by the competent organ for the administration of abandoned property provided under the law relating to the management of abandoned property, irrevocably declares the succession unclaimed, and the property in succession is automatically vested in the State. However, if prescriptions provided under the law on prescription has not yet expired, an heir who shows up may request the return of the property previously escheated to the State; (5) an heir who shows up before the expiry of the above-mentioned deadlines inherits the estate of the *de cujus*, irrespective of the condition in which it is found and expenses incurred are deducted.

F. Role of succession council in liquidation (Art. 84–87 LMDS)

Liquidation is a process of making inventory of the estate so that the heirs or legatees of the *de cujus* may acquire full ownership of the portion of the estate inherited by them.

The Family Council has powers to settle any dispute or issue arising in the family in connection with succession before they are referred to the *Abunzi* Committee or the competent court. When considering issues related to succession, the Family Council designates members of the succession council from among the following people: (1) a representative of heirs if they include those having attained the age of majority; (2) the surviving spouse in case this spouse is called to succeed; (3) the representative of the family of the *de cujus*; (4) two friends of the family, one of whom is from the husband's family and the other of whom is from the wife's family if they were married. The succession council carries out its duties under the supervision of the Family Council.

The succession council has the following responsibilities: (1) to choose and supervise the liquidator, (2) to approve the acts of a liquidator, and (3) to take decisions on any disputes regarding the duties of the liquidator.

Unless otherwise specified in the will, the liquidator is designated by the succession council, which sets out their responsibilities, including presenting and determining the procedure for the repayment of the debts incurred by the *de cujus*, and also sets the deadline for the discharge of such responsibilities. If possible, the liquidator is chosen from among the heirs of the *de cujus*. Upon completion of their responsibilities, the liquidator reports to the succession council for approval of the acts performed.

When paying charges attaching to the estate, the liquidator must comply with the following order: funeral costs incurred by the *de cujus*; the costs associated with the administration, liquidation, and the estimation of expenses related to the partition of the estate; all maturing debts left by the *de cujus*; and legacies created by the *de cujus*.

G. Right to accept or renounce the succession (Art. 88–93 LMDS)

No person is bound to accept a succession or legacy to which they are called. Every heir has the right to accept or renounce a legacy. Acceptance of a succession or legacy is expressed publicly. When the heirs fail to make their opinion known despite being informed that they are heirs, they are deemed to have accepted to succeed. In principle, a person who accepts to inherit acquires both the assets and liabilities of the *de cujus*.

The right of option in succession is exercised within six months after the date from which the liquidator informs the heir or legatee of their right to succeed, or after the date from which they testify to their status as heirs or legatees. The minor's right of option in succession is exercised by the person exercising parental authority over them, while that of an incapacitated person is exercised by the guardian. When a person dies before exercising their right of option in succession, it is exercised by their heirs.

In case of acceptance of the succession, any heir is bound to incur the liabilities of the *de cujus* in proportion to the portion of the estate devolving upon them. A person having paid the total amount of the debt may petition the court to summon other heirs to pay their portion in such debts.

Renunciation of succession must be expressed and done in writing. If the heir cannot write or is unable to write, they may verbally renounce succession within the prescribed period. Renunciation of succession is communicated to other heirs or, if any, to the liquidator before two witnesses. An heir who renounces the succession is considered as having never been called to succeed. They are relieved of the obligation to pay debts attaching to the estate.

The heir or legatee who has exercised the right of option can no longer reverse their choice after the expiration of the time limit for the exercise of their choice, unless such a choice is the result of fraud, violence, or threat, and a legal action is filed before the court within 12 months from the date of cessation of such acts. If the event is valid and justified, such a period of 12 months may be extended.

H. Partition of the estate (Art. 94–99)

The partition of the property is the procedure by which the succession council, the *Abunzi* Committee, or the court distributes the estate among all rightful beneficiaries.

The estate is divided as it is. The value of that estate is determined on the date of partition. Where it is impossible to divide the estate into equal portions of the estate as it is, the heirs agree on the balance payable by the heirs receiving portions of a higher value than their actual portions they are entitled to under law or a will to those receiving smaller portions. In the event of disagreement between co-heirs as to the value of the estate or to the balance, they file the case to the succession council, *Abunzi* Committee, or competent court for the determination of the value. Where it is impossible to conveniently divide some assets, heirs agree upon modalities of administration thereof and the partition of the proceeds. In case of a sale of such assets, heirs enjoy the pre-emptive right to purchase such assets. Where an heir wants to get their portion while the other heirs do not want the estate to be divided into portions, they refer the matter to the competent court by way of ordinary.

Partition ensures an absolute right to property. An heir irrevocably acquires full ownership of their succeeded portion.

If the *de cujus* exceeds in donating the freely disposable portion, (1) the legacy is not executed and (2) rightful heirs may claim for a return of donations in excess of the freely disposable portion starting with the most recent donations. However, any property donated before three years prior to the opening of succession is not subject to return.

Land is inherited in the same way as any other immovable property. The partition of the land is governed by the same rules as those applicable to the partition of other types of property. However, it is prohibited to subdivide plots of land reserved for agriculture and livestock if the result of such subdivision leads to parcels of land less than a hectare in size for each of them. Heirs of land prohibited for subdivision co-own and use the land in accordance with the law.

Notes

1 Filip Reyntjens and Jan F. J. Gorus, *Codes et lois du Rwanda* (Butare: Université Nationale du Rwanda, 1979), 69.
2 Rendered enforceable in Rwanda by Ordonnance du Rwanda Urundi (O.R.U.) No. 11/82 of 21 June 1949 (B.O.R.U, 1950, 195). Ibid., 69–71.
3 For some customary rules that regulated the family, matrimonial regimes, and succession issues, see J. Vanhove, *Essai de droit coutumier du Ruanda.* Mémoires de la Classe des Sciences Morales et Politiques, IRCB. 1941 T. X, 7–73.
4 For example, Articles 7–15 (foreigners), Articles 106 (non-matriculated spouse). Reyntjens and Gorus. Supra.
5 Loi No. 42/88 du 27 Octobre 1988 portant Titre Préliminaire et Livre Premier du Code Civil, Official Gazette No. 1, 1989.
6 See, for example, Charles Ntampaka, "l'Apport de la loi du 27 Octobre 1988 sur les droits de la femme au Rwanda," *Revue Juridique du Rwanda*, XIV, no. 1–2, January–April 1990, 32–39.
7 Official Gazette No. 22 of 15 November 1999.
8 See Law No. 27/2016 of 08/07/2016 Governing Matrimonial Regimes, donations and successions, Official Gazette No. 31 of 01/08/2016.
9 RS/Inconst/Pén.0003/10/CS, Gatera Johnson, Kabalisa Teddy Vs.
10 The judiciary seems to support the view that what the judge needs as a cause for divorce is only the evidence that spouses have lost all their affection and therefore can no longer live together as wife and husband. See Rwanda Law Report 201, No. 8, of January 2011, 35 (KACHELEWA Jonathan v. NYIRARUKUNDO Chantal, RC 0223/08/TB/KCY).

7 Criminal law

Section 1. Historical development of Rwandan criminal law

Rwandan criminal law has evolved in five key phases: the customary criminal law that dominated the pre-colonial period and continued even under the dualist criminal system of the colonial period for some time; the first penal code introduced in 1940 by the Belgian colonial government;[1] the 1977 Penal Code,[2] which was the very first penal code of post-independence Rwanda; the 2012 Penal Code,[3] which was the first post-genocide penal code; and the 2018 Law Determining Offenses and Penalties in General,[4] which has been in force when this chapter was written. The contents and key characteristics of these criminal laws are briefly discussed below.

A. Customary pre-colonial criminal law

As discussed in chapter one on the history of Rwandan law, unlike most pre-colonial African societies, the Rwandan legal and institutional systems were more or less centralized, consistent, and better organized. These features can be observed in the Rwandan traditional criminal law as well. Key offenses and their punishments were widely known across the country and generally applied as if orally codified. Key offenses included, for example, theft, arson, assault or battery, and murder. A number of authors have documented this type of Rwandan oral customary criminal code.[5]

The punishment for theft (*ubujura*) depended on the kinds of stolen objects (cattle or not), the status of the offender (upper class or low class), and whether the offender was caught *fragrant delicto* or not. A person caught *in fragrante delicto* in one's fenced home (*urugo*) could be killed in self-defense. However, to benefit from self-defense justification, the killed thief must have received an instantaneous unexpected mortal hit.[6] The thief apprehended or caught after a chase could not be killed; he had to be tied to a tree while waiting to be brought before the village court (*inteko y'umutware w'umusozi*). To be untied from that tree, his family or his patron (*shebuja*) had to pay a bail (*incamigozi*). The person found guilty was often ordered to pay not only restitution, but also reparation (*ingurano*) and damages for property trespassing (*incacyuho*). The payment was often evaluated in terms of goods such as cows and harvest.

Theft of cattle was known as *ubushimusi*, while the theft of other goods was known as *ubusambo*. Fraud and breach of trust (*ubwambuzi*) were also considered as a form of theft. The Rwandan customary criminal law punished not only *ubujura* but also those who instigated it (*ubugambanyi*) and those who aided and abetted the thief in his act (*ibyitso*).

Ubushimusi was considered as the most severely punished form of theft. The thief had to pay the fee to be untied (*inguramaboko*), restitute the stolen cattle, and pay at least one cow as *incacyuho*. In cases where the thief was too poor to pay his fines and damages, his family or patron had to pay for him. In exchange for this buyout, the thief had to work as a servant (*umugaragu*) for an indefinite period for his patron (*shebuja*). A thief who had no family or patron to bail him out was brought before the royal court (*inteko y'ibwami*), and the king designated one of his notables as the bailer of the thief. In exchange, the thief was placed as the servant (*umugaragu*) of his bailer for an indefinite period that could sometimes last a lifetime. A recidivist thief of cattle could face the death penalty.[7]

The person found guilty of *ubusambo* or *ubwambuzi* by the village court received corporal punishment and was required to restitute the stolen objects plus compensation (*ingurano*). However, in cases where the thief belonged to upper class (*mututsi*), he received a much more severe punishment that included social class degradation.

Arson (*gutwika*) warranted corporal punishment plus restitution or reparation for all that was destroyed by the fire. In the case that the arsonist could not pay, his home (*urugo*) plus all its contents were seized and awarded to the victim of the arson. The person found guilty of assault or battery had to not only pay his fine (*icyiru*) but also pay for medical damages (*indwaza*). The values of *icyiru* and *indwaza* depended on the seriousness of the assault and also the social status of the victim.

Murder was of exclusive jurisdiction of the royal court (*inteko y'ibwami*). In the case that the suspect was found guilty, the king often ordered that the victim's family avenge themselves (*guhora*) either on the person of the offender only or on some members of the victim's family. The determination of the person or persons to fall under this vengeance depended on the social class of the perpetrator and of the victim. For example, the killing of a lower-class person (*muhutu*) by an upper-class person (*mututsi*) could be resolved by compensation to the victim's family, whereas the killing of an upper-class person either by the person in the same social class or the person in the lower class always led to *guhora*. Because vendetta created an interminable chain of vengeance, especially when it involved upper-class families, the king had the power to end it through an act known as *guca inzigo*.[8]

B. Criminal law under colonialism

The Belgian Ordinance Law No. 2/5 of 6 April 1917 had acknowledged the local authorities to continue exercising their judicial powers using customary law.[9] In 1924, a Ruanda-Urundi Ordinance Law ordered that all courts in the colony "must apply the Belgian Congo criminal law."[10] The Belgian Congo criminal law included "the penal code as established by the decree of 19 December 1896 of the Secretary of States" and also other legislative acts rendered applicable on the territory of Ruanda-Urundi.[11] Obviously, in a completely illiterate society, although these legal texts were written in Flemish and French, these legislations remained foreign to indigenous courts. The field of application of customary criminal law in Rwanda started shrinking, however, when the 1896 Penal Code was abrogated and replaced by the 1940 Penal Code of the Belgian Congo.[12]

The 1940 Penal Code was made up of 202 articles, distributed in two books: *Book One*, made up of 42 articles, contained general provisions applicable to all offenses, while *Book Two*, made up of 160 articles, listed offenses and their punishment. Article 1 of this code provided that no offense shall be punishable by a sentence that was not provided by law at the time of the act. Article 2 of this code provided that offenses committed on the territory of the colony are punishable only in accordance with the law. Despite the attempt to define the term "law" in a much broader sense to include not only legislation but also all written law,[13] the question remained, however, regarding offenses provided by customary law only, but not by the 1940 Penal Code. In most cases, the answer to this question came from the ordinance of 14 May 1886 allowing courts to recourse to customary rules, general principles, and equity when there is no statute on the matter at hand.[14] The fact that this provision applied to both civil and criminal matters does not, however, mean that indigenous courts could apply any of their customary law. The aforementioned 1917 Ordinance required that customary laws be applied only under the supervision of the Belgian colonial resident authority,[15] and nothing contrary to the universally accepted public order could be applied.[16] Indigenous courts were also limited to the punishment they could impose on offenses provided by customary law, but not by the written law.[17]

The 1940 Penal Code provided for seven kinds of sentences: (1) the death penalty, (2) imprisonment, (3) a fine, (4) special confiscation, (5) restraining order to reside in a specific place, (6) obligation to reside in a specific place, (6) to be placed under government custody, known in French as *mise a la disposition du gouvernement*.

This penal code punished most acts considered as offenses in any modern society. Some acts seem, however, to have been included for the specific realities of the society of that time in the colonies. For example, Articles 57–62 punished acts of submitting a person to superstitious or barbaric practices, Articles 63–66 punished duels, Article 133 punished rebellion, and Article 143 punished interfering with the freedom of maritime navigation. The last offense seemed to have been copied verbatim from Belgian or Belgian Congo laws because Rwanda had no maritime navigation.

In addition to the 1940 Penal Code, a number of laws provided for other offenses and their sentences, including the 22 January 1903 Ordinance punishing smoking marijuana,[18] the Decree of 15 July 1949 punishing failure to provide alimentary support to one's family,[19] and the Decree of 25 June 1948 punishing adultery and bigamy.[20] With regard to adultery, while the law punished the wife unconditionally, the husband could be punished for adultery only if the wife proves that she was grievously insulted by his adulterous act.[21]

C. Criminal law under the 1977 Penal Code

Sixteen years after independence, Rwanda was still using the criminal law inherited from colonialism. Therefore, only in 1977, a new and first post-colonial penal code was adopted.[22] It abrogated but also built on the 1940 Penal Code while consolidating other criminal laws scattered outside the 1940 Penal Code in force at that time.[23] This penal code made up of 500 articles, contained two key books: *Book One* related to general provisions applicable to all offenses, and *Book Two* defined offenses and their punishment.

Unlike the 1940 Penal Code, *Book One* of the 1977 Penal Code provided more details on the personal and territorial application of the penal code (Arts 6–17), expanded the list of sentences by including the deprivation of civic rights (Arts 26–27), and included a whole title detailing punishable persons under this code (Arts 70–76). It also incorporated provisions related to mitigating excuses (Art. 79); justifying circumstances (Art. 73 and 337–338); causes of criminal irresponsibility, immunity based on family ties in some offenses (Arts 256–258); pardon (Arts 124–133); amnesty (Arts 100–150); end of criminal action (Art. 100); rehabilitation (Art.150); recidivism (Arts 85–88); and the categorization of offenses into three categories: felony, misdemeanor, and petty offense (Arts 18–20).

With regard to *Book Two*, unlike the 1940 Penal Code that started with offenses against persons, the 1977 Penal Code started with offenses against the State. It also contained a new chapter on crimes against State security, punishing with the death penalty and other severe punishment offenses intended to overthrow or to threaten the government and its institutions. Unlike the 1940 Penal Code that protected the colonial institutions with no reference to the kingdom and other indigenous institutions, the 1977 Penal Code sought to protect the republican regime and institutions.

A number of offenses that existed under the 1940 Penal Code were not included in the 1977 Penal Code; they include acts such as dueling, anthropophagy, and abortion. It included, however, new offenses such as vagrancy (Art. 284), begging (Art. 285), and advertising means of abortion (Art. 379). With regard to adultery (Art. 354), although the law removed the requirement for a wife to prove grievous insult in order for her husband to be punished for adultery, it still punished her more severely than her husband for such an act: The wife faced a maximum of one-year imprisonment for adultery, but the husband incurred a maximum term of 6 months of imprisonment or a fine of one thousand francs.

The 1977 Penal Code contained a number of imperfections. For example, it failed to list all causes of justification defense, and with regard to punishments, there was incoherence in the sense that some offenses were punishable by sentences not defined.[24] Furthermore, the 1977 Penal Code imposed much more severe sentences than the 1940 Penal Code.[25]

The biggest imperfection of the 1977 Penal Code was, however, its failure to punish genocide. In 1975, despite the government's commitment to providing in its domestic law the punishment for genocide,[26] crimes against humanity, and war crimes,[27] the 1977 Penal Code failed to determine such punishments. Following the 1994 Genocide against the Tutsi, Rwanda had to, therefore, adopt a creative organic law that connected the crimes of genocide, war crimes, and crimes against humanity to acts punishable by the 1977 Penal Code for the purpose of punishment and to specifically provide that

> until the publication of the general law on the crime of genocide and the crimes against humanity, whoever commits any act constituting one or more of the crimes after 31 December 1994 shall be liable to the penalty provided by the Penal Code.[28]

D. Criminal law under the 2012 Penal Code

In 2012, Rwanda adopted its first penal code since the 1994 Genocide.[29] It was adopted as organic law to make it superior to other ordinary laws, this law was very innovative and more comprehensive than those passed in 1940 and 1977. With its 705 Articles,[30] this code was adopted with the goal of responding to the need for grouping in one document the many and scattered criminal laws that were sometimes hard to find.

Some of the 2012 Penal Code innovations include: For the first time, Rwanda had a penal code that does not include the death penalty;[31] it punished natural persons but also State institutions, public or private companies, enterprises, associations, and other organizations with legal personality; introduced the penalty of life imprisonment without the option of mercy, conditional release, or rehabilitation before 20 years; introduced community service as an alternative penalty to imprisonment; provided penalties for genocide, war crimes, and crimes against humanity; introduced offenses of genocide ideology as well as discrimination and sectarianism practices; reintroduced penalties for abortion and cannibalism;

punished euthanasia, bestiality, sexual torture, exhibition, and sale or distribution of sexual nature; punished child defilement, marital rape, and sexual harassment; introduced several criminal provisions to protect the child; punished denial of freedom to practice family planning and harassment of spouse; punished equally the wife and husband in the case of adultery; introduced offenses related to human trafficking, illegal removal, sale, and use of human body organs; introduced offenses which infringe on human rights, especially those related to marriage and freedom of worship; introduced offenses against intellectual property, offenses against water and electricity resources; environmental degradation and pollution; and introduced several new offenses against the State such as offenses against the established government or the President of the Republic, disrespect of the national anthem, influencing elections; undermining deliberations of the parliament, and press offenses.

It did not take long, however, for the government to find that the goal of creating a more comprehensive and complete penal code as the one intended in the 2012 Penal Code was not realistic and practical. Any small amendments created the difficult choice of either creating an entirely amended code or just adopting a separate amendment law. Also, judges and prosecutors complained that it was difficult to use.

E. Rwandan criminal law under the 2018 law on offenses and penalties

In 2015, the government initiated a new amendment of the 2012 Penal Code aimed at separating general offenses from special ones.[32] The goal was therefore to move the penal code from the level of organic law, as was the case with the 2012 Penal Code, to that of ordinary law. It involved also removing from this code offenses and penalties related to use, conservation, protection, and management of water resources regulations, as well as those related to mining, electricity, election, human trafficking, and some other special offenses while streamlining other general offenses and their punishments.

As a result of the above-mentioned streamlining, unlike the 2012 "Organic Law instituting the Penal Code," the new 2018 law was called the "Law Determining Offenses and Penalties in General," and reduced to 285 Articles.[33] Among other innovations of this law is the decriminalization of defamation, putting an end to solitary confinement as a form of punishment, moving community service from an accessory penalty to principal penalty, removing the judge's say in the decision-making on abortion, and increasing the severity of punishments related to drug trafficking and child defilement.

The 2018 Law is divided into two key parts: the general provisions applicable to all offenses and penalties, and the part related to specific offenses and penalties. The following sections study the contents of each part in detail.

It is worth highlighting that immediately after the publication of this new law, a number of its provisions were challenged before the Supreme Court as it was considered to be in violation of the Constitution.[34] The challenged provisions are Articles 136 (adultery), 138 (concubinage), 139 (desertion of the marital home), 154 (public defamation of religious rituals), 233 (humiliation of national authorities and persons in charge of public service), and 236 (insults or defamation against the President of the Republic). The ruling of the Supreme Court on each of these provisions will be discussed in the specific sections on these provisions.

Section 2. General provisions applicable to all offenses and penalties

A. General principles guiding the Rwandan criminal law (Arts. 3–15)

The Rwandan criminal law is guided by the following constitutional and human rights principles:

- No one can be held guilty of an offense on account of any act or omission which did not constitute an offense under national or international law when it was committed.
- No offense is punished by a penalty that was not provided for by the law before the offense was committed.
- Criminal laws cannot be interpreted broadly; they must be construed strictly. Courts are prohibited from making judgments by analogy.
- When several laws punish the same offense, the specific law takes precedence over the general law, unless the law provides otherwise.
- A penalty may not be imposed if it is heavier than the one that was applicable at the time the offense was committed.
- In the case of conflict of criminal laws involving a former law that was in force when the offense was committed, and a new law published after the commission of the offense and before a final judgment has been rendered, the new law is the only one to be applied if it imposes a less severe penalty.
- Double jeopardy is prohibited: No person may be punished for the same offense more than once.
- A law ceases to apply to an offense committed when the law was still in force when it is repealed before the final judgment in relation to such an offense, unless the new law provides otherwise.
- An offense is considered to have been committed on the territory of Rwanda if at least one of the acts constituting one of its elements, namely, *mens rea*, *actus reus* and its being punishable by law, was accomplished in Rwanda. An offense is also considered to have been committed on the territory of Rwanda if it is committed by or against a

Rwandan citizen in an area that is not subject to the sovereignty of any State or committed by any person on board a vessel flying the flag of Rwanda and in waters which are not subject to the sovereignty of any State or on board a Rwanda registered aircraft in the territory that is not subject to the sovereignty of any State.

- Any offense committed on the Rwandan territory, either by a Rwandan or by a foreign citizen, is punished according to the Rwandan law. This does not, however, apply to people entitled to diplomatic immunity guaranteed by international conventions ratified by Rwanda or by international customs or practices.
- A Rwandan citizen who commits a felony or a misdemeanor outside the territory of Rwanda may be punished in accordance with Rwandan law as if the offense was committed in Rwanda, provided that such an offense is punishable by Rwandan law.
- Any Rwandan or foreign citizen who commits a felony or a misdemeanor against the interests of Rwanda or against a Rwandan citizen outside the territory of Rwanda may be prosecuted and tried in accordance with Rwandan law as if the offense had been committed in Rwanda. Any person on the territory of Rwanda who is an accomplice to a felony or misdemeanor committed abroad may be punished by Rwandan courts if the offense is punishable under the law of the country where the offense was committed under and is punishable by Rwandan law.
- Any person, whether a Rwandan or foreign citizen, a national or foreign non-governmental organization or association, that commits, inside or outside the territory of Rwanda, an international crime or transnational crime may, if apprehended on the territory of Rwanda, be punished in accordance with Rwandan law. International crimes are the following: (1) the crime of genocide, (2) a crime against humanity, (3) war crimes. A transnational crime means a crime, one of whose constituent elements is accomplished outside Rwanda's borders.

B. Categories of offenses; conspiracies; and attempts to commit offenses (Arts. 16–22)

There are three categories of offenses under Rwandan criminal law classified according to their gravity: (1) felony defined as offense punishable under the law by a principal penalty of imprisonment for a term of more than five years or by life imprisonment; (2) misdemeanor defined as an offense punishable under the law by a principal penalty of imprisonment for a term of not fewer than six months and not more than five years; and (3) petty offense defined as an offense punishable under the law only by a principal penalty of imprisonment for a term of fewer than six months, a fine or the penalty of community service.

The Rwandan criminal law punishes conspiracy to commit an offense by the same penalty as the intended offense. However, any person involved in conspiracy but who reports it to administrative authorities, judicial or security organs and disclose to them the names of involved criminals and their accomplices is exempted from the penalty prescribed for conspiracy if they report it before the commission of the offense in respect of which conspiracy takes place.

An attempt to commit an offense is also punishable when the intention to commit the offense has been demonstrated by one or more observable and unequivocal acts that constitute the beginning of the commission of the offense and leading to its execution, and that were suspended or failed in their purpose only because of circumstances beyond the offender's control. An attempt to commit an offense is punishable even if the intended purpose could not be achieved because of factual circumstances unknown to the offender. An attempt to commit a felony or a misdemeanor is punishable with one half the penalty for the felony or misdemeanor itself. For the offense punishable by the penalty of life imprisonment, the attempt is punishable by imprisonment for a term of 25 years. An attempt to commit a petty offense is, however, not punishable.

C. *Categories of penalties (Arts. 23–46)*

In 2007, Rwanda abolished the death penalty.[35] Since then, principal penalties applicable to natural persons include imprisonment, fines, and penalties of community service, whereas accessory penalties applicable to them are special confiscation, a ban on residence or compulsory residence in a particular location, deprivation of civic rights, and publication of the offense committed and the penalty pronounced by the court.

Principal penalties applicable to the institutions and organizations of the State, companies, cooperatives, and non-governmental organizations with legal personality include a fine, the ban on the conduct of one or several professional or social activities for a fixed period of time, confiscation of the object used or intended for use in the commission of the offense or the proceeds thereof, or publication of the penalty pronounced. These entities may also be punishable by the following penalties: dissolution; permanent closure of establishments in which incriminated acts have been committed or which have been used to commit such acts; permanent exclusion from public procurement contracts, either indefinitely or for a fixed period of time provided for by relevant laws; the ban on issuing a check, a credit card, or negotiable instrument; and placement under judicial supervision.

Public institutions, companies, cooperatives, and public or private entities or organizations with legal personality are held liable for offenses committed on their behalf by their organs or representatives. Criminal liability is established when the offenders have acted by virtue of the power of representation, decision-making power, or the power of supervision. The criminal liability of such entities or organizations does not exclude the criminal liability of their representatives, those who hold leadership posts within them or their co-offenders and accomplices.

The penalty of imprisonment may be for a fixed term or for life. Fixed-term imprisonment is imposed for at least one day and at most 25 years, unless the law provides otherwise. Fixed-term imprisonment is calculated on the basis of days, months, or years of the Gregorian calendar. An imprisonment of one day is equal to 24 hours, an imprisonment of one month is equal to 30 days, and an imprisonment of one year is equal to 12 months. The term of imprisonment runs from the day on which the judgment of conviction becomes final. The length of the period of detention by legally competent organs is deducted from the term of imprisonment imposed by the court. In calculating the term of imprisonment, no account is taken of the period during which the convict has voluntarily avoided serving the penalty. When a person is given more than one penalty of imprisonment, the next imprisonment penalty starts to run upon the expiration of the previous one.

The penalty of life imprisonment implies a jail term for the rest of the convict's life.

A fine is at least one Rwandan franc. A fine is imposed individually on each of the convicts on the basis of the gravity of the offense. The court sets the time limit for payment of a fine. This time limit cannot exceed one year from the day the judgment has become final. The court may order that the fine be paid in installments or commuted to community service. When the convict's property is insufficient for the payment of the fine, restitutions, and damages, priority is given to the payment of restitutions and damages. All persons convicted of the same offense are held jointly responsible for restitutions, damages, and court fees.

In case the penalty of community service is imposed as the principal penalty, the court sets the time limit for serving such a penalty. Such a time limit does not exceed six months. The penalty of community service may be imposed in lieu of another principal penalty. In that case, it is imposed as follows:

1 When an offense is punishable by imprisonment for a term of more than six months and not more than five years, the court may order that the convict serve half of the term of their penalty in serving the penalty of community service.
2 When an offense is punishable by imprisonment for a term of less than six months, the court may order that the convict serve the penalty of community service for a period not exceeding the maximum imprisonment provided by the law for such an offense.

In the case of the convict's failure to properly serve the penalty of community service, they are forced to serve the remainder of the penalty in prison.

When the court orders restitutions or payment of damages for the benefit of the victim, community service imposed does not preclude the victim's right to such restitutions or damages. A convict is exempted from serving the penalty of community service if they effect payment.

In case a felony or a misdemeanor is committed, confiscation of items regarded as forming the *corpus delicti*, those used or intended for use in the commission of the offense, or those regarded as the proceeds from the commission of the offense is imposed as an accessory penalty in addition to the principal penalty if such items belong to the convict. If such items do not belong to the convict or if the offense committed is a petty offense, the confiscation is ordered only in cases specified by the law. The general confiscation of all the convict's current and future property is prohibited.

Unless the law provides otherwise, the court may order a ban on residence or compulsory residence in a particular location in the following cases: (1) if a person is sentenced to imprisonment for a term of more than five years; (2) if a person who, having been sentenced to imprisonment for a term equal to or more than six months, is sentenced again to imprisonment for a term equal to or more than six months within five years of the execution of such a penalty or when its enforcement has become time-barred. The duration of ban on residence or compulsory residence in a particular location may not exceed a period of one year. The penalty of ban on residence or compulsory residence in a particular location commences on the day of completion of the penalty of imprisonment by the convict. If the convict is released on parole, the penalty of ban on residence or compulsory residence in a particular location commences on the day of release.

If the convict released on parole is re-incarcerated, the period of ban on residence or compulsory residence in a particular location is deducted from the penalty imposed on them by the court.

The deprivation of civic rights consists of removal or prohibition from any public service, deprivation of all or part of political rights, deprivation of the right to wear decorations of honor, prohibition to act as an expert witness or a witness to deeds and to testify in court, except in the case of providing information, loss of legal capacity to act as a family council member, a guardian, a trustee, a guardian replacement, a guardian of intellectually disabled persons except in the case of their own children, deprivation of the right to possess arms, prohibition to use a negotiable instrument or a credit card, debarment from participating in public procurement, deprivation of the right to leave the national territory, and deprivation of the right to perform such functions as may be specified by the court.

Life imprisonment automatically entails the permanent deprivation of all civic rights. Except for persons sentenced to life imprisonment, no person may be deprived of all civic rights. The deprivation of civic rights may be imposed only as an accessory penalty in addition to the principal penalty of imprisonment that is equal to or more than five years. With the exception of convicts sentenced to life imprisonment, the deprivation of civic rights cannot exceed ten years. The deprivation of civic rights may be suspended, lifted, or reduced in the same manner as in the case of the penalty of imprisonment. The deprivation of civic rights may be lifted if the convict has performed an exceptional act of good citizenship or highly committed themselves to promoting social development.

D. Imposition and extinction of penalties (Art. 47–82)

A judge determines a penalty according to the gravity, consequences of, and the motive for committing the offense, the offender's prior record and personal situation, and the circumstances surrounding the commission of the offense. In the event of concurrence of grounds for judgment, the judge must consider the aggravating circumstances and the mitigating circumstances. In any case, no penalty may be reduced except in cases and under circumstances provided by law.[36]

Aggravating circumstances are exclusively provided for by law. They are not determined by the judge.

The law accepts only the following mitigating circumstances: minority age, provocation, and mitigating circumstances decided by the judge.

With regard to mitigating circumstances decided by a judge, the latter may reduce penalties, especially when (1) the accused, before the commencement of prosecution, pleads guilty and sincerely seeks forgiveness from the victim and the Rwandan society and expresses remorse and repairs the damage caused as much as would be expected from them; (2) the accused turns themselves in to competent judicial authority before or during the pre-trial proceedings; (3) at the outset of the trial in the first instance, the accused pleads guilty by a sincere confession; (4) the offense has minor consequences.

A sentence can be suspended. Suspension of a sentence is a court decision which orders the stay of execution of a penalty of imprisonment not exceeding five years. Suspension of a penalty is ordered on the basis of the gravity of the offense. A suspended penalty is considered void if, within the period set out in the decision and not less than one year and not exceeding five years, the convict has not subsequently been convicted of a felony or misdemeanor from the date when the decision ordering the suspension of penalty has become final. Otherwise, the suspended penalty and the penalty subsequently imposed for the new offense are combined and executed at the same time.

A penalty can be extinct following its execution, the convict's death, amnesty, presidential pardon, or due to its prescription. A penalty can also be subject to prescription. A penalty of imprisonment of fewer than six months is subject to prescription after two years has elapsed. A penalty of imprisonment for a term equal to or more than six months and not more than five years is subject to prescription after ten years has elapsed. A penalty of imprisonment of more than five years other than the penalty of life imprisonment is subject to prescription after 20 years has elapsed. A penalty of life imprisonment for prescriptible offenses is subject to prescription after 30 years has elapsed. A penalty of community service is subject to prescription after ten years has elapsed. Finally, a penalty of a fine not exceeding five hundred thousand Rwandan francs is subject to prescription after two years has elapsed while that of a fine exceeding 500,000 Rwandan francs is subject to prescription after ten years has elapsed. The period of prescription of penalties commences from the day on which the decision imposing the penalty or revoking the suspension of penalty has become final. However, if the convict has evaded the execution of the penalty, the period of prescription commences when they turn themselves in to the organs in charge of execution of court decisions. The arrest or detention of a convict interrupts the period of prescription of penalties for which the convict was not detained. The period of prescription of a penalty is suspended whenever the execution of the judgment is impossible for reasons arising from the law or *force majeure*.

E. Criminal liability for natural persons (Art. 83–87)

Criminal liability is incurred by the offender, their co-offender, or accomplice. Only a person who intentionally commits an offense is punishable. However, if the law so provides, a person commits an offense as a result of their recklessness, clumsiness, negligence, or any other form of carelessness.

There is no criminal liability if the accused is a child under the age of 14 years, or the accused was insane during the commission of the offense. However, a person who deliberately deprives themselves of mental faculties during the commission of an offense is criminally liable, even if such deprivation was not intended to commit an offense.

Grounds for exemption from criminal liability that are inherent to the offender are admitted if a person commits an offense under the effect of a force or under duress to such an extent that they cannot resist; a person commits an act under orders of a legitimate authority, unless such an act is evidently unlawful; a person commits an offense as a result of an error of law or an error of fact if such an error entirely removes the intention to commit an offense.

Grounds for exemption from criminal liability that are inherent to the act are admitted if a person acts in self-defense resulting from fending off a person who breaks into or enters by force or trickery an inhabited place, defending oneself against thieves or other wrongdoers, defending oneself or another person in case of danger, or interrupting the commission of an offense of damage to property.

Section 3. Specific offenses and their penalties

Rwandan criminal law demarcates four categories of offenses: offenses against persons, offenses against property, offenses against the State, and military offenses.[37]

A. Offenses against persons

1. Crimes of genocide, crimes against humanity, and war crimes (Art. 91–106)

Rwandan criminal law adopted the same definitions of genocide, crimes against humanity, and war crimes as those in the Rome Statute of International Criminal Court. While allowing the possibility for a term imprisonment in some crimes against humanity and war crimes, the criminal law imposes the penalty of life imprisonment for genocide that cannot be mitigated under any circumstances.

Companies, cooperatives, and private entities with legal personality that, by any means, support the crime of genocide and crimes against humanity are liable to the penalty of dissolution, or that of being subject to revocation of their authorization to carry out their activities in Rwanda.

2. Homicide, assault or battery, bodily harm, and abortion (Art. 107–127)

The following acts are considered punishable under the provisions of Art. 107–127: voluntary murder, infanticide committed by a woman against a child under 12 months while in postpartum depression or by effect of lactation, euthanasia, poisoning, manslaughter, torture, sexual torture, administering to another person a substance that may cause death or seriously alter the person's health, incitement to and assistance with suicide, transmission of an illness to another person, unintentional bodily harm, throwing an object at a person that may inconvenience or dirty him, intentional assault or battery, unintentional assault or battery, neglecting care for the person entrusted into one's care, self-induced abortion, performing an abortion on another person, and advertising the means of abortion.

There is no criminal liability for abortion; however, if the pregnancy originates from rape, forced marriage, incest up to the second degree, or when the pregnant person is a child or her health or that of the fetus is in danger, the abortion must be performed by a recognized medical ob-gyn.

3. Providing false statement, threat to harm a person, and inhuman acts on a dead body (Art. 128–132)

The offenses that are punishable under this category include the following: providing a false statement, the use of threat with the intent to harm another person, blackmailing, cannibalism, and hiding or exhuming, mutilating, or inflicting dehumanizing treatment on a dead human body.

4. Sexual offenses and offenses against morality (Art. 133–143)

The offenses that are punishable under this category include the following: child defilement, rape, indecent assault, adultery, desertion of marital home, concubinage, bigamy or officiating at bigamy, bestiality, and public indecency. The prosecution of adultery, concubinage, and desertion of the marital home is initiated only upon complaint by the offended spouse.

The criminalization of adultery, desertion of marital home, and concubinage were challenged before the Supreme Court for violating Article 18 of the Constitution.[38] The applicant argued that these acts should not be considered as offenses because they result from contracts and therefore should constitute contract violations rather than criminal offenses, and that criminalizing them could jeopardize family stability and undermine spouses' freedom to reconcile and forgive each other following such acts. The Supreme Court found that the fact that "adultery, desertion of marital home and concubinage result from a contract is not a valid argument not to make them punishable offenses."[39] The court also ruled that punishing such acts does not undermine family stability because its aim is rather to shelter the family from such acts that could jeopardize its foundation and stability.[40] With regard to the freedom of parties to forgive each other and reconcile after such acts, while the court found that the law allows parties such freedom in the sense that Article 40 of the same law conditions the prosecution of such acts on the complaint of the offended spouse and allows the latter to withdraw the complaint and end the procedure at any stage of the prosecution, it agreed with the applicant that this freedom ends when the case reaches the judge;[41] therefore, the paragraph of this provision limiting this freedom is unconstitutional.[42]

5. *Offenses against persons unable to protect themselves (Art. 144–145)*

The offenses that are punishable under this category include the abandonment of a dependent unable to protect themselves and stigmatizing against a sick person.

6. *Offenses against human rights and freedom of worship (Art. 146–154)*

The offenses that are punishable under this category include the following: forcing a man and a woman to cohabitate, harassment of a spouse, denial of freedom to practice family planning, sexual harassment, fraudulent use of family property, abduction and unlawful detention of a person, false accusations, obstruction of smooth running of religious rituals, and public defamation of religious rituals.

Article 154 on public defamation of religious rituals was challenged in the *Mugisha* case[43] where the applicant argued that such criminalization violates Article 38 of the Constitution on the freedom of press, expression, and access to information. The court agreed with the applicant and argued that such a criminalization that is common in religious states has no place in Rwanda where there is a distinction between religion and the State.[44]

7. Offenses against privacy (Art. 155–162)

The offenses that are punishable under this category include the following: the violation of domicile, secretly listening to conversations, taking photos or disclosing them, publication of edited statements or images, breach of professional secrecy, using fraudulent means to open, remove, delay, or divert a correspondence or such other documents, collecting an individual's personal information on a computer, and public insult. Offenses against privacy are prosecuted only at the request of the victim or their representatives.

8. Crimes of discrimination and instigating division (Art. 163–164)

Punishable acts of discrimination constitute the following: (1) acts that inconvenience a person or a group of people or cause division among persons or a group of people on the basis of race, ethnicity, origin, clan, family connection, color of skin, sex, region, nationality, religion, political ideology, economic classes, culture, language, social status, physical or mental disability, or physical appearance; (2) acts aimed at denying a person or a group of people their rights granted under Rwandan law or international conventions ratified by Rwanda, on the basis of race, ethnicity, origin, clan, family connection, color of skin, sex, region, nationality, religion, political ideology, economic classes, culture, language, social status, physical or mental disability, or physical appearance; or (3) act instigating a person to deny another person or a group of people their rights granted under Rwandan law or international conventions ratified by Rwanda, on the basis of race, ethnicity, origin, clan, family connection, color of skin, sex, region, nationality, religion, political ideology, economic classes, culture, language, social status, physical or mental disability, or physical appearance.

Instigating division happens when a person makes use of speech, writing, or any other act that divides people or may set them against each other or cause civil unrest on the basis of discrimination.

B. Offenses against property

1. Fraudulent appropriation of the property of others (Art. 165–178)

This category includes theft, extortion, fraudulent retention of another person's found property, forging or alteration of keys, fraud, non-payment of bills, breach of trust, selling or pledging as a security a property of another person, and embezzlement or destruction of a mortgaged property.

2. *Arson, demolition, and degradation of property (Art. 179–190)*

This category includes the offenses of arson by the property owner, arson against another person's house, transportation, means, or any other places, setting fire to another person's property, deliberate demolition or damaging of another person's construction, demolition of monuments, demolition of tombs, memorials, symbols, or defilement of tombs or graveyards, sale or use properties resulting from offenses, damaging or plundering another person's property, damaging or plundering of trees, crops, and agricultural tools, removal or displacement of signs or geodetic land marks, removal, displacement or plundering of land marks, and mistreatment, injuring, or killing domestic animals.

C. *Offenses against the State*

1. *Offenses against State security (Art. 191–223)*

This category includes the offenses of (1) treason; (2) maintaining relations with a foreign government with an intent to wage a war; (3) spreading false information or harmful propaganda with an intent to cause a hostile international opinion against the Rwandan government; (4) handing over a territory, troop, or arsenal to a foreign country; (5) supporting a foreign country at war with the government of Rwanda; (6) causing Rwanda to be at war or in hostility with another country; (7) offering and accepting a price to cause war in Rwanda; (8) obstruction to national defense; (9) formation of an irregular group or joining it; (10) carrying out any act to harm the established government or overthrowing it by use of military force or any other means; (11) carrying out any act against the President of the Republic with an intent to harm the established government or overthrow it; (12) conspiracy against the established government or the President of the Republic; (13) causing uprising or unrest among the population; (14) attack on the force of law, devastation, looting of the nation, or massacre; (15) self-styled commander of a criminal gang; (16) membership in a seditious group or gang; (17) providing accommodation or sanctuary to seditious gangs; (18) obstruction to the fight against an insurrection movement; (19) commanding insurrection movements; (20) non-disclosure of plans of treason, espionage, or any other act that could impede national defense; (21) assaulting foreign heads of states or representatives of foreign states or representatives of international organizations in Rwanda; (22) humiliation or insult against foreign heads of states or representatives of foreign states or representatives of international organizations in Rwanda; (23) desecrating of the flag or symbols of a foreign state; (24) discrediting the value of national currency; (25) inciting the public to undermine the financial sector, and (26) illegal operations of currency sale or exchange.

Any member of a seditious group who voluntarily withdraws from the group or who withdraws after a warning or order issued by civil or military authorities is not punished for the offense of sedition. The same applies to a member caught elsewhere other than in the seditious group who showed no resistance and was not armed. However, they are punished for any other offenses committed individually.

Any person who threatens State security benefits from mitigating circumstances if the denunciation comes after the commission of the offense. But before or after the commencement of criminal investigations, one of the offenders assists in the arrest of co-offenders and accomplices or other persons who committed other similarly grave offenses.

2. *Offenses against public security (Art. 224–229)*

This category includes the offenses of formation of a criminal association, illegal demonstration or public meeting, detainee or prisoner escape, helping a detainee or prisoner to escape, and breach of a sentenced restriction of movement.

3. *Offenses against the government (Art. 230–268)*

This category includes the offenses of (1) rebellion against the authority; (2) disrespect of employment badges; (3) humiliation of national authorities and persons in charge of public service; (4) assault or violence against public authorities; (5) assault or violence against the President of the Republic; (6) insult or defamation against the President of the Republic; (7) interfering with the smooth running of the activities of the Parliament; (8) entry into the premises of the Parliament with an intention to harm; (9) interference with the activities within the premises of the Office of the President of the Republic or the cabinet; (10) unlawful break of seals; (11) breaking seals affixed by judicial organs or bailiffs on seized property; (12) refusal to appear before the organ in charge of investigation, public prosecution, or other authority; (13) non-disclosure of a felony or misdemeanor; (14) failure to assist a person in danger, obliteration of evidence; (15) concealing objects used or meant to be used to commit an offense; (16) concealment of objects obtained from an offense; (17) intentional destruction or embezzlement of seized or confiscated property; (18) hiding a corpse of a murdered person; (19) use of threat or intimidation to influence a complaint; (20) refusal to testify; (21) refusal to answer questions from judicial authorities; (22) refusal to answer questions of the intelligence or security organs; (23) giving false testimony; (24) misleading witnesses or judges; (25) refusal to take oath before judicial or intelligence organs;

(26) influencing assistants in judicial organs; (27) false declaration by an expert before judicial organs; (28) insulting or causing violence to personnel in judicial organs; (29) threat against judicial personnel; and (30) discrediting a decision of judicial organs.

Criminal law also punishes carrying out acts related to the use of narcotic drugs or psychotropic substances, facilitating a person to use narcotic drugs or psychotropic substances, production, selling, or prescription of prohibited substances in medicine, noise nuisance, and public drunkenness in the category of offenses against the government.

With regard to refusal to answer questions of judicial, intelligence, and security organs, such an act may not constitute an offense when the person requested to answer considers that it may result in self-incrimination.

The offense of humiliation of national authorities and persons in charge of public service provided in Article 233[45] was challenged in the *Mugisha* case because it violates the principle of equality and equal protection guaranteed in Article 15 of the Constitution and freedom of press, expression, and access to information guaranteed in Article 38 of the Constitution. The court agreed with the applicant that this provision is unconstitutional mainly because it categorizes people and does not give them equal protection[46] and stiffens the freedom of the media and everyone's freedom of expression.[47] The most controversial sentence in this Article 233 was "any other person in charge of a public service." The court found that that term was too vague and did not define who was in or out of that category.[48]

With regard to Article 236 (insults or defamation against the President of the Republic), the Supreme Court ruled that this provision does violate Article 15 (equal protection) and Article 38 of the Constitution (freedom of press, expression, and access to information) because the distinction made by this provision between the president and others and the protection of the president is based on protecting the presidency, but not the individual.[49] This supreme court position is, however, different from that of the Office of the President, which considers humiliation of public officials, including the President of the Republic, as a civil rather than a criminal matter.[50]

4. *Offenses against public credibility (Art. 269–285)*

This category includes the offenses of counterfeiting and falsification or alteration of currency or monetary signs or their distribution, damaging monies, counterfeiting negotiable instruments, their use or circulation, falsification of official marks, of individuals, institutions, or private associations with or without legal personality, illegal use of marks, forgery, falsification, and use of forged documents, fraudulent acquisition or production and the use of forged documents and papers issued by a competent authority, issuance of a document to a person who is not entitled, usurpation of titles and wearing a uniform with an intention to mislead the public, wearing badges, a ribbon, or any other decoration by an unauthorized person, claiming to be attached to a profession, a certificate, an official diploma, or any other entitlement granted to a person not meeting requirements.

The following are also included in the category of offenses against public credibility when committed by civil servants: taking a decision which hinders the enforcement of the law, continued use of authority after the termination of a service in accordance with the law, commission of an act which violates individual liberty, and unlawful detention.

Notes

1 Decree of 30 January 1940 instituant le Code Penal du Congo Belge (B.O, 193) made applicable on the Rwanda by Ordonnance du Ruanda-Urundi (O.R.U.) No. 43/Just of 18 May 1940 (B.O.R.U. 86).
2 Decree-Loi No. 21/77 of 18 August 1977 instituant le Code Penal (J.O. 1978, No 13bis).
3 Organic Law No 01/2012/OL of 02/05/2012 instituting the penal code (Official Gazette Special No. of 14 June 2012).
4 Law no 68/2018 of 30/08/2018 determining offenses and penalties in general (Official Gazette Special No. of 27 September 2018).
5 J.Vanhove, Essai de Droit Coutumier du Ruanda, Memoire couronne au Concours Annuel de 1940, Brussels, Library Falk fils, 1941, the following section is based on this essay, 107–122.
6 Ibid., 107.
7 Ibid.
8 Ibid., 112.
9 See Article 4 of this decree.
10 See Article 2 of the Ruanda-Urundi Ordinance Law No. 45 of 30 August 1924, in Pierre Leroy and Jacques Westhof, Legislation du Ruanda-Urundi, Textes Receullis et Annotes, 2nd edition, Brussels, 1954, 34.
11 See the Ordinance Law No. 1/J. of 22 January 1929, in Leroy and Jacques Westhof, idem.
12 The Code Penal du Congo Belge of 30 January 1940 (B.O. 193) was rendered enforceable on the territory of Ruanda-Urundi by the Ordinance of Ruanda-Urundi (O.R.U) No. 43/Just. Of 18 May 1940. See Leroy and Jacques Westhof, supra. 34. The text of this code can be found in Pierre Piron and Jacques Devos, Codes et Lois du Congo Belge, Tome 1, Maison Ferdinand Larcier, Brussels, 1960, 308–338.
13 See 1st Inst. Kat. 18 November 1953 (J.T.O., 1955, 44, No. 59) cited in Pierre Piron and Jacques, supra. 311.
14 See Robert Kint, Notes du Cours de Droit Penal Special, Universite National du Rwanda, Publication de la Faculte de Droit No. 22. Butare, 1985, 6.
15 Byanafashe and Paul Rutayisire, surpa. 262.
16 See Article 20 of the Ordinance No. 348 of 5 October 1943 regulating the indigenous courts of Ruanda-Urundi.
17 Ibid. Article 2 of this ordinance provided that such offenses can only be punished by whipping. In cases of imprisonment, this could not be more than two months, and if it was a fine, it could not be of more than two thousand francs.
18 Pierre Piron and Jacques Devos, supra. 343.
19 Ibid., 341.
20 Ibid.
21 Article 3 of the same decree.

22 See Decret-Loi No. 21/77 of 18 August 1977, J.O., No. 13bis, 1978. It was rendered effective on 1 January 1980 by the presidential decree No. 462/07 of 1 October 1979. J.O.R.R. 1979, No. 22, 671.

23 These scattered criminal laws made a total of 40 articles and covered issues such as family desertion, adultery and bigamy, cannabis, drunkenness in public, and issuing bouncing checks. see Rene de Wolf, Quelques considerations sur la legislation penale Rwandaise, Revue Juridique du Rwanda, Vo. XII, No. 1, 1 January 1988. 3.

24 Rene de Wolf, Quelques considerations sur la legislation penale Rwandaise, supra note. 3.

25 Ibid., 32.

26 See Article 5 of the International Convention on the repression of the Crime of Genocide of 9 December 1948. Rwanda adhered to it by the Decree-law No. 8/75 of 12 February 1975 (J.O. 1975, 230).

27 See Article 4 of International Convention on non-application of statute limitations to War Crimes and Crimes against Humanity of 26 November 1968. Rwanda adhered to this Convention by the Decree-Law No. 8/75 of 12 February 1975 (J.O. 1975. 230).

28 See Article 39 of the Organic Law No. 08/1996 on the organization of Prosecutions for Offenses constituting the Crime of Genocide or Crimes against Humanity committed since 1 October 1990. J.O. No. 17 of 1 September 1996.

29 Organic Law No 01/2012/OL of 02/05/2012 instituting the penal code, Official Gazette No Special of 14 June 2012.

30 The whole penal code summed up to 766 articles if those related to military offenses were added.

31 Rwanda abolished the death penalty. See Article 2 of the Organic Law No. 31/2007 of 25 July 2007 relating to the abolition of the death penalty, O.G no Special of 25 July 2007.

32 See statement of the Minister for Constitutional and Legal Affairs when tabling the bill before the Parliament in October 2017, quoted in Eugene Kwibuka, Parliament Agrees to Penal Code Amendment, New Times, 19 October 2017.

33 Not counting those related to military offenses.

34 See *Mugisha* case No. RS/Inconst/Spec 00002/2018/SC.

35 Organic Law No. 31/2007 of 2007 Relating to the Abolition of the Death Penalty.

36 See Supreme Court decision to the contrary.

37 Because of their limited application, military offenses are not covered in this chapter.

38 Article 18 provides that

> The family, being the natural foundation of the Rwandan society, is protected by the State. Both parents have the right and responsibility to raise their children. The State puts in place appropriate legislation and organs for the protection of the family, particularly the child and mother, in order to ensure that the family flourishes.

39 *Mugisha* case. para. 40.

40 Ibid., para. 46 and 48.

41 Para 3 of Article 40 provides that. However, if the matter is already brought before court or if a decision thereon has been taken, retraction does not stop the consideration of the case or the execution of the judgment. The judge considers the case after which he/she can accept and refuse such a retraction upon justification.

42 *Mugisha* case Para. 55.

43 Ibid.
44 Ibid., para. 71–72.
45 This article provides that

> any person who, verbally, by gestures or threats, in writings or cartoons, humiliates a member of Parliament when exercising their mandate, a member of the Cabinet, security officers or any other person in charge of a public service in the performance or in connection with the performance of their duties, commits an offence.

46 Mugisha case, para. 92.
47 Ibid., para. 100–101.
48 Ibid., para. 91.
49 Ibid., para. 113 and 123.
50 See statement from the Office of the President following the above-mentioned Supreme Court ruling

> The President of the Republic respects the independence of the judiciary and the recent Supreme Court decision to decriminalize the offences related to humiliation of public officials. The President, however, takes issue with the decision to retain as criminal offences, insults or defamation against the Head of State, who is also a public official. His position has always been that this should be a civil not a criminal matter. The President trusts that there will be further debate on this important matter.
>
> Rwanda Broadcasting Agency at https://rba.co.rw/post/Statement-on-Decision-of-the-Supreme-Court

Bibliography

A. Books and Articles

Ackerman, Bruce. *We the People*. Cambridge: Belknap Press of Harvard University Press, 1991.

Akhayan, Payam. "Justice in the Hague, Peace in the Former Yugoslavia- A Commentary on the United Nations War Crimes Tribunal." *Human Rights Quarterly* 20, no. 2 (1998): 737–816.

Anson, William R. *Principles of the Law of Contracts: With a Chapter on the Law of Agency*. Edited by Arthur L. Corbin. 3rd Am. ed. New York: Banks Law Publishing Co., 1919.

Amstutz, Mark R. *The Healing of Nations: The Promise and Limits of Political Forgiveness*. Lanham: Rowman and Littlefield Publishers, 2005.

Barak, A. "The Role of Judges in a Democracy." in *Human Rights, Democracy and Rule of Law*, edited by Liber Amicorum and Luzius Wildhaber. Zurich: Dike Verlad, 2007. 939–960.

Barber, Nicholas W. *The Principles of Constitutionalism*. Oxford: Oxford University Press, 2018.

Bashoga, Bernard, Quelques lacunes de la Constitution de la Republic Rwandaise du 10 Juin 1991, in Revue Jurique du Rwanda, Vol. XVI, No. 1, January 1992. 62–65.

Bassiouni, M. Cherif. *International Crimes: Digest/Index of International Instruments, 1815–1985*. New York, London, Rome: Oceana Publications, Inc., 1986.

Bgoya, W. and Hyden, G. "State and the Crisis in Africa: In Search of a Second Liberation." *Development Dialogue* 2 (1987): 5–29.

Bornkamm, Paul Christoph. *Rwanda's Gacaca Court: Between Retribution and Reparation*. Oxford; New York: Oxford University Press, 2012.

Booth, David and Cammack, Deana. *Governance for Development in Africa, Solving Collective Action Problems*. London: Zed Books Ltd, 2013.

Brehm, Hollie Nyseth, Christopher Uggen, and Jean-Damascene Gasanabo. "Genocide, Justice and Rwanda's Gacaca Courts." *Journal of Contemporary Criminal Justice* 30, no. 3 (August 2014): 333–352.

Byanafashye, Deo and Rutayisire, Paul. *Histoire du Rwanda, Des origins a la fin du XXe siècle*. Huye: Universite Nationale du Rwanda, 2011.

Clark, Phil. "The Gacaca Courts and Abbreviated Criminal Procedure for Genocide Crimes in Rwanda." in *Abbreviated Criminal Procedures for Core International Crimes*, edited by Morten Bergsmo, 189–208. Brussels: Torkel Opsahl Academic Publisher, 2017.

Cousineau, Marc. "L'Établissement de L'État de Droit au Rwanda: Un but Irrealisable." *Ottawa Law Review* 28, no. 1 (1997): 171–190.

Des Forges, Alison. *Leave None to Tell the Story: Genocide in Rwanda.* New York: Human Rights Watch, 1999.

DesForges, Alison. *Defeat is the Only Bad News: Rwanda under Musing, 1896–193.* Edited by David Newbury. Madison: University of Wisconsin Press, 2011.

De Brouwer, Anne-Marie and Ruyebana, Etienne. "The Legacy of the Gacaca Courts in Rwanda: Survivors' Views." *International Criminal Law Review* 13, no. 5 (2013): 937–976.

De Lacger, Louis. *Ruanda.* Kabgayi, 1961.

Delmas, L. *Généalogies de la Noblesse du Rwanda.* Kabgayi: Vicariat apostolique du Ruanda, 1950.

De Winne, Ruben and Pohu, Anne-Ael. *Mediation in Rwanda, Conceptions and Realities of Abunzi Justice (2011–2014).* 1st ed. Belgium.

De Wolf, Rene Apercu de la Constitution Rwandaise, Revue Juridique du Rwanda, Vol. V, No. 1, 1 January 1981.

De Wolf, Rene. "Quelques considerations sur la legislation penale Rwandaise." *Revue Juridique du Rwanda* 7, no. 1 (January 1988).

Digneffe, Francoise and Fierens, Jacques, ed. *Justice et Gacaca, l'experience rwandaise et le genocide.* Namur: Press universitaires de Namur, 2003.

Dugan, Marie. "A Nested Theory of Conflict." *Women in Leadership* 1, no. 1 (Summer 1996): 14–15.

Gacaca Report Summary, "Summary of the Report Presented at the closing of Gacaca Court Activities: National Service of Gacaca Jurisdictions" (Kigali, 2012).

Gahima, Gerald, *Transitional Justice in Rwanda, Accountability for Atrocity.* London: Routledge 2013.

Gardner, Jane F. *Women in Roman Law and Society.* London: Routledge, 1986.

Garner, Bryan A. and Black, Henry Campbell. *Black's Law Dictionary*, 8th ed. St. Paul: Thomson/West, 2004.

Hagenimana, F.X. *La separation des pouvoirs et l'histoire constitutionnelle Rwandaise.* Kigali: UNR, 1990.

Human Rights Watch. "Justice Compromised: The Legacy of Rwanda's Community-Based Gacaca Courts." *Human Rights Watch* (May 2011): 27–80. https://www.hrw.org/sites/default/files/reports/rwanda0511webwcover_0.pdf

Hyse, T. *Le Mandat Belge sur le Ruanda-Urundi.* Bruxelles: la Renaissance de l'Occident, 1930.

Ingelaere, Bert. *Inside Rwanda's Gacaca Courts: Seeking Justice after Genocide.* Madison: University of Wisconsin Press, 2016.

Kaitesi, Usta and Haveman, Roelof. "Prosecution of Genocidal Rape and Sexual Torture before the Gacaca Tribunals in Rwanda." in *Victimological Approaches to International Crimes: Africa*, edited by Rianne Letschert, Roelof Haveman, Anne-Marie de Brouwer, and Antony Pemberton, 385–411. Cambridge: Intersentia, 2011.

Kagame, Alexis. *Code des institutions du Rwanda precoloniale.* Brussels: Institute Royal Colonial Belge, 1952.

Kagame, A. Le Code Esotherique de la Dynastie du Rwanda, in Zaire, Revue Congolese, April 1947. 364–374.

Kagame, Alexis. *Un abrégé de l'Ethno-Histoire du Rwanda.* Butare: Editions Universtaires du Rwanda, 1972.

Kagame, Alexis. *Les milices du Rwanda precolonial.* Bruxelles, 1963.

Kamatali, Jean-Marie. "Accountability for Genocide and Other Gross Human Rights Violations: The Need for an Integrated and Victim-based Transitional Justice." *Journal of Genocide Research* 9, no. 2 (June 2007): 275–295.

Kamatali, J.M. "State-Building in Rwanda." in *Reconstructing the Authoritarian State in Africa*, edited by George K. Kieh, Jr. and Pita O. Agbese, 154–179. New York: Routledge, 2013.

Kamatali, J.M. "Ethnicity and Constitutionalism in Post-Genocide Rwanda." in *Constitutionalism in Africa, Creating Opportunity, Facing Challenges*, edited by J. Oloka-Onyango, 103–127. Kampala: Fountain Publishers, 2001.

Kamatali, J.M. "The Challenge of Linking International Criminal Justice and National Reconciliation: The Case of the ICTR." *Leiden Journal of International Law* 16 (2003): 116–133.

Kamatali, J.M. "From the ICTR to ICC: Learning from the ICTR Experience in Bringing Justice to Rwandans." *New England Journal of International and Comparative Law* 12, no. 1 (2005): 89–104.

Kint, Robert. *Notes du Cours de Droit Penal Special.* Butare: Universite National du Rwanda, Publication de la Faculte de Droit, 1985.

Kwibuka, Eugene. "Parliament Agrees to Penal Code Amendment." *New Times*, October 19, 2017.

Lederach, John Paul. *Building Peace: Sustainable Reconciliation in Divided Societies.* Washington, DC: United States Institution for Peace Press, 1997.

Lemarchand, Rene. *Rwanda and Burundi.* New York: Praeger Publishers, 1970.

Leroy, Pierre and Westhof, Jacques. *Legislation du Ruanda-Urundi, Textes Receullis et Annotes*, 2nd ed. Brussels: R. Louis, 1954.

Lock, John. *Second Treaties on Civil Government.* Edited by Peter Laslett. New York: New American Library, 1965.

Lugan, Bernard. *Histoire du Rwanda, de la Préhistoire à nos jours.* Paris: Editions Bartillat, 1997.

Mohmood, Malik Khalid. *Human and Institutional Capacity Development Handbook, a USAID Model for Sustainable Performance Improvement.* Washington, DC: USAID, October 2010.

Malfeyt, J. "Note sur le Rapport Politique du Rwanda, 1920–1921." *African Archives* AE/II, no. 1847.

Mamdani, M. *Politics and Class Formation in Uganda.* London: Heinemann, 1976.

Mamdani, Mahmood. "Amnesty or Impunity? A Preliminary Critique of the Report of the Truth and Reconciliation Commission of South Africa (TRC)." *Diacritics* 32, no. ¾ (2002): 32–59.

Maquet, Jacques J. *The Premise of Inequality in Rwanda.* London; New York: Oxford University Press, 1961.

McDougal, Myres. "The Impact of International Law upon National Law: A Policy-Oriented Perspective." *South Dakota Law Review* 4 (1959): 25–92.

Maquet, Jacques J. *The Premise of Inequality in Ruanda: A Study of Political Relations in a Central African Kingdom.* New York: Routledge, 2018.

Muberanziza, Aloys. "Quelques Réflexions sur la Loi fondamentale Actuelle a la Veille de la Mise en Place d'une Nouvelle Constitution au Rwanda." *Revue Scientifique de Droit* 5 (June 2000): 1–132.

Murego, Donat. "La Revolution Rwandaise 1959–1962, Essa d'interpretation." Master's thesis, University of Louvain, 1975.

Mutisi, Martha. "Local Conflict Resolution in Rwanda: The Case of Abunzi Mediators." *Integrating Traditional and Modern Conflict Resolution: Experiences from Selected Cases in Eastern and the Horn of Africa*, edited by Martha Mutisi and Kwesi Sansculotte-Greenidge, 50–54. Umhlanga Rocks: ACCORD, 2012.

Newbury, David. *The Land Beyond the Mists: Essays on Identity and Authority in Precolonial Congo and Rwanda.* Athens: Ohio University Press, 2009.

Nkundabagenzi, F., ed., *Rwanda Politique 1958–1960.* Bruxelles: The Centre, 1961.

Ntampaka, Charles. "Le Retour à la tradition dans le jugement du génocide rwandais: Le Gacaca, justice participative." *Bulletin des Séances de l'Académie Royale des Sciences d'Outre-Mer* 48 (2002): 419–456.

Ntampaka, C. l'Apport de la loi du 27 Octobre 1988 sur les droits de la femme au Rwanda, Revue Juridique du Rwanda Vol. XIV, No. 1–2, January-April 1990, 32–39.

O'Connell, Mary Ellen, Richard F. Scott, and Naomi Roht-Arriaza. *The International Legal System, Cases and Materials.* 6th ed. St. Paul: Foundation Press, 2010.

Okereke, Chukwumerije and Agupusi, Patricia. *Homegrown Development in Africa: Reality of Illusion?* London: Routledge, 2015.

Palmer, Nicola. *Courts in Conflict: Interpreting the Layers of Justice in Post-genocide Rwanda.* Oxford: Oxford University Press, 2015.

Perugia, Paul Del. *Les derniers rois mages.* Paris: Editions Phebus, 1993.

Piron, Pierre and Devos, Jacques. *Codes et Lois du Congo Belge.* Brussels: Maison Ferdinand Larcier, 1960.

Reyntjens, Filip La Nouvelle Constitution du 20 Decembre 1978, Revue Juridique du Rwanda, Vol. IV, No. 2, of April 1st, 1980.

Reynjens, Filip and Gorus, Jan F. J. *Codes et lois du Rwanda.* Butare: Université nationale du Rwanda, 1979.

Reyntjens, Filip. "Le gacaca ou la justice du gazon au Rwanda." *Politique Africaine* 40 (1990): 30–41.

Reyntjens, Filip. *Pouvoirs et Droit au Rwanda: droit public et evolution politique, 1916–1973.* Tervuren: Musée royal de l'Afrique centrale, 1985.

Rwanda Women's Network. *Experience of Women in Asserting their Land Rights: The Case of Bugesera District.* Rwanda: Rwanda Women's Network, 2011.

Sadat, Leila Nadya. "The Contribution of ICTR to the Rule of Law." in *Promoting Accountability under International Law for Gross Human Rights Violations in Africa: Essays in Honour of Prosecutor Hassan Bubacar Jallow*, edited by Charles C. Jalloh and Alhagi B.M. Marong, 118–129. Leiden: Nijhoff, 2015.

Sadat, Leila Nadya. "The Legacy of the International Criminal Tribunal for Rwanda." Paper presented at the ICTR, July 3, 2012.

Sarkin, Jeremy. "The Tension between Justice and Reconciliation in Rwanda: Politics, Human Rights, Due Process and the Role of Gacaca Courts in Dealing with the Genocide." *Journal of African Law* 45, no. 2 (2001): 143–172.

Scher, Daniel and Macaulay, Christine. "How Tradition Remade Rwanda: The Secret Ingredient in Rwanda's Effort to Rebuild Its Nation After the Violence of Genocide." *Foreign Policy.* January 2014.

Sohier, A. "Le marriage en droit coutumier Congolais." Institut Royal colonial Belge, Section des Sciences Morales et Politiques, Memoires, T.XI, fasc. 3, 1943.

Totten, Samuel and Bartrop, Paul R. *Dictionary of Genocide*. London: Greenwood Press, 2008.

Tutu, Desmond. *No Future without Forgiveness*. 1st ed. New York: Doubleday, 1999.

Vanhove, J. *Essai de Droit Coutumier du Ruanda, Memoire couronne au Councours Annuel de 1940*. Brussels: Library Falk fils, 1941.

Vandeginste, Stef. "Rwanda: Dealing with Genocide and Crimes Against Humanity in the Context of Armed Conflict and Failed Political transition." in *Burying the Past: Making Peace and Doing Justice after Civil Conflict*, edited by Nigel Biggar, 251–286. Washington, DC: Georgetown University Press, 2001.

Vandeginste, Stef "A Truth and Reconciliation Approach to the Genocide and Crimes against humanity in Rwanda." Working Paper 1998/1. Center for the study of the Great Lakes Region of Africa, University of Antwerp, May 1998.

Vansina, J. *L'évolution du royaume rwanda des origines à 1900*. Bruxelles: Académie Royale des Sciences d'Outre- Mers, 1962.

B. Key Cases

1 *Democratic Green Party of Rwanda v. Republic of Rwanda*, RS/SPEC/002/15, (2015).
2 *Nicaragua v. United States*, 1986 I.C.J. Rep. 14, (ICJ 1986).
3 *BRD v. Mwubahamana*, Rwanda Law Report vol. 2 (2015).
4 *The Government of Rwanda (Minecofin) v. Vuzimpundu*, Rwanda Law Reports vol. 1 (2017).
5 Armed Activities on the Territory of the Congo (New Application: 2002) (*Democratic Republic of the Congo v. Rwanda*).
6 *Mugisha case* No. RS/Inconst/Spec 00002/2018/SC.
7 *Akayesu*, ICTR, Trial Chamber I, Judgment of 2 September 1998, case no. ICTR-96-4-T.
8 *Mulindahabi Fidele v. Republic of Rwanda*, App. No 008/2017 (2017).
9 *Rutabingwa Chrysanthe v. Republic of Rwanda*, App. No. 003/2013 (2013).
10 *Ingabire Victoire Umuhoza v. Republic of Rwanda*, App. No. 003/2014 (2018).
11 RS/Inconst/Pén.0003/10/CS, Gatera Johnson, Kabalisa Teddy Vs. (2011).
12 *General Kayumba Nyamwasa and others v. Republic of Rwanda*, App. No. 016/2015 (2017).
13 The Prosecutor v. Ferdinand Nahimana, Jean-Bosco Barayagwiza, Hassan Ngeze (Judgment and Sentence), ICTR-99-52-T.
14 Supreme Court of Rwanda, Decree No. 1/2000 of March 20, 2000.
15 Kachelewa J. v. Nyirarukundo Ch., RC 0223/08/TB/KCY.

Index

For Product Safety Concerns and Information please contact our EU
representative GPSR@taylorandfrancis.com
Taylor & Francis Verlag GmbH, Kaufingerstraße 24, 80331 München, Germany

www.ingramcontent.com/pod-product-compliance
Lightning Source LLC
LaVergne TN
LVHW011126300926
849160LV00008B/529

* 9 7 8 1 0 3 2 1 7 5 7 4 4 *